THE DISCOURSE OF SOVEREIGNTY, HOBBES TO FIELDING

In this new study the authors examine a range of theories about the state of nature in seventeenth- and eighteenth-century England, considering the contribution they made to the period's discourse on sovereignty and their impact on literary activity. Texts examined include *Leviathan*, *Oceana*, *Paradise Lost*, *Discourses Concerning Government*, *Two Treatises on Government*, *Don Sebastian*, *Oronooko*, *The New Atalantis*, *Robinson Crusoe*, *Dissertation upon Parties*, *David Simple*, and *Tom Jones*. The state of nature is identified as an important organizing principle for narratives in the century running from the Civil War through to the second Jacobite Rebellion, and as a way of situating the author within either a reactionary or a radical political tradition. *The Discourse of Sovereignty* provides an exciting new perspective on the intellectual history of this fascinating period.

The Discourse of Sovereignty, Hobbes to Fielding

Hobbes to Fielding

The State of Nature and the Nature of the State

STUART SIM
University of Sunderland

and

DAVID WALKER
University of Northumbria

ASHGATE

Published by
Ashgate Publishing Limited
Gower House
Croft Road
Aldershot
Hampshire GU11 3HR
England

Ashgate Publishing Company
Suite 420
101 Cherry Street
Burlington, VT 05401-4405
USA

Ashgate website: http//www.ashgate.com

British Library Cataloguing in Publication Data
Sim, Stuart, 1943-
    The discourse of sovereignty - Hobbes to Fielding : the
    state of nature and the nature of the state. - (Studies in
    early modern English literature)
    1.English literature - Early modern, 1500-1700 - History
    and criticism 2.English literature - 18th century - History
    and criticism 3.Soveriegnty in literature 4.Philosophy of
    nature 5.Nature in literature 6.Great Britain - Politics
    and government - 1603-1714 7.Great Britain - Politics and
    government - 1714-1760
    I.Title II.Walker, David
    820.9'358'09032

Library of Congress Cataloging-in-Publication Data
Sim, Stuart
    The discourse of sovereignty, Hobbes to Fielding : the state of nature and the nature of
    the state / Stuart Sim and David Walker.
        p. cm.-- (Studies in early modern English literature)
    Includes bibliographical references and index.
    ISBN 0-7546-0455-1 (alk. paper)
    1.English literature--Early modern, 1500-1700--History and criticism. 2. Politics and
literature--Great Britain--History--17th century. 3. Politics and literature--Great
Britain--History--18th century. 4. English literature--18th century--History and criticism.
5. Hobbes, Thomas, 1588-1679--Influence. 6. Sovereignty in literature. 7. State, The, in
literature. 8. Monarchy in literature. 9. Nature in literature. I. Walker, David, 1960- II.
Title. III. Series.

PR438.P65 S58 2002
820.9'358--dc21   2002027908

ISBN 0 7546 0455 1

Printed and bound in Great Britain by MPG Books Ltd, Bodmin, Cornwall

Contents

Acknowledgements

Our thanks go to Iona D'Souza for the production of the camera-ready copy of the manuscript.

General Editor's Preface

Studies in Early Modern English Literature

The series focuses on literary writing of the seventeenth and eighteenth centuries. Its objectives are to examine the individuals, trends, and channels of influence of the period between the Renaissance and the rise of Romanticism. During this period the English novel was invented, poetry began to tackle its unsteady relationship with non-literary discourse, and post-Shakespearean drama reinvented itself.

Alongside studies of established figures, the series will include books on important but lesser-known writers and those who are acknowledged as significant but given slight attention: typically, William Cartwright, James Shirley, John Denham, Edmund Waller, Isaac Watts, Matthew Prior, William D'Avenant, Mark Akenside and John Dyer. Also of particular interest are studies of the development of literary criticism in this period, monographs which deal with the conditions and practicalities of writing – including the practices of the publishing trade and financial and social circumstances of writing as a profession – and books which give special attention to the relationship between literature and other arts and discourses.

Monographs on a variety of writers and topics will be accepted; authors are invited to combine the best traditions of detailed research with astute critical analysis. The use of contemporary theoretical approaches will be acceptable, but every book will be founded upon historical, biographical and textual scholarship.

Professor Richard Bradford,
University of Ulster

Introduction:
From Revolution to Rebellion

Political sovereignty was a keenly-contested issue throughout the seventeenth century and then into the eighteenth, with English society experiencing two full-scale revolutions (the Civil War of 1640-49, and the 'Glorious Revolution' of 1688-9), as well as several rebellions (the Monmouth, and the two Jacobite) over that period. Religious sectarianism was a critical factor in such political conflict, ensuring that sovereignty became an issue right down to the level of the personal. The nature of the relationship between the individual and authority (political and theological), and the very nature of the state itself, altered quite radically between 1640 and the Hanoverian succession, generating a wide range of responses from thinkers across the political spectrum.

Various theories of the state of nature were put forward during this period as contributions to the debate on sovereignty. In the case of the contrasting theories of Thomas Hobbes and John Locke, these had a far-reaching influence on intellectual life in general, with echoes to be found in the work of a diverse range of authors. We can recognise something like the Hobbesian state, for example, when self-interest is in the ascendance, as in the work of such early novelists as Delarivier Manley and the Fieldings, Henry and Sarah; whereas Locke's version informs the narrative of *Robinson Crusoe*, one of the great myths to emerge from the debate on the state of nature. Other, more biblically-oriented formulations of the state of nature can be located in the work of writers such as Gerard Winstanley, John Milton, and John Dryden. This study examines a range of such theories, considering the contribution they made to the period's discourse on sovereignty, as well as their impact on literary activity; taking on board A.O. Lovejoy's point about the overlapping senses of the concept – anthropological, cultural and political – in the period.[1] The enquiry is divided into three parts, covering the period from the outbreak of Civil War through to the immediate aftermath of the second Jacobite Rebellion: 'From Revolution to Restoration' (1640-60); 'From Restoration to Revolution' (1660-90); 'Post-Restoration and the Hanoverian Settlement' (1690-1750s). Texts to be covered in detail include: *Leviathan, Oceana, Discourses Concerning Government, Two Treatises on Government, A Defence of the People of*

England, Don Sebastian, Oroonoko, Love Letters from a Nobleman to his Sister, The New Atalantis, Robinson Crusoe, Roxana, Dissertation upon Parties, David Simple and *Tom Jones*. The state of nature will be identified as an important organising principle for narratives, ranging through both philosophy and literature, and as a way of situating the author within either a reactionary or a radical political tradition.

We should emphasise that our forays into the literature of this period have, of necessity, to be very selective, and that we make no pretensions to a general survey of literary activity from Hobbes to Fielding. The authors and texts chosen are the ones deemed most conducive to our theme, and this has meant swerving away from canonical texts on occasion, and leaving some chronological gaps on others. In the main we have opted for a case study approach rather than trying to gloss over the entire oeuvres of our chosen authors. Thus Milton's prose features at the expense of *Paradise Lost* (although this is dealt with briefly), and Aphra Benn's prose at the expense of her plays. Dryden's *Don Sebastian*, a very striking drama written in the immediate aftermath of the Glorious Revolution (and arguably Dryden's most underrated work), provides a more fertile site for our analysis than does the more famous, yet also Hobbesian-influenced, *Absalom and Achitophel*. As with *Paradise Lost*, however, we do engage with the canonical work briefly, when appropriate to establishing the importance of Dryden's contribution to the debate about the the state of nature in the later *Don Sebastian*. The latter work was also considered by us to have far more interesting and provocative things to say about the state of nature's political implications than are to be found in any of Dryden's Restoration playwright peers, for all their acknowledged awareness of Hobbesian ideas.[2] The fact that we have had to be selective, is evidence of just how deeply the state of nature infiltrated the consciousness of our period of enquiry.

In a recent study we examined the impact of the seventeenth century's 'crisis of sovereignty' on the work of John Bunyan, suggesting that he was caught up in a 'conflict of narratives', whereby his own nonconformist narrative could only remain incommensurable to the establishment narrative of the Restoration regime.[3] In Bunyan's case, much of this crisis hinged on religious issues (always bearing in mind that religious positions entailed political ones in this period), and it was never likely to be resolved to his satisfaction, given his more than somewhat fundamentalist outlook. Bunyan comes to symbolise the nonconformist position under the Restoration settlement, where issues of personal and political sovereignty become inextricably intertwined, and in that sense he is very much a creature of conflict. As we noted, it is hard to imagine him operating in the context of toleration, and his death in 1688 seems to signal the end of a certain kind of hard-line nonconformist narrative, almost fanatically resistant to the art of compromise.

Yet Bunyan was only one voice in a much larger, and extremely complex, 'discourse of sovereignty' that gathers momentum as the seventeenth century progresses: a discourse in which the concept of the state of nature comes to play a critical role. At the heart of this discourse is the Stuart monarchy. It is a Stuart monarch who is beheaded in 1649; a Stuart monarch who returns to the throne in 1660; a Stuart monarch who is chased from the throne in 1688; a Stuart monarch who succeeds to the throne in 1704 and leaves yet another succession problem behind; and would-be Stuart monarchs whose scheming underpins the Jacobite rebellions of 1715 and 1745. For over a century, therefore, the Stuarts generate a series of crises over sovereignty (their talent for that remains unrivalled in British public life), and they constitute a frame for this enquiry into the ensuing discourse.

It is against this background of conflict, therefore, that we must judge the various theories of the state of nature put forward in this period. Those of Hobbes and Locke are the best known, and, in conjunction with that of Locke's Whig contemporary Algernon Sidney, philosophically the most heavyweight; but there are others of varying degrees of sophistication to be considered also. The Bible was a particularly fruitful source for such theories, with Genesis, for example, providing Winstanley with the basis for his primitive agrarian communist ideas in a series of pamphlets written during the Commonwealth period; as well as acting as a spur to the imagination of Milton in the creation of *Paradise Lost*. It was the Bible, too, that lay behind the divine right theories of Sir Robert Filmer, whose ideas were so admired by the Stuart monarchy and its Tory supporters in the turbulent period of the 1680s, which culminated in the Glorious Revolution of 1688-9. Divine right for Filmer was grounded in the situation in Eden, that original state of nature which continued, for this thinker anyway, to dictate the human condition.

At this point it would be helpful to consider the nature of the English state between 1640 and 1750 (from 1707 the British state, of course). England in 1640 was a close approximation to an absolute monarchy, in that Charles I had ruled without Parliament since 1629. The close of the civil war issued in a republican Commonwealth for the first, and so far only, time in modern English life. Oliver Cromwell's ambivalent status in English history (hate figure to some, hero to others) is an indication of the problematical status of the Commonwealth, both then and since. There is nothing to compare to that episode in subsequent British history, and constitutionally it remains an anomaly – as the use of the phrase 'interregnum' suggests. Succession proved to be its weakest point, and it did not long survive Cromwell's death, with his son Richard never commanding the loyalty or respect of his illustrious father. Despite its 'failure', however, we can trace a discourse, albeit often somewhat disguised, of republicanism for much of our period of enquiry: a point to which we shall be returning later. The uneasy nature of the Restoration 'settlements' has been extensively documented, and the sovereignty issue continued to bedevil English political life throughout the reign of Charles II, to break out into open revolution once again in the events of 1688-9, when his brother James II was driven from the throne in favour of a Protestant succession.[4] At least part of the problem with the later Stuart monarchy was the attraction that absolute monarchy held for them, and that proved a critical element in the emergence of party politics in this period, with the Tories, broadly speaking, supporting the absolutist ideal and the Whigs opposing it.[5]

The legacy of the Stuart monarchy was felt in British political life well beyond the settlement of 1689, in the form of two Jacobite rebellions in 1715 and 1745, which served to prove just how live the succession issue remained despite the apparent 'resolution' achieved by the 'Glorious Revolution'. Perhaps even beyond that latter date and the defeat of the Young Pretender, in the sense that another rebellion remained at least an objective possibility: a situation which Sir Walter Scott turned to such good effect in his novel *Redgauntlet*, which postulates a third Jacobite rebellion in the 1760s. We find Henry Fielding complaining in late 1748 that a 'strange spirit of Jacobinism, indeed of Infatuation, discovered itself at the latter End of the Year 1747, in many Parts of this Kingdom'.[6] Charles Edward Stuart even made a secret visit to London in 1750 in the hopes of gaining support for a new uprising, so Fielding's fears and Scott's premise are not without some foundation.[7]

Even with the apparent guarantee of a Protestant succession, sovereignty remains a critical issue, with nonconformism envisaging a different relationship between the individual (and particularly the individual *conscience*) and the state than the establishment tended to. The relationship between human nature and the nature of the state comes to constitute a fascinating dialogue, where issues of personal and political sovereignty are intertwined. Defoe's nonconformism argues a very different kind of state, and form of political legitimacy, than does Henry Fielding's arguably Hobbesian-tinged conception of self-interested human nature (as we shall see in chapter 12, Fielding was no particular fan of Hobbes, but he does seem to have imbibed a fair measure of the latter's cynicism regarding individual conduct). Manley will show us how female sovereignty is simply occluded by the larger discourse of self-interest that is beginning to exert its cultural dominance over British society: a dominance against which both Henry and Sarah Fielding will align themselves in their narrative projects. To be for or against self-interest is to position oneself ideologically, and it becomes arguably the most critical topic in the debate over the relationship between the state of nature and the nature of the state.

Republicanism does not disappear after the collapse of the Protectorate and the restoration of the monarchy in 1660. Indeed, it continues to be a significant factor in political debate well into the eighteenth century, both at home and abroad. Its canonical texts formed during the mid- and later seventeenth century are instrumental in understanding the ideological direction taken by the Whig party after its failure to bring about Exclusion in 1682, and are central to an appreciation of world events such as the American Revolution.[8] Historians of later eighteenth-century America make this clear. In a very influential study Bernard Bailyn informs us that the texts of Milton, 'the radical tractarian', Harrington and the like-minded Henry Neville, and above all Algernon Sidney, were part of the intellectual furniture of radical colonials in revolutionary America. In Gordon Wood's view, American colonists in the second half of the eighteenth century drew from 'British culture its most republican and whiggish strains'.[9]

Republicanism underwent a period of adaptation, an evolving process that was continually being tailored to suit the prevailing circumstances. Rather than advancing an alternative political system republicanism was transformed into an idiom, a language calling for probity and reform in public life, and a redirected emphasis appeared on the relationship between king and subject. At the forefront of this relationship was the consent of a free-born people willing to place themselves under the sovereignty of a just prince.[10] Theories of contract lie at the heart of much republican and quasi-republican political writing in the seventeenth and eighteenth centuries. Changes in the way that republican texts from the 1650s were interpreted later in the century led to corresponding changes of emphasis. Such texts were figured most often as defences of the ancient constitution and the rights of Parliament; of limiting the powers of the monarchy and placing them within and not above the law. Later writers in this tradition were often monarchists for pragmatic reasons. They share characteristics with puritans, now classified as nonconformists and dissenters, with whom they were often allied during crises generated by heightened anti-Catholicism and the exclusion of James, Duke of York, from the throne.[11] The experience of defeat was not as debilitating as Christopher Hill has suggested, and republicanism and nonconformity continued to be powerful discourses in the political history of the nation for some time to come after Charles II's triumphant return to London in May, 1660.[12] The later seventeenth century abounds with plots and political crises that even now, after two decades of revisionism in the historiography of the later Stuarts, are still overshadowed by the mid-century civil wars, commonwealth and protectorate.

In an extremely large body of writing, some of which is the richest literature in the canon of English political thought, the ideas associated with republicanism from the Restoration through to the Jacobite rebellion of 1745, became weapons in the fight to restrain the arbitrary claims to absolute rule of both the Stuarts and the Hanoverians. Much of what was written by Milton, Harrington, Neville, Sidney, and Molesworth, to confine ourselves merely to the well-known, were keynote texts in the opposition rhetoric of those like Bolingbroke, Trenchard, Gordon, and Thomson in the age of Walpole. The nature of republican thought changed its hue in the years after 1660. The Earl of Shaftesbury's *Letter from a Person of Quality* (1675), occasionally thought to have been penned by Locke, is a neo-Harringtonian document that is aimed specfically at the attempt by government to pass a 'non-resisting test' in the mid-1670s. Such a bill would have made it treasonous for subjects to rebel against their monarch regardless of the cause. As Molesworth would in the 1690s, Shaftesbury in the 1670s blames 'Churchmen' for trying to hatch a bill that would constrain the liberty of the subject:

> The ecclesiastical establishment 'design to *have the Government of the Church Sworne to as Unalterable*, and so Tacitly owned to be of Divine Right ... Then in requital to the Crown, they declare the Government *Absolute* and *Arbitrary*, and allow Monarchy as well as Episcopacy to be *Jure Divino*, and not to be bounded, or limited by human Laws.[13]

Shaftesbury's opening remarks in this biting tract on arbitrary rule touch on issues that were to the fore regarding the fears and anxieties that many felt about the fate of the political nation. Richard Ashcraft describes the *Letter* as 'the most important tract [in the] propaganda war waged against the government by Shaftesbury and others' for toleration for nonconformists, the maintenance of parliamentary privilege, 'and as a defense against popery, arbitrary power and tyranny'.[14] The maintenance of parliamentary privilege and the ancient constitution enshrined in law, were themes that were to recur time and again between the reign of Charles I and the second Jacobite rebellion.

From the late 1630s through to the regicide of Charles I, there were attempts made to convince the monarch that his position within the constitution was one that should be considered as a partnership with Parliament. The Constitutional Royalists of the 1640s, like Edward Hyde, the future Earl of Clarendon and chief minister under Charles II until he fled the country in 1667, believed firmly that the king was *not* above the law. Many of these men identified as Constitutional Royalists in a recent study spoke against the king in the Short Parliament, where they demanded redress of grievances before they granted supply. They were driven to the king's side in the Civil War because they believed that this was the best way to safeguard the common law against the godly zeal of Presbyterians and sectaries. Constitutional Royalists were committed to Charles I because they considered him to be a viable constitutional monarch.[15] Clearly, such men believed that the king could not rule arbitrarily within the constitution and the common law. When the monarchy was restored, and the euphoria that accompanied the event was replaced by resistance to what were perceived as attempts to place the monarchy on a French footing, the arguments about the king's role within the constitution once more became current.

Shaftesbury's *Letter* emphasises that the citizen has not just an entitlement, but also a responsibility to safeguard his rights from the encroachment of arbitrary rule. The *Letter* consists of a running series of objections to attempts made by the government to prescribe oaths of unquestioning obedience to the crown. Throughout the document Shaftesbury makes it clear that Parliament has ancient privileges that must be respected by the monarchy, and that the kings and queens of England are accountable to the law. The oath that is central to the non-resisting test is systematically taken apart by Shaftesbury in a pamphlet that caused a great public uproar when it was published. The oath demanded that 'I A. B. *do declare that it is not lawful upon any pretence whatsoever, to take up Armes against the King*'. It required unquestioning obedience to the monarchy, begging a question that Shaftesbury immediately dismisses:

> but it is an idle question at best to ask whether Armes in any case can be taken up against a lawful Prince, because it necessarily brings in the debate in every man's mind, how there can be a distinction then left between Absolute and Bounded Monarchies, if *Monarchs* have only the fear of *God*, and no fear of human Resistance to restrain them.[16]

Shaftesbury explicitly refers to the fact that this is simply a disguise to usher in arbitrary government masked by declarations of obedience, as the pamphlet's progression makes clear: '*Arbitrary Government* appeared barefaced', supported by the establishment of a standing army is to be recognised by act of parliament. Such oaths, according to Shaftesbury, do the prince little service in that 'every deviation of the Crown towards Absolute power, lessens the King in the love, and the Affection of his People, making him become less their Interest'.[17]

As Shaftesbury brings the pamphlet to its conclusion he insists that the nobility are the guardians of liberty against the forces of absolutism. English history has proven that whenever the power of the nobility has been diminished tyranny follows shortly afterwards. The weakening of aristocratic power is the precursor of 'Military and Arbitrary government'.[18] In this respect Shaftesbury's text is pivotal in the development of a revised and adapted republican discourse. The text itself appears at a time when dissent against the government was becoming more pronounced, and echoes the constitutional arguments between king and Parliament in the 1640s and 1650s. English republican writers, and those who adapted their works, continually drew upon their heritage and history as well as the history of Greece and Rome to validate their arguments. The 'antiquity of English laws and liberties' was a constant refrain in the works of those writers addressed below. As J.G.A. Pocock has convincingly argued, post-Elizabethan man was imbued with a civic consciousness which was accompanied by a strong sense of historical awareness: 'the claim was being made that the English possessed a historical and immemorial sovereignty over themselves; they were not, and they had never been anything which was not of their own making'.[19]

The fear of standing armies, popery and arbitrary government, the French, the pretensions of the Anglican establishment to interfere in secular politics through their support for providentialism, patriarchy and divine right, are constant themes in the political literature of writers focused upon throughout this volume. How these occur in a wide variety of contexts, and the impact they have on the discourse of sovereignty, forms the subject of the following chapters.

Notes

1   See A.O. Lovejoy, *Essays in the History of Ideas*, Baltimore, Johns Hopkins University Press, 1948, pp. 14-15.

2   For a brief survey of this topic, see chapter 1, 'Hobbes and the Libertines', of Warren Chernaik, *Sexual Freedom in Restoration Literature*, Cambridge: Cambridge University Press, 1995. Chernaik notes a highly selective interpretation of Hobbes on the part of Restoration playwrights, and apologists for libertinism such as Rochester, who chose 'to emphasise certain aspects of his philosophical system and ignore others as it suited them' (p. 24).

3   Stuart Sim and David Walker, *Bunyan and Authority: The Rhetoric of Dissent and the Legitimation Crisis in Seventeenth-Century England*, Bern and New York, Peter Lang, 2000.

4   For analyses of the Restoration 'settlements', see, for example, John Miller, *Restoration England: the Reign of Charles II*, London and New York: Longman, 1985; Ronald Hutton, *The Restoration: A Political and Religious History of England and Wales, 1658-1667*, Oxford, Oxford University Press, 1986; Paul Seaward, *The Cavalier Parliament and the Reconstruction of the Old Regime 1661-1667*, Cambridge, Cambridge University Press, 1989; Tim Harris, Mark Goldie, and Paul Seaward (eds), *The Politics of Religion in Restoration England*, Oxford, Blackwell, 1990; and Jonathan Scott, *Algernon Sidney and the Restoration Crisis, 1677-1683*, Cambridge, Cambridge University Press, 1991.

5   For a discussion of the debate about absolutism from the Treaty of Dover (1670) onwards, see Richard Ashcraft, *Revolutionary Politics and Locke's Two Treatises of Government*, Princeton, NJ, Princeton University Press, 1986, chapter 1.

6   Henry Fielding, *The Jacobite's Journal and Related Writings*, W.B. Coley (ed.), Oxford, Clarendon Press, 1974, p. 424.

7   Scott, drawing on Dr. William King's *Political and Literary Anecdotes of His Own Times* (posthumously published in 1818) refers to this event in his Introduction to *Redgauntlet*, Kathryn Sutherland (ed.), Oxford, Oxford University Press, 1985, pp. 6-8.

8   It should be acknowledged that the nature of the Exclusion crisis is still being debated by historians. Jonathan Scott's revisionist account, for example, questions the validity of the term itself: 'The "exclusion crisis" was not ... about exclusion at all. ... The crisis of 1678-83 was about the rebirth, in the reign of Charles II, of those ugly sisters Popery and Arbitrary Government' (*Algernon Sidney and the Restoration Crisis, 1677-1683*, p. 8). But since the designated successor to the throne, being a Catholic, seemed even more identified with 'those ugly sisters' than his brother Charles II was, the term may not be quite so problematical as Scott is claiming.

9   Bernard Bailyn, *The Ideological Origins of the American Revolution*, Cambridge, MA, Harvard University Press, 1982; Gordon S. Wood, *The Radicalism of the American Revolution*, New York, Vintage, 1993, p. 110. See also Caroline Robbins, *The Eighteenth-Century Commonwealthmen: Studies in the Transmission, Development and Circumstance of English Liberal Thought from the Restoration of Charles II until the War with the Thirteen Colonies*, Cambridge, MA, Harvard University Press, 1959; J.G.A. Pocock, *The Machiavellian Moment: Florentine Political Thought and the Atlantic Republican Tradition*, Princeton, NJ, Princeton University Press, 1975; idem., *Politics, Language and Time: Essays on Political Thought and History*, London, Methuen, 1972, particularly chapter 4, 'Machiavelli, Harrington and English Political Ideologies in the Eighteenth Century'.

10 Pocock, *The Machiavellian Moment*; Blair Worden, 'English Republicanism', in J.H. Burns and Mark Goldie (eds), *The Cambridge History of Political Thought 1450-1700*, Cambridge, Cambridge University Press, 1994, pp. 443-75. The literature on this subject is considerable. The reader is referred to the relevant chapters and references.

11 See the following: Ashcraft, *Revolutionary Politics*; John Miller, *Popery and Politics in England, 1660-1688*, Cambridge, Cambridge University Press, 1973; Richard L. Greaves, *Deliver Us from Evil: The Radical Underground in Britain, 1660-1663*, Oxford, Oxford University Press, 1986; idem., *Enemies Under his Feet: Radicals and Nonconformists in Britain, 1664-1677*, Stanford, CA, Stanford University Press, 1990; idem., *Secrets of the Kingdom: British Radicals from the Popish Plot to the Revolution*

of 1688-89, Stanford, CA, Stanford University Press, 1992; Jonathan Scott, *England's Troubles: Seventeenth-Century English Political Instability in European Context*, Cambridge, Cambridge University Press, 2000; N.H. Keeble, *The Literary Culture of Nonconformity in Later Seventeenth-Century England*, Leicester, Leicester University Press, 1987.

12   Christopher Hill, *The Experience of Defeat: Milton and Some Contemporaries*, London, Faber, 1984.

13   Anthony Ashley Cooper, Earl of Shaftesbury, *A Letter From a Person of Quality, To His Friend in the Country*, in Joyce Lee Malcolm (ed.), *The Struggle for Sovereignty: Seventeenth-Century English Political Tracts*, Indianapolis, IN, Liberty Fund, 1999, I-II, vol. II, pp. 603-49 (p. 607).

14   Ashcraft, *Revolutionary Politics*, pp. 117, 120.

15   David L. Smith, *Constitutional Royalism and the Search for Settlement, 1640-1649*, Cambridge, Cambridge University Press, 1994, pp. 63-5, 79.

16   *A Letter*, p. 626.

17   *Ibid.*, pp. 629, 642.

18   *Ibid.*, p. 646.

19   Pocock, *The Machiavellian Moment*, p. 341.

PART I

REVOLUTION TO REPUBLIC

Chapter 1

Hobbes:
Absolutism and the State of Nature

'And the life of man, solitary, poore, nasty, brutish, and short'.[1] Hobbes' famous words in *Leviathan* about the condition of mankind in the state of nature reverberate down the centuries, communicating as they do a keen sense of the fragility of the social bond that separates us from that desperate condition. There was every reason to draw attention to that fragility in a time of civil war, when the breakdown in central authority in England left individuals uncertain as to where political legitimacy lay, and conflicting political narratives competed aggressively for their attention. Hobbes' drastic prescriptions to resolve the 'disorders of the present times' are well known: absolute sovereignty, preferably in the person of a monarch, who could not be divided against himself, and absolute obedience on the part of the state's subjects, who could not question the sovereign's actions (or would be severely punished if ever they dared to do so). The sovereign's remit even extended over the practice of religion, with obedience to his will being demanded in this area no less than in the political: an aspect of Hobbes' thought which helped to fuel the charges of atheism brought against him soon after the publication of *Leviathan* in 1651. In this instance the state of nature really did dictate the nature of the state, with absolutism being presented as a remedy to the all-too-human tendency to regress to a pre-social condition of the 'warre of every man against every man'.[2] The Hobbesian nation state is designed to deal with perceived defects in human psychology rather than proceeding from any idealistic motives: 'expediency, not morality', as Christopher Hill has noted, constituting its real basis.[3] One might say that the writing of *Leviathan* is first and foremost a damage limitation exercise on behalf of an inherently flawed mankind, and Hobbes is deeply pessimistic as to what happens when we leave individuals to their own devices.

Not everyone was as pessimistic about either human nature or the mid-century political situation as was Hobbes. Millenarians, of whom there were no shortage in this turbulent period, saw the collapse of the existing social order as a prelude to the second coming, where fallen human nature, would finally be redeemed.

For Levellers and Diggers, the same event held out the possibility of a new social order with expanded powers for the individual vis-à-vis institutional authority. In the case of the Ranters, these powers were to be more or less unlimited and subject to no official curb. Abiezer Coppe's writings give us some notion of what to expect in this latter regard, with their threats to '*overturn, overturn, overturn*' all established authority in a ruthless levelling exercise.[4] Hobbes' ideas about human nature struck a chord nevertheless, and continued to influence thought well into the eighteenth century (in some respects right through to the present day), even if later seventeenth-century monarchists were more likely to draw on Sir Robert Filmer's theories for inspiration than those of Hobbes – a topic we shall explore in more detail in chapter 5. Henry Fielding's jaundiced vision of human nature, as well as his prescriptions as to what to do about it to make social life tolerable, owe at least something to Hobbes and the notion of the appetite-driven, essentially self-seeking individual (aversion being the other defining trait to note of this figure). It is also worth pointing out that some commentators see more of Hobbes' ideas in the practice of the Restoration regime than that regime is prepared to admit openly. This is despite the later popularity of Filmer in monarchical circles in the 1680s, and the fact that Charles II refused permission for Hobbes' late work *Behemoth* (a diatribe against the Long Parliament) to be published for fear it would stir up yet more unwelcome controversy. Catherine Gimelli Martin, for example, has argued that, under the Restoration regime, 'the Anglican clergy adopted an essentially Hobbesian position' when it came to the relation of church and state.[5] Samuel I. Mintz has noted the impact of Hobbes' ideas on the 'libertines' of the Restoration period, although he also maintains that such figures generally misinterpreted what their supposed mentor was saying, in order, as Hobbes' contemporary critic John Eachard put it, to 'furnish themselves with some of your little *slender Philosophical pretences* to be wicked'.[6] Mintz may conclude that 'Hobbes' influence on his countrymen during his own lifetime and for almost a century after was negative', but that influence can be detected none the less.[7]

But Hobbes is doing more than commenting on the particular political situation of his time, he is putting forward a theory of human nature which has implications for our entire social system. The Hobbesian individual has a natural disposition towards anti-social behaviour that must be checked for the public good: as Hobbes put it as early as 1642 in *De Cive*, we are motivated, 'either for Gain, or for Glory; (i.e.) not so much for love of our Fellowes, as for the love of our Selves'.[8] Authoritarianism, far from being the evil that someone like Winstanley or Coppe pictures it to be, holds the key to our collective salvation in the Hobbesian scheme of things, therefore, in the limits that it imposes on what we might be moved to do 'for the love of our Selves'.

Hobbes' model of human nature precludes him from seeing anything worth preserving from the pre-social state. Without curbs on his behaviour, the individual in the state of nature, no matter what his powers, is condemned to a life that is 'solitary, poore, nasty, brutish, and short'. The individual is pictured as dominated by his appetites (Hobbes is often accused of being a determinist in this respect), a state of affairs that inevitably leads to conflict over resources with the rest of his fellows: a process later to be dubbed 'possessive individualism' by the political philosopher C.B. Macpherson, for whom it is a characteristic of a free-market society of the kind that England was already turning into in Hobbes' day.[9] Although short-term gains might be made by the more powerful individuals, no-one is ever powerful enough to protect themselves, and the resources they have gained in conflict with others, indefinitely. Looked at in the mass we are not so dissimilar from each other:

> Nature hath made men so equall, in the faculties of body, and mind; as that though there bee found one man sometimes manifestly stronger in body, or of quicker mind then another; yet when all is reckoned together, the difference between man, and man, is not so considerable, as that one man can thereupon claim to himselfe any benefit, to which another may not pretend, as well as he. For as to the strength of body, the weakest has strength enough to kill the strongest, either by secret machination, or by confederacy with others, that are in the same danger with himselfe.[10]

The message is that none of us can ever consider ourselves safe as long as this natural condition prevails: absolutism rescues us from the anarchy of personal sovereignty.

Civil society, as Hobbes observes in his earlier statement of his political philosophy, *De Cive* , has its origin in 'the mutuall fear [men] had of each other'.[11] Even *in* civil society we continue to fear each other's natural drives; hence, as Hobbes notes, we arm ourselves on journeys and lock our doors at night. Our fellow human beings are never completely to be trusted, and will revert to pre-social type given the slightest opportunity to do so: as *De Cive* pithily summarises the situation, '*except they be restrained through feare of some coercive power, every man will distrust and dread each other*'.[12] Hobbes argues that we cannot help ourselves from following these drives: 'The Desires, and other Passions of man, are in themselves no Sin. No more are the Actions, that proceed from those Passions, till they know a Law that forbids them'.[13] Again, one can see how the charge of atheism would come about, given such a morally-neutral view of human action. To his contemporaries it must have seemed as if Hobbes was turning a blind eye to the fall. We are to be restrained for our own good, therefore, and only an absolute sovereign has the power to ensure that such restraint can be enforced and the experience of distrust and dread at least minimised. Although it is intriguing to note that this political absolutism, as Mintz has pointed out, puts into doubt the existence of 'such absolutes as divine providence, good and evil, and an immortal soul'.[14]

We move out of the state of nature by making a contract to transfer our natural rights (to survive, to protect ourselves, etc.) to a central sovereign authority. Such a transfer, initiating what has been called 'alienation social contract theory', is considered by Hobbes to be unconditionally binding: 'In Contracts, the right passeth, not onely where the words are of the time Present, or Past; but also where they are of the Future'.[15] Once that sovereign authority is in place we have no right to contest its wishes, since it is presumed to represent the will of us all:

> as if every man should say to every man, *I Authorise and give up my Right of Governing my selfe, to this Man, or to this Assembly of men, on this condition, that thou give up thy Right to him, and Authorise all his Actions in like manner*. This done, the Multitude so united in one Person, is called a COMMON-WEALTH, in latine CIVITAS. This is the Generation of that great LEVIATHAN.[16]

While Hobbes does allow the possibility of an Assembly (such as Parliament) wielding sovereign power, he is temperamentally drawn to the monarchical concept as the best method of achieving his objectives. Power is for Hobbes indivisible, and a monarch is proof against any slippage in this respect, since 'in Monarchy, the private interest is the same with the publique'.[17] Assemblies, on the other hand, are only too likely to break up into warring factions, and factions problematise succession, putting the commonwealth's very future at risk. It might be objected that indivisibility raises the spectre of the arbitrary exercise of power, but Hobbes sees this as a negligible threat compared to those attendant on the absence of a strong central power. Where absolute sovereignty is wanting, civil discord will follow, and from Hobbes' perspective no-one gains from that state of affairs.

Sidney and Locke will later reach the opposite view about sovereign power, arguing that its *divisibility* will better ensure the survival of the commonwealth. The executive, legislative, and judicial functions of government are separated out in the theories of these thinkers, a formula subsequently adopted in the American political constitution. Such a system of checks and balances is precisely what Hobbes is striving to avoid, however, and the abuse of power it is designed to prevent is for him hardly an issue at all. If one starts from Hobbesian premises about human nature, checks and balances can only be regarded as destabilising influences on the proper exercise of sovereign authority within the commonwealth.

Hobbes can see no alternative to absolute sovereignty but a 'perpetuall warre of every man against his neighbour', and on those grounds he is willing to countenance what to us are severe limitations on individual liberty.[18] In fact, individual liberty in the Hobbesian commonwealth is reduced to whatever the sovereign sees fit to grant: 'The Liberty of a Subject, lyeth therefore only in those things, which in regulating their actions, the Sovereign hath praetermitted'. Furthermore, the sovereign retains the right of life or death over his subjects: 'nothing the Soveraign Representative can doe to a Subject, on what pretence soever, can properly be called Injustice, or Injury; because every Subject is Author of every act the Soveraign doth'.[19] Dissent becomes a logical impossibility under such a dispensation: a case of contradicting one's own contractual decisions. Impeccable though the logic may be, the implications for individual freedom of action are more than somewhat alarming – especially in a period when conscience, on religious matters particularly, was becoming such an important factor in social and political life; but Hobbes' fear of civil discord transcends all such considerations: 'To resist the Sword of the Common-wealth, in defence of another mañ, guilty, or innocent, no man hath Liberty; because such Liberty, takes away from the Soveraign, the means of Protecting us'.[20] Once that power to protect fails, however, the individual is returned to a state of nature, and regains the liberty to protect himself as circumstances dictate.

Anything that reduces sovereign power in any way tends, in Hobbes' reading of the political process, to undermine the commonwealth, and he is adamant that power must never be distributed across various individuals or institutions within the state. Separation of power equates to weakness in Hobbes' model of government. It is the sovereign's duty to ensure that such division never occurs, and he would be going against that duty if he were to transfer any of the rights he holds on behalf of the nation at large to any others. The minute that sovereign power is divided we are at risk of sliding back to 'the greatest evill that can happen in this life' – the state of nature.[21] All of Hobbes' efforts as a political theorist are directed towards the prevention of that evil, and he can see no alternative to the absolutist prescriptions that he makes. For all that he talks up the role of reason in human affairs, Hobbes seems to view the bulk of mankind as largely irrational in its political behaviour, unable to see where its own best interests lie and only too easily seduced by the evils of the state of nature. Given that humankind *is* so easily seduced, the sovereign state has to be backed up by force: 'Covenants, without the Sword, are but Words',[22] No amount of social conditioning, it would seem, can overcome our natural inclinations without some threat of punishment: human nature must be endlessly, and very strictly, policed.

Despite our natural disposition towards self-serving behaviour we can recognise the need for checks on it, and Hobbes outlines various 'laws of nature' by which we come to appreciate the virtues of peace as opposed to war; these taking the form of,

> a Precept, or generall Rule, found out by Reason, by which a man is forbidden to do, that, which is destructive of his life, or taketh away the means of preserving the same; and to omit, that, by which he thinketh it may be best preserved.[23]

Given that the state of nature is a state of permanent insecurity, it is undeniably rational to wish for an end to this, since peace obviously will preserve our persons better than a condition of open conflict (although Bruno Latour looks less kindly on the social contract as the abruptly-conceived collective act of 'terrorized citizens'[24]). It becomes a 'Fundamental Law' of nature, therefore, '*to seek Peace, and follow it*'; from which follows a further law that we ought to be content to accept the restrictions this imposes on our natural rights if our fellow human beings accept them also.[25] The collective desire for peace involves a general surrender of personal rights to the absolute sovereign, and Hobbes' severely logical bias enables him to argue that it would be to enter into 'absurdity' for anyone ever to reclaim those rights, or 'voluntarily to undo that, which from the beginning he had voluntarily done'.[26] 'Ought' is derived from 'is', on the basis of the law of non-contradiction, although that does seem to underestimate our ability to encompass paradox and contradiction within our individual personalities.

Hobbes can easily become a hate figure for defenders of liberal democracy, in that his totalitarianism can seem the antithesis of virtually everything that they stand for; in C.B. Macpherson's pithy summary, 'His postulates about the nature of man are unflattering, his political conclusions are illiberal, and his logic appears to deny us any way out'.[27] Yet Hobbes can also be claimed as a moderniser in his secularisation of the political process. It has even been argued that the 'stringent separation of religious from political thought' that we find in Hobbes' political philosophy paves the way for 'modern constitutional democracy'.[28] Christopher Hill speaks approvingly of Hobbes' ability to 'cut right through the religious smoke screen' of much seventeenth-century political thought in this regard.[29] With his demystification of political power and self-consciously pragmatic approach to the practice of government, Hobbes can seem closer to us than most of his religiously-oriented contemporaries with their need to justify their political beliefs with constant reference to scripture.[30] Filmer's work, for example, with its lines of monarchical succession traced back to Adam and the account of his creation in *Genesis*, seems hopelessly dated now ('quaintly absurd' to one commentator[31]), whereas Hobbes is still saying highly pertinent, if often also highly uncomfortable, things about human nature and the attractions of power. Even when Hobbes does delve into scripture for reinforcement, he does so in a clinical manner at variance with the literalism of a Filmer, informing us that 'we are not to renounce our Senses, and Experience; nor (that which is the undoubted Word of God) our naturall Reason', when engaging in scriptural exegesis.[32]

More than somewhat against the grain of the time, religion has only a subsidiary role to play in Hobbes' discourse of sovereignty, and for many of his contemporaries this was enough to justify his description as an atheist. Bishop Bramhall, for example, unequivocally asserted, 'That no man who is thoroughly an Hobbist can be a good Christian'.[33] Hobbes is highly critical of the Christian Church, claiming that it has contributed in no small measure to the political divisions that have scarred human history:

> Whence comes it, that in Christendome there has been, almost from the time of the Apostles, such justling of one another out of their places, both by forraign, and Civill war? such stumbling at every little asperity of their own fortune, and every little eminence of that of other men? ... wee are therefore yet in the Dark.[34]

Hobbes devotes parts 3 and 4 of *Leviathan*, 'Of a Christian Common-Wealth' and 'Of the Kingdome of Darknesse', to a demolition of the Church's claim to have any significant role to play, as God's representative on earth, in the discourse of political sovereignty. He is adamant that any pact made between God and his chosen people, the Jews, has long since lapsed, and that it is an error to assume 'that the present Church is Christs Kingdome'. Such a belief is dismissed as an 'abuse of Scripture', which has given rise to a host of socio-political problems that can still be seen to plague Hobbes' world.[35] Certainly, the religious extremists of the 1640s and

1650s were very prone to make just such claims, and to interpret 'Christs Kingdome' in a very narrow sense that could only lead to further social division. Exclusionary tactics are the norm in such debates, and the notion of the 'gathered church' favoured by so many of the sects hardly promotes a sense of national unity. This is not, however, a theological problem *per se* for Hobbes, but a political one, requiring a political solution. Only an absolute sovereign can prevent the decline into anarchy that such scriptural disputes inevitably generate. 'True religion', as he points out in his *Treatise of Liberty and Necessity*, 'consists in obedience to Christ's lieutenants', and Hobbes makes it clear that kings are the foremost of 'Christ's lieutenants'.[36] As Bruno Latour has succinctly summarised it, 'Hobbes wanted to wipe the slate clean of all appeals to entities higher than civil authority. He wanted to rediscover Catholic unity while at the same time closing off any access to divine transcendence'.[37]

Hobbes makes it clear that sovereigns have the last word in the matter of scriptural interpretation, by linking scriptural authority to law. We are not to ask *'From whence the Scriptures derive their Authority'*, therefore, but rather *'By what Authority they are made Law'*.[38] The shift of emphasis is highly significant, since law is the province of the sovereign, not the church, enabling Hobbes to dispense with all possibility of theological dispute of the kind that, in his opinion, had helped to tear mid-seventeenth century England apart:

> So that the question of the Authority of the Scriptures, is reduced to this, *Whether Christian Kings, and the Soveraigne Assemblies in Christian Common-wealths, be absolute in their own Territories, immediately under God; or subject to one Vicar of Christ, constituted over the Universall Church; to bee judged, condemned, deposed, and put to death, as hee shall think expedient, or necessary for the common good.*

At a stroke, the church is removed from the political equation: as usual in Hobbes, power is not to be divided in any way. He goes on to insist that 'whosoever hath a lawfull power over any Writing, to make it Law, hath the power also to approve, or disapprove the interpretation of the same': and since that power belongs to the sovereign, and to the sovereign alone, theology is unceremoniously subordinated to the sovereign will.[39] Scriptural disputation is turned into a political, rather than a religious issue, and at that point it can be dealt with swiftly, and, in the Hobbesian scheme, quite ruthlessly too. Once again the logic is impeccable, but it does underestimate the emotional investment most people of the time had in religion – an investment that went well past the narrow confines of philosophical logic.

Behemoth, Hobbes' later meditation on the 'disorders' of the 1640s and 50s (1668, although not published until 1679), continues the attack on religious sectarianism, condemning the situation that arose where 'every man became a judge of religion, and an interpreter of the Scriptures to himself'.[40] Sectarianism is presented as an enemy within, that is instrumental in eroding the authority of the rightful sovereign and plunging the nation into political chaos. To have observed England in the period 1640-60, Hobbes maintains, is to 'have had a prospect of all kinds of injustice, and of all kinds of folly, that the world could afford, and how they were produced by their dams hypocrisy and self-conceit, whereof the one is double iniquity, and the other double folly'.[41] Soon a Presbyterian-leaning Parliament is openly contesting sovereignty with Charles I, and, in Hobbes' reading of events, the slide to disaster is well under way. Again he is adamant that there can be no sharing of power. There is an 'ethics of subjects' and an 'ethics of sovereigns', and '[t]he virtue of a subject is comprehended wholly on obedience to the laws of the commonwealth'.[42] The notion that parliament can aspire higher than this obedience is treated with disdain by 'A', the leading light in Hobbes' dialogue. The other protagonist, 'B', is reduced to exasperation by sectarian squabbling: 'What needs so much preaching of faith to us that are no heathens, and that believe already all that Christ and his apostles have told us is necessary to salvation, and more too? Why is there so little preaching of justice?'.[43] The answer is that, in Presbyterian hands, such preaching is being used as a cover for sedition, and the case for absolute sovereignty is merely strengthened for Hobbes by such plain evidence of human malice.

Behemoth treats at length of the struggle between the monarchy and Parliament, finding in it a classic case of the dangers inherent in the doctrine of the separation of powers. For Hobbes, it is a struggle for supremacy that admits of no compromise between the respective parties, and the parliamentary side is pictured as being entirely in the wrong. When Parliament claims to be the guardian of 'the fundamental laws and government of the realm', it is chastised for its presumption by 'B':

> What are those laws that are called fundamental? For I understand not how one law can be more fundamental than another, except only that law of nature that binds us all to obey him, whosoever he be, whom lawfully and for our own safety, we have promised to obey; nor any other fundamental law to a King, but *salus populi*, the safety and well-being of his people.[44]

The notion of failure at the level of the monarch cannot be countenanced by Hobbes, for whom that individual, by virtue of the covenant that establishes civil society, must be considered to incorporate all the desires of his subjects and thus to stand beyond judgement by them. Under no circumstances can a body like Parliament ever have the right to challenge the conduct of the sovereign: if they do, the best that can be said of the accusations they make is that they are 'pretended faults'.[45] It is not a question of weighing up the rights and wrongs of the situation in the early 1640s – Parliament can *never* be in the right. The verdict of 'A' and 'B' can only be that the Long Parliament was guilty of sedition, and of the desire to turn England into an oligarchy ruled by its members. Monarchy has no case to answer – then or ever.

The state of nature is an abstract concept, 'a logical not an historical hypothesis' as Macpherson has put it, and it cannot be proved that mankind ever existed in such a condition, let alone covenanted itself out of it as Hobbes is suggesting.[46] Even Hobbes himself concedes this point: 'It may peradventure be thought, there was never such a time, nor condition of warre as this; and I believe it was never generally so'.[47] Michael Oakeshott encourages us to appreciate the creative side of Hobbes' endeavour, emphasising that *Leviathan* 'is a myth, the transposition of an abstract argument into the world of the imagination'.[48] Yet such theoretical abstraction cannot mask the most disturbing implication of Hobbes' concept, and that is that each of us carries the state of nature *within us*; that it describes our inner psychology. Left to our own devices we would most likely act *as if* we were in a state of nature, competing aggressively for resources and exploiting others as much as we could along the way: this 'kingdom within' promotes social turmoil rather than personal equilibrium. No matter how absolute sovereignty may be, therefore, the state of nature remains a latent threat to our society, since the competitive drive is encoded so deeply within all of us – as well as the distrust and fear of others that accompanies it. Macpherson's possessive individualism proceeds from just such a realisation, although here the suggestion is that Hobbes' vision is based on the character traits required for success in the developing market economy of the time: 'Hobbes' explicit postulates (notably, that labour is a commodity, that some men want to increase their level of delight, and that some have more natural power than others) are essentially those of a possessive market society'.[49] Hobbes, we might say, is reading off the state of nature from the condition of early capitalism, and for commentators like Macpherson that makes him less of an abstract theoretician and more our contemporary.

To resort to postmodernist thought, there is a cultural differend declaring itself at this point. We have two phrase regimes which cannot accommodate each other's imperatives, and Hobbes' objective, as so often is the case in such clashes, is to suppress the other phrase regime by imposing his own legitimation procedures on it, insisting, as he does in *Behemoth*, for example, that monarchy is never under any obligation to justify its conduct. Thus the state of nature, and everything that it stands for in terms of human behaviour, is to be eclipsed by the greater power of the absolutist state. If we do carry the state of nature within us as individuals, however, this can never be more than a temporary victory – and a perpetually uneasy one as far as the absolutists are concerned. As the civil war demonstrated, the state of nature can reassert itself with very little warning, and the absolutists can never assume the wholehearted support of those under their rule – for all the coercive power they can bring to bear on the nation's subjects. Beneath apparent social harmony lurks the ever-present threat of anarchy.

Part of the problem is that Hobbes is extremely reductive about what the opposing phrase regime involves. For him, it is a political issue only, and in the restricted sense that the 'personal is political' he is right; but Hobbes refuses to acknowledge just how complex the personal is, and how resistant it can be to macro-political resolution – essentially what he is offering us in *Leviathan*'s prescriptions. Hobbes banishes everything he dislikes about the individualism of his time to the state of nature, which enables him to offer a seductively simple solution to the threat it poses to national unity; but political absolutism cannot eradicate, as a case in point, conflict over religious sovereignty at the level of the individual. Political absolutism falters when confronted by the phenomenon of conscience – if anything, as the case of someone like John Bunyan would seem to suggest, political absolutism merely stiffens the resolve of conscience. Excision from the formal political process is not enough to silence a dissident phrase regime; especially one as complex as individual conscience proved to be in this period. Bunyan, for example, will spend twelve years in prison over what is essentially a matter of conscience (whether or not he can bring himself to give up lay preaching, as commanded by the state's representatives in the Bedford judiciary). Hobbes may subordinate religious matters to political ones, but for religious enthusiasts of the mid- to late seventeenth century, this was completely unacceptable – unless toleration could be arranged on terms suitable to them (as, ultimately, it was in the aftermath of the 'Glorious Revolution', if on the most basic of levels). The sincerity of religious belief, as well as the depth of commitment it could inspire in the individual, effectively escapes Hobbes, who can only see the political implications and never the personal; the macro-perspective but not the micro. Emotional needs are rationalised away by this remorselessly logical thinker, but in his failure to provide for these needs lies the essential weakness of his response to the 'disorders of the present times'. The personal cannot simply be banished by the operations of logic – and nor can the spiritual. For a significant section of the population of Hobbes' England, disorder is actually preferable to an order where they forfeit the right to act according to the dictates of their conscience – especially in matters of religion.

The Hobbesian state of nature, therefore, contains not just the drive towards survival, but the drive towards market-economy competitiveness, the drive towards freedom of religious expression, the drive towards the cultural institutionalisation of conscience – in summary, the drive towards personal autonomy that we now recognise as an integral part of our cultural ethos. Autonomy is the real enemy that Hobbes is fighting, and it is a much more slippery enemy than he supposes; one less easily brought into line by ideological authoritarianism than his prescriptions would imply, more resourceful and more resilient. The sheer clarity of Hobbes' thought fails to capture the complexity, indeed, the messiness, of the personal, where contradictions can be encompassed and paradoxes tolerated without causing system breakdown – as Hobbes' logical training insists must occur in such cases.[50] Far from providing a resolution for the disorders of the period, Hobbes' prescriptions merely serve to mark the persistence of the differend entrenched within English culture.

Hobbes' was not the only solution put forward to the 'disorders of the present times' of course, and the spectrum of response ranged from absolute monarchy at the one end through to unrepentant republicanism and primitive agrarian communism at the other. We shall go on to consider some key points on this spectrum in the chapters that follow.

Notes

1   Thomas Hobbes, *Leviathan, Or, The Matter, Forme, and Power of a Common-wealth Ecclesiasticall and Civill,* Richard Tuck (ed.), Cambridge, Cambridge University Press, 1991, p. 89.
2   *Ibid.,* p. 90.
3   Christopher Hill, *Puritanism and Revolution: Studies in Interpretation of the English Revolution of the Seventeenth Century,* London, Secker and Warburg, 1958, p. 277.
4   Abiezer Coppe, *A Fiery Flying Roll,* in *Selected Writings,* Andrew Hopton (ed.), London, Aporia Press, 1987, p. 21.
5   Catherine Gimelli Martin, 'The Phoenix and the Crocodile: Milton's Natural Law Debate with Hobbes Retried in the Tragic Forum of *Samson Agonistes*', in Claude J. Summers and Ted-Larry Pebworth (eds), *The English Civil Wars in the Literary Imagination,* Columbia, MO and London, University of Missouri Press, 1999, pp. 242-70 (p. 253). Samuel Parker's *Discourse of Ecclesiastical Polity* (1669) is a notable

defence of the principle of absolute monarchical sovereignty from within Anglicanism in this period (for a discussion of the impact of Parker's work, see Ashcraft, *Revolutionary Politics*, chapter 2).

6   See Samuel I. Mintz, *The Hunting of Leviathan*, Cambridge, Cambridge University Press, 1962, chapter 7; John Eachard, *Mr Hobbs's State of Nature Considered*, London, 1672, p. 9. Hobbes' effect on Restoration libertinism is also covered in chapter 1 of Chernaik, *Sexual Freedom in Restoration Literature*.

7   Mintz, *The Hunting of Leviathan*, p. 147. For an argument claiming a more positive impact for Hobbes' thought, see G.A.J. Rogers, 'Hobbes's Hidden Influence', in G.A.J. Rogers and Alan Ryan (eds), *Perspectives on Thomas Hobbes*, Oxford, Clarendon Press, 1988, pp. 189-205.

8   Thomas Hobbes, *De Cive: Philosophicall Rudiments Concerning Government and Society*, Howard Warrender (ed.), Oxford, Clarendon Press, 1983, p. 43.

9   See C.B. Macpherson, *The Political Theory of Possessive Individualism: Hobbes to Locke*, Oxford, Oxford University Press, 1962. For an argument playing down the economic aspect of that individualism, see Alan Ryan, 'Hobbes's Individualism', in Rogers and Ryan, *Perspectives on Thomas Hobbes*, pp. 81-105.

10   *Leviathan*, pp. 86-7.

11   *De Cive*, p. 44.

12   *Ibid.*, p. 32.

13   *Leviathan*, p. 89.

14   Mintz, *The Hunting of Leviathan*, p. 23.

15   David Gauthier, 'Hobbes's Social Contract', in Rogers and Ryan, *Perspectives on Thomas Hobbes*, pp. 125-52 (p. 126); *Leviathan*, p. 95.

16   *Ibid.*, p. 120.

17   *Ibid.*, p. 131.

18   *Ibid.*, p. 145.

19   *Ibid.*, p. 148.

20   *Ibid.*, p. 152.

21   *Ibid.*, p. 231.

22   *Ibid.*, p. 117.

23   *Ibid.*, p. 91.

24   Bruno Latour, *We Have Never Been Modern*, Catherine Porter (trans.), Hemel Hempstead, Harvester Wheatsheaf, 1993, p. 19.

25   *Leviathan*, p. 92.

26   *Ibid.*, p. 93.

27   Macpherson, *Possessive Individualism*, p. 9.

28   Martin, 'The Phoenix and the Crocodile', p. 247. See also Latour, *We Have Never Been Modern*, chapter 2, and Hill, *Puritanism and Revolution*, chapter 9.

29   *Ibid.*, p. 277.

30   For an argument relating Hobbes' thought to pragmatic currents in his own time, see Quentin Skinner, 'Conquest and Consent: Thomas Hobbes and the Engagement Controversy', in G.E. Aylmer (ed.), *The Interregnum: The Quest for Settlement 1646-1660*, London and Basingstoke, Macmillan, 1972, pp. 79-98. Skinner draws parallels between *Leviathan's* prescriptions and those of the 'Engagers', whose line was that 'it was not unlawful to obey such an unlawful power' as the Commonwealth government could appear to be to traditionalists (p. 83). Richard Tuck, on the other hand, argues that Hobbes' thought is closer to that of John Selden and his followers (such as the

Tew Circle) than the Engagers (see *Natural Rights Theories: Their Origin and Development*, Cambridge: Cambridge University Press, 1979).

31   Alan Craig Houston, *Algernon Sidney and the Republican Heritage in England and America*, Princeton, NJ, Princeton University Press, 1991, p. 68.

32   *Leviathan*, p. 255.

33   Quoted in Mintz, *The Hunting of Leviathan*, p. 55. For a survey of the contemporary response to Hobbes, and the many accusations of atheism made against him, see *Ibid.*, chapter 3. The vexed question of the relationship between Hobbes' philosophical and theological beliefs is further analysed in Arrigo Pacchi, 'Hobbes and the Problem of God', in Rogers and Ryan, *Perspectives on Thomas Hobbes*, pp. 171-87.

34   *Leviathan*, p. 418.

35   *Ibid.*, p. 419.

36   Thomas Hobbes, *Treatise of Liberty and Necessity*, in Vere Chappell (ed.), *Hobbes and Bramhall on Liberty and Necessity*, Cambridge, Cambridge University Press, 1999, pp. 15-42 (p. 42).

37   Latour, *We Have Never Been Modern*, p. 19.

38   *Leviathan*, p. 267.

39   *Ibid.*, p. 269.

40   Thomas Hobbes, *Behemoth, or The Long Parliament*, Ferdinand Tonnies (ed.), London, Frank Cass, 1969, p. 22.

41   *Ibid.*, p. 1.

42   *Ibid.*, p. 44.

43   *Ibid.*, p. 63.

44   *Ibid.*, pp. 67-8.

45   *Ibid.*, p. 83.

46   Macpherson, *Possessive Individualism*, p. 20.

47   *Leviathan*, p. 89.

48   Michael Oakeshott, Introduction to Hobbes, *Leviathan, Or, The Matter, Forme, and Power of a Commonwealth Ecclesiastical and Civil*, Michael Oakeshott (ed.), Oxford, Blackwell, 1946, p. xviii.

49   Macpherson, *Possessive Individualism*, p. 68.

50   For a reading emphasising paradox and contradiction in Hobbes' thought, however, see François Tricaud, 'Hobbes's Conception of the State of Nature from 1640 to 1651: Evolution and Ambiguities', in Rogers and Ryan, *Perspectives on Thomas Hobbes*, pp. 107-23.

Chapter 2

Harrington: *Oceana* and the State of Nature

James Harrington's *Oceana* provides us with an alternative rendering of man in a state of nature than that offered by Hobbes and Milton. Harrington was the most historical of political thinkers writing in the mid-seventeenth century. Whereas Hobbes, as we shall see, gave as one reason the excessive preoccupation with classical history and literature for the current lamentable state of affairs in the 1640s and 1650s, Harrington's thought was deeply obliged not only to classical historiography and political theory, but also its sixteenth-century application by continental republican historians and political thinkers. The most notable of these is Machiavelli, whose analysis of past and present political behaviour in the *Discourses* and *The Prince* exercised a profound influence on Harrington's works. *Oceana* is a utopian text, and although all such writings are to a greater or lesser extent indebted to Plato's *Republic*, above all Harrington's republicanism is indebted to Machiavelli: 'In *The Commonwealth of Oceana* [Harrington] found means of depicting England as a classical republic and the Englishman as a classical citizen'. Reacting to an 'historic constitution' that had collapsed, 'Harrington's classical republicanism' was one of many attempts in the 1650s designed 'to formulate various moral, political and theoretical problems' faced for the first time in England.[1] On the other hand Jonathan Scott has argued that the affinity between Harrington and Machiavelli has been overstated. On every major issue that concerns the organisation of the commonwealth along republican principles, Harrington is in contradiction with Machiavelli and in closer accord with Hobbes than previous commentators have been willing to allow. The argument of the 'Preliminaries' is not based upon irreconcilable differences between the two; rather, it is 'the rivalry of siblings'. The root of this difference is that 'Harrington thought the ancients had perceived the principles of nature, Hobbes did not'. *Oceana*, by this reckoning, demonstrates that 'ancient prudence is conformable with Hobbes' metaphysics'.[2] Scott's analysis is powerfully argued, yet does not render a convincing account of the basic points of disagreement that Harrington has with Hobbes on the nature of fear and the law.

Oceana is the most sophisticated republican treatise to be written in the 1650s; arguably it is the most sophisticated republican treatise to be written by an Englishman in the early modern period. Unlike many utopian texts written in the sixteenth and seventeenth centuries, *Oceana* has sometimes been perceived as standing outside the tradition of early modern utopian writing. This, says J.C. Davis, is because Harrington's republicanism has been seen to obstruct the generic constituents of utopian literature, especially as they relate to political behaviour. There can be little doubt that Harrington was committed to participatory politics achieved through a reconciliation of classical republicanism with that practised by modern adherents in sixteenth-century Italian states. The problem was one of assimilating this into the contemporary situation. How does one reconcile a political theory based on a polity that is overwhelmingly urban and mercantile, with one that is rural and agrarian? Especially a rural society in which 'political institutions, practices and traditions had collapsed in the aftermath of a bewildering civil war and an abortive revolution'. In truth, as Davis goes on to suggest, the rules of participation in political life are discernibly different in utopian and classical republican writing. The former appears to be deterministic and lacking in opportunity to exercise civic virtue, whilst the latter continually emphasises choice and the presence of laws that guarantee the freedom of the subject, which in turn give the individual the opportunity to contribute to public life.[3] On the other hand, and again to quote Scott, Harrington has been accused of restricting access to the political process: 'The truth is that we see in Harrington's *Oceana*, no less than in Hobbes' *Leviathan*, the abolition of the participatory basis of classical citizenship'.[4]

In *The Art of Lawgiving* (1659), Harrington states that 'The ways of nature require peace. The ways of peace require obedience unto laws'.[5] The question of the law and its relationship to the state of nature in Harrington's political writings is important, indeed crucial. In much of 'The Preliminaries showing the Principles of Government' that precedes the text of *Oceana*, Harrington is concerned with refuting the argument of Hobbes' *Leviathan*, particularly as it relates to the law and the laying of methodological foundations:

> Government (to define it *de jure* or according to ancient prudence) is an art whereby a civil society is instituted and preserved upon the foundation of common right or interest, or (to follow Aristotle and Livy) it is the empire of laws and not of men. And government (to define *de facto* or according unto modern prudence) is an art whereby some man, or some few men, subject a city or a nation, and rule it according to his or their private interest; which,

because the laws in such cases are made according to the interests of a man or some few families, may said to be the empire of men and not of laws.[6]

From here Harrington distinguishes between conflicting political doctrines with reference to two modern thinkers. Government according to laws is best understood through a reading of Machiavelli, 'whose books are neglected'; government according to the fear of men and not of laws, Harrington ascribes to Hobbes, whom he quotes in relation to Aristotle. According to Hobbes Aristotle is wrong to suggest that 'in a well ordered Commonwealth not Men should govern, but the Laws'. Men are governed, says Hobbes, by fear, not legality. The law is only sufficient insomuch as the sword supports it.[7] Might, put crudely, is right, and theories of civic virtue merely serve to muddy the waters of what is a straightforward social contract. Harrington is much closer to Milton in relation to the checks and balances that must be maintained between the sword and sovereign power. To place the power of the sword in the hands of one man is to invite disaster:

> For if the power of the sword were anywhere separate and undepending from the power of law, which is originally seated in the highest Court, then would that power of the Sword be soon maister of the law, & being at one man's disposal, might when he pleas'd controule the Law, and [in derision of our *Magna Charta*, which were but weak resistance against an armed Tyrant might absolutely] enslave us.[8]

From the outset then, Harrington takes issue with Hobbes' sovereignty-through-fear thesis. *Contra*-Hobbes and the use of force to administer power, Harrington argues that the sword is useless without the hand that feeds it: 'and what pastures you have will come into the balance of property, without which the public sword is but a name or mere spitfrog'. The key to power therefore lies through the ownership of land; between the extremes of absolute monarchy and commonwealth, lies the Gothic balance. Insofar as small republics such as Holland or Genoa are concerned, 'the balance of treasure may be equal to that of land'.[9] Whereas in *Leviathan* Hobbes states, says Harrington that the law is but words and paper without the supporting power of the 'public sword', Harrington emphatically states 'that the hand or sword that executeth the law is *in it and not above it*'. This is all very different from Hobbes who maintains in his *Elements of Law* that 'it is an error to think: that the power which is virtually the whole power of the commonwealth, and in which whomsoever it resideth, is usually called supreme or sovereign, can be subject to any law but that of God

Almighty'.[10] For Harrington, however, the law is the executive hand of the magistrate and its head 'is answerable to the people'. Thus Glenn Burgess has argued convincingly that Harrington was concerned above all 'with producing a constitutional structure of orders (*ordini*) that would be characterised by sovereign closure, the rule of law, and thus the maintenance of peace'.[11] Such an argument is drawn out of nature; accordingly, Harrington puts forward historical examples from Israel, Sparta, Athens, Carthage, Rome and Venice.[12] Interestingly, and like Milton, Harrington sees no incongruity in mixing classical and biblical sources in order to make his point:

> But that we may observe a little further how the heathen politicians have written, not only out of nature, but as it were out of Scripture: as in the commonwealth of Israel God is said to have been king, so the commonwealth where the law is king is said by Aristotle to be the kingdom of God. And where, by the lusts or passions of man, a power is set above that of the law, deriving reason which is the dictate of God, God in that sense is rejected or deposed that he should not reign over them as he was in Israel.[13]

True to the methodology that will guide him throughout *Oceana* – the continual recourse to historical precedent – Harrington lambasts Hobbes for denying the authority of ancient sources. The argument rests on the 'nature' of nature. Hobbes would have it that men have been influenced to an unacceptable extent by the writings of the classical past, particularly the republican writings of Aristotle and Cicero, figures whom, like Milton, Harrington reveres. In *Leviathan* Hobbes argues that the rights of men living in commonwealths have been falsely constructed according to principles that are alien to contemporary society. Such rights are derived 'not from the Principles of Nature' but out of the 'Practise of their own Common-wealths, which were Popular'. There is little use, says Hobbes, in referring, as Harrington and Milton were to do later in the 1650s, to Aristotle and Cicero, when these two standard authorities had simply got things wrong. Athenian freedom as espoused by Aristotle was not natural to Athenian men; rather it was taught to them 'to keep them from desire of changing their Government'. Hobbes is similarly dismissive of Cicero and the legacy of Roman freedom, whereby successive writers have 'grounded their Civill doctrine, on the opinions of the Romans, who were *taught* to hate Monarchy, at first, by them that having deposed their Soveraign, shared amongst them the Soveraignty of *Rome*'. Hobbes wraps up this point with the oft-quoted observation that 'there was never anything so deerly bought, as these Western parts have bought the learning of the Greek and Latine tongues'.

Hobbes, of course, despite his pronouncements on classical rhetoric, is massively indebted to it in his writings. The analogy Hobbes makes in this passage between the assimilation of political principles to the system learned from the 'Rules of Poetry', taken primarily 'out of the poems of Homer and Virgil', is significant, and points forcibly to the literariness of seventeenth-century republican thought.[14]

As Nigel Smith has pointed out, 'Despite his elevation of his materialist and geometric vision over authorities, the political passions (the passions in the body politic) are registered for Hobbes through and in classical literature and rhetoric'.[15] Fundamentally, Harrington differs from Hobbes on what constitutes man's political condition in a state of nature. Hobbes appears to regard freedom as being unnatural to man – it is taught and therefore artificial, contrived and man-made. Harrington's response to this is to state that one might just as well tell 'famous Harvey that he transcribed his circulation of the blood not out of the principles of nature, but out of the anatomy of this or that body'. Later in *Oceana*, Harrington returns to the metaphor of blood circulation to illustrate a point about the structure of the constitution, where such an analogy is seen to be perfectly natural:

> And the constitution of the senate and the people being shown, you have that of the parliament of Oceana, consisting of the senate proposing and of the people resolving which amounts to an act of parliament. So the parliament is the heart which, consisteth of two ventricles, the one greater and replenished with a grosser store, the other less and full of a purer, sucketh in and gusheth forth the life blood of Oceana by a perpetual circulation.[16]

This begs questions about what one considers natural. For Harrington the principles of government are twofold: in the first instance there are 'goods of the mind – wisdom, prudence and courage'; in the second there are external goods, or 'goods of fortune', defined by Harrington as riches. Goods of the body – health, strength and beauty – do not enter into the equation as these may reside in a conquered or subjugated people who may enjoy such virtues 'and yet find little remedy'. As he develops this line of thought Harrington takes further issue with Hobbes, and in the process of doing so begs questions about the nature of authority and the origins of governmental power.

> The principles of government then are in the goods of the mind, or in the goods of fortune. To the goods of the mind answers authority; to the goods of fortune, power or empire. Wherefore Leviathan though he be right when he

saith that "riches are power", is mistaken where he saith that "prudence, or the reputation of prudence, is power".

According to Harrington, prudence, or learning, is defined by books and authors and does not have power intrinsic to it. Consequently, a man may have authority without power if he is learned; by the same token, ignorance and power can go quite easily together, as in the figure of the foolish magistrate. 'Such a figure', says Harrington quoting Livy, 'has ruled rather by authority than by power'.[17]

Although the utopian fiction that is *Oceana* is recognisably England in the 1650s, Harrington continually has recourse to classical models in order to ground his discourse. In this he is emphatically humanist in his methodology. It is not simply that Harrington holds up the political theories and practice of Greece and Rome as benchmarks of excellence. He is also an incisive critic of their failings and shortcomings. The most serious of these is their inequality in agrarian matters and the lack of rotation in government office that proved to be the ruin of classical government. Greece fell because the people had too much 'headiness'; Rome fell because the nobility 'had too much ambition' and also because 'a negligence committed in their agrarian laws, let in the sink of luxury, and forfeited the inestimable treasure of liberty for themselves and posterity'.[18] The proper balance of class is an important constituent of Harrington's political thought. In an ideal or natural condition, the people and the gentry recognise that theirs is a mutually supportive relationship. The upper hand, however, invariably lies with those who are able properly to govern. There has been no leader of republican government worthy of the name that did not have nobility in his blood. Harrington cites many examples in support of this assertion. The gentry is his ideal class: 'There is something in the making of a commonwealth, then in the governing of her, and last of all in the leading of her armies, which, though there be great divines, great lawyers, great men in all professions, seems to be peculiar unto the genius of a gentleman'. The founders of commonwealths, says Harrington, were all recognisably gentle in their condition: Moses, Theseus, Solon, the Gracchi, Brutus and Publicola were nobles. Olphaus Megalator, 'sole legislator (as you will see) of the commonwealth of *Oceana*, was derived from a noble family'. Without a politically active nobility and gentry suffused with civic virtue, freedom is impossible: 'For where there is not a nobility to bolt out the people, they are slothful, regardless of the world and the public interest of liberty, as even that of Rome had been without her gentry'.[19] As John Pocock and Gordon Schochet have remarked, 'Harrington is the Gerrard Winstanley of the gentry'.[20] Similarly, J.C. Davis has argued that the entire premise of the agrarian law has been enacted in *Oceana* 'as a device to preserve a propertied aristocracy, as well as to prevent the balance of dominion in land tipping over into the hands of the few'.[21] Given such a view, it is little wonder that Harrington's brand of republicanism found favour later in the century, and in the one following, with the aristocratic Whigs.

As the 'Preliminaries' develop into their second part, Harrington writes a fictional history of Oceana that is a thinly veiled account of England since the invasion of the Romans. Much of what follows from this point is an attempt to explain the 'Gothic balance' and the manner in which this was destabilised by the baronial wars of the early and high Middle Ages. Harrington has it that the Gothic balance in its original state was a tripartite division of fealty and obligation:

> The first of nobility distinguished by dukes, marquesses and earls … . Feuds of the second order were such as by the consent of the king were bestowed by these feudatory princes upon men of inferior quality, called their barons, on condition that next unto the king they should defend the dignities and fortunes of their lord in arms. The lowest order of feuds were such as those being conferred by those of the second order upon private men, whether noble or not noble, obliged them in the like duty to their superiors; these were called *vavasors*.

The ideal Gothic balance of *Oceana* and the foundation upon which it rests is soon disturbed, however, by 'the ambition of Turbo [William I]', aided by the first rank of the feudal order, and maintained by those kings who succeeded him. The political power struggle between kings with absolutist intentions was checked by the growing political consciousness of the third order, the baronial class, who had gone native and assimilated the political beliefs of their Saxon predecessors. As a consequence of this a long running ideological war developed between the king's desire for 'absolute power', and his nobility who had grown fierce in the defence of their 'immunities', 'ancient rights and liberties'. The end result was that in the reign of Aldous [John], open war between these two by now irreconcilable foes broke out in earnest.

As he moves his narrative into the sixteenth century Harrington follows closely Francis Bacon's *History of Henry VII*, perhaps the most Machiavellian and Tacitean of all seventeenth-century works of history. Panurgus' [Henry VII] humbling of the Oceanic nobility, and his elevation of the commons leads to a growing imbalance of power that is exacerbated during the reign of Queen Parthenia [Elizabeth I], who by 'converting her reign through the perpetual love tricks that passed between her and her people into a kind of romance, wholly neglected the nobility'. Such a weakening of this lynch-pin class was crucial and fatal to the monarchy: 'And by these degrees came the house of commons to raise that head, which since hath been so high and formidable unto their princes that they have looked pale upon those assemblies'.[22] Harrington's final point is that without an effectual and supportive class of nobles, or a victorious army at their back, monarchies must fall. The conclusion for Oceana and any other state that neglects the structural importance of the nobility, is that they must needs exist without a monarchy. Indeed, under Oceanic property laws a monarchy would seem to be out of the question: 'For where there is equality of estates, there must be equality of power, and where there is equality of power, there can be no monarchy'.[23] The equitable division of property amongst the right class is crucial to political liberty. Where property is concentrated in the hands of a very small number of people, dispossessing them is a relatively easy business; 'where the people have equal shares', however, dispossession becomes 'not only dangerous, but fruitless'.[24] Equality in possessions is essential to political security by creating a common bond that men will fight to defend.[25] Property rights then, are central to an internally peaceful polity. Moreover, such rights are in accord with the law of nature.

The commonwealth of Oceana stands at a crucial point in its history, one that requires a stable and continuous political architecture to replace the Gothic balance that has been thrown radically out of kilter by civil conflict. Extraordinary means require extraordinary measures. As a book or a building reaches perfection if its author or architect is solely responsible for its design, so too is the political organisation of a commonwealth 'of the like nature':

> And thus it may be made at once, in which there be great advantages: for a commonwealth made at once taketh her security at the same time she lendeth her money, trusteth not herself to the faith of men but launcheth immediately forth into the empire of laws and, being set straight, bringeth the manner of her citizens into her rule.

Crucially Harrington grounds his discourse in law and not men. He argues against Hobbes in stating that a commonwealth is best conserved if its citizens are not battered into submission through fear of the sword, but instead have a vested interest in the preservation of an equitable political structure that best serves their own interests. In this respect the arbitrary will of an unscrupulous individual cannot subvert the constitution. Thus, liberty is maintained.[26]

Notes

1   J.G.A. Pocock (ed.), *The Political Works of James Harrington*, Cambridge, Cambridge University Press, 1977, p. 15. Harrington describes Machiavelli at the outset of *Oceana* as 'the only politician of later ages', p. 162. All references to Harrington's works are to this edition and are hereafter referred to as *Political Works*.

2   Jonathan Scott, 'The Rapture of Motion: James Harrington's Republicanism', in Nicholas Phillipson and Quentin Skinner (eds), *Political Discourse in Early Modern Britain*, Cambridge, Cambridge University Press, 1993, pp. 139-63 (p. 159).

3   J.C. Davis, *Utopia and the Ideal Society: A Study of English Utopian Writing, 1516-1700*, Cambridge, Cambridge University Press, 1981, p. 207.

4   Scott, 'The Rapture of Motion', p. 151.

5   *Political Works*, p. 660.

6   *Ibid.*, p. 161.

7   Hobbes, *Leviathan*, p. 471; cited by Harrington, *Ibid*, pp. 161-62.

8   John Milton, *Eikonoklastes*, in *The Complete Prose Works of John Milton*, Don Wolfe, *et. al.* (eds), New Haven, CT, and London, Yale University Press, 1953-1982, I-VIII; III, p. 454. All references to Milton's prose are to this edition and are abbreviated as *CPW*.

9   *Political Works*, p. 165.

10   *Political Works*, p. 165; *Leviathan*, p. 123; Thomas Hobbes, *The Elements of Law* (1640), in J.C.A. Gaskin (ed.), *Human Nature and De Corpore Politico*, Oxford, Oxford University Press, 1994, Part Two, XXVII. 6, p. 166. Hobbes' view of the sovereign power and the law is developed much more systematically in *Leviathan*. However, the principles underpinning this view remain consistent from the earlier writings.

11   Glenn Burgess, 'Repacifying the Polity: the Responses of Hobbes and Harrington to the "Crisis of Common Law"', in Ian Gentles, John Morrill and Blair Worden (eds), *Soldiers, Writers and Statesmen of the English Revolution*, Cambridge, Cambridge University Press, 1998, pp. 202-29; pp. 222-23.

12   *Political Works*, pp. 174-77 (emphasis added).

13   *Ibid.*, p. 178.

14   *Leviathan*, pp. 149-50, (emphasis added.). See Quentin Skinner, *Reason and Rhetoric in the Philosophy of Hobbes*, Cambridge, Cambridge University Press, 1996; Nigel Smith, *Literature and Revolution in England, 1640-1660*, New Haven, CT, and London, Yale University Press, 1994, pp. 154-72.

15   Smith, *Literature and Revolution*, p. 159.

16   *Political Works*, pp. 162, 287.

17   *Ibid.*, p. 163.

18   *Ibid.*, pp. 184; 188.

19   *Ibid.*, p. 183.

20   J.G.A Pocock and Gordon J. Schochet, 'Interregnum and Restoration', in J.G.A. Pocock (ed.), with the assistance of Gordon J. Schochet and Lois G. Schwoerer, *The*

Varieties of British Political Thought, 1500-1800, Cambridge, Cambridge University Press, 1993, pp. 146-79 (p. 168).

21   J.C. Davis, 'Equality in an unequal commonwealth: James Harrington's republicanism and the meaning of equality', in Gentles, *et. al.*, (eds), *Soldiers, Statesmen and Writers*, pp. 229-42; p. 231.

22   *Political Works*, pp. 191, 195-98.

23   *Ibid.*, p. 201.

24   *Ibid.*, p. 199. On the same page Harrington cites Nero's frustration at not being able to sever the singular political neck of the Roman people. As Pocock's note makes clear, it was the wish of Caligula and not Nero.

25   *Ibid.*, pp. 203-4.

26   *Ibid.*, p. 207.

Chapter 3

Diggers, Levellers, and Ranters: The Bible and the State of Nature

Winstanley presents us with a significantly more benign vision of the state of nature than Hobbes does, one which in many ways prefigures that of Locke in its commitment to personal freedom and equality:

> In the beginning of Time, the great Creator Reason, made the Earth to be a Common Treasury, to preserve Beasts, Birds, Fishes, and Man, the lord that was to govern this Creation; for Man had Domination given to him, over the Beasts, Birds, and Fishes; but not one word was spoken in the beginning, That one branch of mankind should rule over another. And the Reason is this, Every single man, Male and Female, is a perfect Creature of himself.[1]

Yet again the state of nature will dictate the nature of the state: this time around, a primitive agrarian communistic society that will replace the corrupt one associated with the '*Norman* yoke', where hierarchy has supplanted natural equality.[2] The 'Norman yoke' might be regarded as a secular equivalent of the 'fall': the point at which we are forcibly ejected from our political state of grace. The primitive agrarian communism being advocated by Winstanley and the Digger movement is designed to reinstate that condition of grace, where the Hobbesian competitive instinct is noticeable by its absence. Cooperative endeavour rules instead in Winstanley, who wishes to reveal to his fellow citizens, as the title page of *The True Levellers' Standard Advanced* has it, 'The State of Community opened'.[3] For Hobbes, the exercise of personal sovereignty divided us from each other, leading to even greater levels of insecurity for each individual. Personal sovereignty in this instance, however, is to be expressed within a communal setting, for the benefit of humankind as a whole; with Winstanley's vision of the individual as 'a perfect creature' cutting across both class and gender lines.[4]

The Digger movement saw itself, as the pamphlet above indicates, as 'True' Levellers, with the implication being that other levelling theories, of which the 1640s featured a host of examples, had somehow missed the mark or lost their sense of momentum by the latter part of the decade. Levelling in the period could mean things as diverse as a demand for the extension of the franchise or a call for anarchy in the streets. In the former case we have the Leveller movement itself, and its representations to the Army Council at the Putney Debates of 1647 for 'the freeborn at the age of 21 yeares and upwards' to 'be the electors' of biannual parliaments; in the latter, the rabble-rousing rhetoric of Ranters like Abiezer Coppe, for whom levelling goes well beyond mere reform of the existing political system:

> 4 And now thus saith the Lord:
> Though you can as little endure the word LEVELLING, as could the late slaine or dead *Charles* (your forerunner, who is gone before you --) and had as live heare the Deville named, as heare of the Levellers (Men-Levellers) which is, and who (indeed) are but shadows of most terrible, yet great and glorious good things to come.
> 5 Behold, behold, behold, I the eternall God, the Lord of Hosts, who am the mighty Leveller, am comming (yea even at the doores) to Levell in good earnest, to Levell to some purpose, to Levell with a witnesse, to Levell the Hills with the Valleyes, and to lay the Mountaines low.[5]

Men-Levellers are threatening enough to the political establishment of the time, but a God-Leveller offers the prospect of a return to our natural state with a vengeance. In the interim before this millenarian event arrives, the Ranters are determined to be as confrontational as possible with regard to the social norms of their time:

> we had as live be dead drunk every day of the weeke, and lye with whores i'th the market place, and account these as good actions as taking the poore abused, enslaved ploughmans money from him (who is almost every where undone, and squeezed to death ...).[6]

Such an anarchic life-style is, Coppe contends, more natural than one that involves economic exploitation of one's fellow men. Whether women (such as the whores mentioned by Coppe above) would find it as natural is, however, another question, but the anti-establishment intent of Coppe's sentiments is clear enough. Personal sovereignty is to replace the existing concept of sovereignty based on hierarchy, and even a republican government found that hard to accept as baldly stated as it was by Coppe, with the Council of State ordering his arrest shortly after the publication of *A Fiery Flying Roll* (1650). Coppe's protestation that, 'To the pure all things are pure', falls on deaf ears therefore, and to the authorities he may be said to represent the unacceptable face of personal sovereignty.[7]

The Leveller movement itself can look somewhat conservative compared to their Digger and Ranter counterparts, but they were pursuing a politically radical programme by the standards of their time nevertheless; one concerned with extending the scope for personal sovereignty for 'the freeborn' at least, even if this was a more restricted social category than it might at first appear (the issue being the worth of one's property, thus narrowing down those eligible). Exactly how radical the Levellers were is still a matter of considerable debate. Macpherson saw their demands as stopping well short of full manhood suffrage, although his line has been contested by several other historians of the period.[8] It is worth pointing out that some Leveller spokesmen at the Putney Debates, such as Colonel Rainborough, *were* willing to argue the case for full manhood suffrage: 'I do think that the poorest man in England is not at all bound in a strict sense to that government that he hath not had a voice to put himself under'.[9] The Debates brought the Levelling movement, a strong force within the Army by this point, up against an Army Council of conspicuously conservative intent on such social matters as the protection of existing property rights: in General Ireton's words,

> All the main thing that I speak for, is because I would have an eye to property. I hope we do not come to contend for victory – but let every man consider with himself that he do not go that way to take away all property. For here is the case of the most fundamental part of the constitution of the kingdom, which if you take away, you take away all by that.[10]

The exchanges between Rainborough and Ireton crystallise around the property issue, with Ireton maintaining that any move towards universal suffrage would represent a threat to property.[11] Rainborough claims that a vote is a natural right; that we should not be subjected to arbitrary power; that government must be consensual. For Ireton, however, the implications of such egalitarianism go well beyond the electoral process:

> For thus: by that same right of nature (whatever it be) that you pretend, by which you can say, one man hath an equal right with another to the choosing of him that shall govern him – by the same right of nature, he hath the same [equal] right in any goods he sees – meat, drink, clothes – to take and use them for his sustenance. He hath a freedom to the land, [to take] the ground, to exercise it, till it; he hath the [same] freedom to anything that any one doth account himself to have any propriety in.[12]

Arguments from our natural condition failed to impress the Army Council in general, with Cromwell informing Rainborough at one point that, 'the consequence of this rule tends to anarchy, must end in anarchy'; indicating a fear of the state of nature not far short of that found in Hobbes.[13] Natural right and socio-political right are kept separate, with the Army Council making clear its determination to resist any move towards reconstruction of the nation state on the basis of the former right. Thus we find Ireton warning participants in the debate that, '[i]f you will resort only to the Law of Nature, by the Law of Nature you have no more right to this land, or anything else, than I have'.[14] For True Levellers that realisation is enough to sanction a communistic socio-political project, with the Bible providing further reinforcement for their decision to return to the land and resist the trend towards enclosure; but for the Army Council, no less than for Hobbes, that way lies only trouble for the nation at large. There may have been several years of civil war by the time of the Debates, but the Army Council is still operating largely within the parameters of the old discourse of sovereignty with its commitment to a social hierarchy based on property ownership. Communism is certainly not on their agenda.[15]

If not communistic, the Levellers nevertheless conceive of us as social beings who recognise the need to cooperate with each other, and this is held to be a fundamental aspect of our natures:

> no man is born for himself only, but obliged by the Laws of Nature (which reaches all) of Christianity (which ingages us as Christians) and of Publick Societie and Government, to employ our endeavours for the advancement of a communitive Happinesse, of equall concernment to others as our selves.

This is to see us as having what amounts to a natural disposition towards social existence, rather than the innate selfishness posited by Hobbes, for whom we have to be forced into cooperation since that runs against our true, appetite-driven, natures. In *A Manifestation* (1649), the Leveller leaders Lilburne, Overton, and Walwyn agree that civil war creates risk and insecurity in our lives: "'Tis a very great unhappinesse we well know, to be always strugling and striving in the world, and does wholly keep us from the enjoyment of those contentments our several Conditions reach unto'.[16] Nevertheless, they accept this as a necessary step towards the removal of the despised Norman yoke. They are careful to distance themselves, however, from any radical concept of levelling; describing themselves in the title as 'commonly (though unjustly) stiled *Levellers*', and going on to insist that:

We profess therefore that we never had it in our thoughts to Level mens estates, it being the utmost of our aime that the Common-wealth be reduced to such a passe that every man may with as much security as may be enjoy his propriety.[17]

Leveller radicalism stops well short of 'overturning', therefore, and while it may disagree with certain forms of government, and the encroachment on personal sovereignty these involve, it is still firmly in favour of the civil state: 'we are for Government and against Popular Confusion'. We may have a natural disposition towards social existence, but given 'the pravity and corruption of mans heart', government is essential to our well-being.[18] Reform rather than a new beginning is what is being preached.

The Norman yoke theory plays a critical role in the development of the Leveller discourse of sovereignty throughout the 1640s. Thus we find Overton arguing in *A Remonstrance of Many Thousand Citizens and Other Freeborn People of England to their Own House of Commons* (1646) that:

The History of our Fore-fathers since they were Conquered by the *Normans*, doth manifest that this Nation hath been held in bondage all along ever since by the policies and force of the Officers of Trust in the Common-wealth, amongst whom, wee always esteemed Kings the chiefest.[19]

Overton's many appeals to the interests of 'the people' are somewhat misleading, in that they refer to the political nation (that is, the freeborn 'electors') rather than the nation at large, but there is nevertheless a clear sense of a desire significantly to extend the scope of personal sovereignty in his writings. Parliament is reminded that 'Yee only are chosen by Us the People', and that it must respect and even facilitate the people's desire to exercise their personal sovereignty.[20] There is a resistance to authoritarian grand narratives being imposed on the populace, and when it comes to religious belief, for example, personal sovereignty is paramount:

Whereas truely wee are well assured, neither you, nor none else, can have any into Power at all to conclude the People in matters that concerne the Worship of God, for therein everyone of us ought to be fully assured in our owne mindes, and to be sure to worship him according to our Consciences.[21]

Conscience is precisely what Hobbes cannot tolerate in his commonwealth, and the more it is emphasised, as here in Overton, the less chance there is of there being any consensus to accept a Hobbesian solution to the 'disorders of the present times' – no matter what the drawbacks of civil war might prove to be. The political dimension of religious belief becomes obvious in the way that the state's power to regulate individual behaviour is being challenged. Limits are being set to political sovereignty at the macro-level, and a division between the public and private is being insisted upon, with religion providing the test case of where the boundaries lie. As the Army Council is to be informed by Leveller radicals, 'to enforce us to a human conformity never enjoined by Christ' is the best way to ensure that those boundaries will be vigorously defended by the sectarian movement.[22] Religious nonconformity inevitably takes on a political dimension.

The biblical state of nature, crucially for Winstanley, contains no mention of property ownership, the evil from which almost all our current social and political ills stem for this thinker – hence the 'true leveller' tag to differentiate himself from the mainstream Leveller movement, which, as we have seen, is at pains to emphasise its property-supporting credentials. Winstanley is significantly more radical on this issue, and, prefiguring Proudhon, we have property defined as theft:

> And likewise Thirdly a breach of the Eighth Commandement, *Thou shalt not steal*; but these landlords have thus stoln the Earth from their fellow Creatures, that have an equal share with them, by the Law of Reason and Creation, as well as they.[23]

As Christopher Hill has noted, 'Winstanley had grasped a crucial point in modern political thinking: that state power is related to the property system and to the body of ideas which supports that system'.[24] The fact that the Bible is silent on such matters enables Winstanley, who, like so many of his peers, can be quite literal in his reading of that text, to construct an attack on the entire property-owning ethos of the England of his day; including the freeborn-oriented Levellers, who from this perspective are no less part of the problem that is demanding radical solution than the Army Council is. The goal instead becomes communal living in which no one individual has any greater status, or right of access or possession, than any other. We are to regard the earth as a 'Common Treasury' donated to mankind by God, and Winstanley and his Digger colleagues intend to make use of it in just that fashion: 'The Work we are going about is this, To dig up *Georges-Hill* and the waste Ground thereabouts, and to Sow Corn, and to eat our bread together by the sweat of our brows'.[25]

It is a 'back to nature' movement, whereby the intervening period in English culture of the 'Norman yoke' is simply bracketed out. Pre-Norman society is, for Winstanley, by implication a prelapsarian society, and thus closer to the biblical ideal that we are presented with in Genesis. Since the

Norman conquest the state has been engaged in 'imprisoning, robbing and killing the poor enslaved English Israelites': hence Winstanley's continual recourse to what Nigel Smith has called 'narratives of dispossession' to radicalise his compatriots.[26] It is on behalf of this 'poor oppressed people', as another of Winstanley's pamphlets describes them, that the Diggers are making their representations to the powers-that-be – Parliament, the Army, and the City of London all being appealed to over the course of his writings.[27] Whereas civil society protects us from our own natures in Hobbes, in Winstanley it is little more than a condition of slavery that prevents us from realising what is best in our natures. '*Let Israel go Free*' becomes the watchword of those in opposition to both Army and king.[28]

The 'poor, oppressed people' are oppressed by a regime which denies the claims of personal sovereignty, and with that, humankind's natural desire to share equally in the benefits of the world's 'Common Treasury'. Social relations are structured on the principle of hierarchy instead, and Winstanley is insistent that this is against the natural order of things as ordained by God: 'the King of Righteousness, our Maker, hath inlightened our hearts so far, as to see, That the earth was not made purposely for you, to be Lords of it, and we to be your Slaves, Servants, and Beggers'.[29] Winstanley's argument homes in on the evil of '*Particular Propriety*' (that is, property), which acts as a barrier to the return to the biblical state of nature.[30] Between the conception of 'particular property' as the bulwark of the state, 'which if you take away, you take away all by that', and that where it is an iredeemable evil, there lies a massive differend which can only be overcome by the triumph of one side or the other. There can be no middle ground between property-owners and squatters.

While Winstanley relies heavily on the bible for his political theory, it is a very selective reading of it that we find in his early pamphlets; one that avoids, for example, the problem of original sin that was exercising so many of his contemporaries. Winstanley's conception of the fall of mankind is political: a problem that arises in the aftermath of the Norman conquest, and which is therefore amenable to human solution without the need for any divine intercession. Through our own actions the sin of human greed, the 'inward covetousnesse' that Winstanley continues to rail against over the course of his writings, can be overcome, and we can return to the world as it was in Genesis – the world of a 'Common Treasury' for us all to share. There is another 'kingdom within' in operation here; the kingdom within of a prelapsarian human nature, which even the Norman yoke, despite being in force for several centuries, cannot eliminate from our consciousness. Once we recognise that a return to this prelapsarian nature is within our grasp, then we have the makings of a new political narrative that will rewrite the discourse of sovereignty; but for that new narrative to be constructed, Winstanley must turn a blind eye to the rest of the biblical narrative. Ultimately, he does address this longer narrative in *Fire in the Bush*, a message, as he bleakly describes it in 1651 after the officially-sanctioned destruction of Winstanley's Surrey commune, from one '*wading through the bondage of the world*'.[31]

Fire in the Bush pictures the individual as a site of bitter conflict between two forces: our innocent, cooperative prelapsarian nature (our kingdom within) and 'the selfish imaginary power within you' that proceeds from the devil.[32] Original sin is conceived of in primarily economic terms, and when we give in to its appeal and allow an 'inward covetousness' to develop, we exile *ourselves* from the state of nature:

> These are cast out of the Garden, they live out of themselves upon the Earth; they live upon riches, honors, pleasures, Ministers, Lawyers, Armies, wife, children, Ordinances, customes and all outward formes of worship, or in that beastly community with women; nowadayes cryed up by the lust of the flesh. ... For they have no peace nor Kingdome within.[33]

In order to protect this kingdom within such that we can express our 'true' natures, we have to overturn existing institutions, and Winstanley can sound almost as radical as Coppe on this issue by this stage in his career, arguing that 'all government and ministry that is lifted up by imagination is to be thrown down and plucked up, that Christ alone may be exalted in the day of his power'. Once again, the problem is deemed to lie *within* humankind, and to be curable *by* humankind, with Winstanley urging us to recognise that the solution lies in our own hands: 'Looke back into Ages past, and see what overturnings, and pluckings up there hath been of the Authority, power, and government of Nations'.[34] Just as Winstanley has been conducting a campaign on behalf of 'true' levelling, so he sets about prosecuting the cause of 'true' government, whose concern must always be with 'the poore despised ones of the Earth' rather than just the freeborn.[35] The serpent is seen metaphorically as comprising all those forces which prevent true government from being practised in our culture; in which case we can redeem ourselves from original sin by resisting the devious schemes of 'false' government. At such points Winstanley is moving dangerously close to heresy, and for a period which was so attracted to determinist doctrines (predestinarian soteriology, Hobbesian materialism, etc.) he is conspicuously anti-determinist in his outlook. Personal sovereignty is about making choices in Winstanley, rather than being driven by internal or external forces beyond our power to control. 'True' or 'false' government takes on something of the character of an existential choice for the individual in this setting. We are neither condemned to a brutish state of nature nor the workings of a repressive state apparatus – other possibilities exist, and they are within our power to initiate.

The worst sins are, for Winstanley, to appropriate more than one's share of the earth's common treasury, and then to defend one's appropriation by force. Together these constitute the cause of the fall of humankind in his historical narrative, 'the greatest sinne against universall Love'; but it is interesting to note that, in defiance of standard Christian dogma, not all of us are to be held responsible for this fall – only those complicit in the process of appropriation will be.[36] Winstanley has succeeded in politicising the fall; turning it into an issue of sovereignty where the English state is to be condemned for taking the side of the serpent, and preventing humankind from developing as God wanted it to do. The weak point of his argument is that once the Bible is read metaphorically in this way, then it is opened up to a range of conflicting interpretations by other sectarian thinkers, and thus to a potentially bewildering array of competing new narratives: in our reading here, to a proliferating series of differends. Winstanley relies very heavily on a notion of consensus that the events of the 1640s would seem to challenge. The explosive growth of sectarianism offers little hope that any general social movement can be put together in this period (the parliamentarian cause being, as a case in point, a fairly loose coalition of interests, as the Putney Debates make clear), and the Digger philosophy is only one of many narratives claiming biblical justification. The more the Bible is used to construct political positions, however, the more confusing the overall situation becomes, and one can appreciate why Hobbes felt it necessary to subordinate religion to politics – even if one might feel uneasy about the ruthlessness of the projected solution.

Winstanley goes on to offer his version of what government should be in more detail in *The Law of Freedom in a Platform*, whose subtitle, 'True Magistracy Restored', indicates yet another campaign to overturn contemporary institutional authority (although as J.C. Davis has pointed out, Winstanley was not against authority as such, his criticism being directed rather against its abuse[37]). 'The great searching of the heart in these days', he tells us, 'is to finde out where true Freedom lies, that the Commonwealth of *England* might be established in Peace' – and that freedom is not to be found in any defence of the property system.[38] Again, the Bible is appealed to for reinforcement of the argument against property consciousness: 'All that a man labors for, saith *Solomon*, is this, That he may enjoy the free use of the Earth, with the fruits thereof. *Eccles.* 2.24'.[39] It is a message which has gone unheeded by those in authority, with disastrous consequences for humankind. Winstanley sets about constructing a model of the state that will protect that basic right to share in the world's resources: *'the Government of the Earth without buying and selling'*.

The objective is a society where all labour for the common good, and where surpluses are stored for distribution in times of need – a 'commonwealth' in its most literal sense. While the family system is retained, *'Every Family shall live apart, as now they do; every man shall enjoy his own wife, and every woman her own husband, as now they do'*, individuals essentially owe their allegiance to the collective.[40] Winstanley's synoptic view of history reveals to him that from the time of the Scriptures to the Norman conquest, 'free enjoyment of the Earth' was the norm.[41] In what by now is a well-worn argument, all of this changes dramatically after the arrival of the Normans, who commandeer English common land for their own private use: a system to be maintained down the centuries to the Stuart monarchy, who are no less culpable than their predecessors of revoking our natural rights as free individuals. Although the church ought to have been decrying this offence against God's will, they betray the populace in their turn by siding with the conquerors, the reward for their support being the right to levy tithes. The clergy are to be considered little better than hypocrites, part of the repressive state apparatus that is the Normans' unfortunate legacy to English culture.

Monarchical government is seen to run counter to God's natural order in various ways. First of all, by being based on 'that cheating Art of buying & selling', whereby individuals are forced into ruthless competition with each other to the detriment of public security (Hobbes' state of nature transposed into civil society as it were).[42] Then, by encouraging the construction of social hierarchies, whose existence challenges the very nature of God as depicted in the Bible:

> And whereas the Scriptures say, That the Creator of all things (God) is no Respecter of persons, yet this Kingly Power doth nothing else but respect persons, preferring the rich and the proud; therefore he denies the Scriptures and the true God of Righteousness.

From here, it is but a short step to describing monarchy as 'the great Antichrist', with Winstanley insisting on a reformulation of the discourse of sovereignty on supposedly 'egalitarian' scriptural lines.[43] The scope for divergent readings is graphically illustrated at such points; Winstanley finding an argument *against* hierarchy in Scripture, while Filmer, equally confidently, finds an argument conclusively *for*. Far from resolving cultural differends, the Bible proves to be a fruitful source of them.

Winstanley's commonwealth is certainly firmly grounded in the Bible, in that it assumes that 'the spirit of universal Righteousness' within each of us, by which we are moved to do unto others as we would be done to by them, will be enough to constitute *'The great Lawgiver in Commonwealth Government'*.[44] Hierarchy will be abolished in this projected new state, as will all the old figures of authority (monarchs, the aristocracy, landlords, the clergy, etc.) who kept the people oppressed. We will be ruled instead by the law of righteousness. Magistracy's role in the commonwealth is to ensure that this law is kept, rather than, as is generally the case under the Norman yoke, to protect the rights of property-holders and the socio-political elite; indeed, the magistrate's primary responsibility is 'to help the weak and the foolish'.[45] In Winstanley's idealised view of the Bible, this was what figures such as Adam were doing in their own society, and it is this function of magistracy above all that we need to recover if we are to re-create biblical social models in our own time. Magistrates are to be conceived of as 'overseers', and to be elected annually, in order to prevent them entrenching themselves in power and seeking to exploit their position for their own benefit. Although there is full manhood suffrage (with the exception of law-breakers), candidates for the magistracy must meet stringent criteria before being allowed to stand for office: to be peaceable, courageous, over 40, and to 'have suffered under Kingly Oppression', for example.[46]

Winstanley admits that not all men are trustworthy: aside from the weak and the foolish there are also 'uncivil livers', 'drunkards', 'quarrelers', and 'fearful ignorant men' to contend with.[47] Yet he has a more optimistic view of humankind than Hobbes, and is confident that his commonwealth will have no need of authoritarian power structures. An extended network of overseers, each with specific areas of responsibility (public order, trade, or manufacture, for example) is felt to be adequate to guarantee the smooth functioning of the commonwealth, with Parliament – again, elected annually – as the 'Court ... to oversee all other Courts' in the land.[48] The weakness of the system is that, the weak and foolish, etc., notwithstanding, it assumes general consent to Winstanley's notion of freedom, and has no clear policy for dealing with dissent: indeed, it assumes that dissent could hardly exist in such a rationally-ordered society with an unequivocal commitment to human freedom. Even his supporters admit such gaps in Winstanley's thought, with David W. Petegorsky noting that what he presents us with is 'less an integrated, doctrinal system than a series of brilliant perceptions and profound insights'.[49] Hobbes does not make the same mistake, although he is no more capable of allowing a place for dissent within his commonwealth: it will be dealt with decisively – by means of 'swords'. Winstanley grants the power to overseers to punish wrongdoers, but the implication is that the new state will help to engineer a change in public consciousness so that dissent will wither away: the hope of utopian-minded social reformers through the ages (see the work of Marx, for example).

Religion, too, is to be reorganised to fit Winstanley's conception of social freedom, with ministers being annually-elected overseers on the principle of all the commonwealth's public officers. They are to have both a propagandist and an academic role: celebrating the state's achievements on the one hand, and disseminating useful knowledge in the arts and sciences on the other. Any other member of society is permitted to lecture in the same fashion if moved to do so, somewhat along the lines of Quaker worship, to ensure that the ministry does not become too professionalised and elitist. Doctrinal difference is held to be a consequence of a power-seeking clergy, and the assumption is made that if the old style of ministry is removed, doctrinal difference will disappear along with it: 'divining spiritual Doctrine is a cheat', Winstanley concludes, although that is to fail to recognise the possibility that the clergy may be as much symptom as cause of the period's doctrinal controversy.[50] Winstanley finds a basis for consensus on such matters that contemporary sectarian division would seem to mock.

Winstanley's 'free' commonwealth looks like an idealised version of early biblical society, therefore, with all reference to the fall removed and the positive aspects only of such a condition emphasised. All socio-political problems are traced back to the rise of institutions under monarchical government, and once that evil has been removed from the scene, it is claimed that humanity as a whole will revert to its 'true' cooperative nature. Communal sovereignty replaces monarchical, and absorbs the more extreme forms of personal sovereignty that sectarian division had promoted in the 1640s: everyone in the commonwealth is deemed to be an integral part of its 'ruling army', which 'is called Magistracy in times of Peace'.[51] *The Law of Freedom* represents a blueprint for a state based on our natural, pre-monarchical – and emphatically, pre-Norman yoke – condition. For Winstanley, the disorders have provided us with an opportunity to take stock of our discourse of sovereignty, and by so doing to theorise a new socio-political beginning. In this respect he goes much further than his Leveller contemporaries, and, by Cromwell's standards, is far more deserving of the charge of being anarchistic in outlook.[52] Winstanley's is an attractive social vision in its movement away from authoritarian institutional structures, although in its insistence on ideological conformity it is perhaps not as far away from absolutism as it would like to claim. J.C. Davis' point about Winstanley's general 'respect for patriarchal authority' is worth noting in this context.[53] A kingdom within that includes a concept of collective magistracy might be just as oppressive in its way, we might conjecture, as monarchical absolutism.

Notes

1   Gerrard Winstanley, *The True Levellers Standard Advanced*, in *The Works of Gerrard Winstanley*, Georg H. Sabine (ed.), New York, Russell and Russell, 1965, pp. 245-66 (p. 251).

2   *Ibid.*, p. 259. Others to make a similar point include David W. Petegorsky, for whom the Diggers' 'social doctrine was wholly a proletarian ideology' (*Left-Wing Democracy in the English Civil War: A Study of the Social Philosophy of Gerrard Winstanley*, New York, Haskell House, 1972, p. 13).

3   Reprinted in Gerrard Winstanley, *The Law of Freedom and Other Writings*, Christopher Hill (ed.), Harmondsworth, Penguin, 1973, p. 75. For an argument emphasising this public orientation to Winstanley's thought, see Warren Chernaik, 'Civil Liberty in Milton, the Levellers and Winstanley', *Prose Studies*, 22 (1999), pp. 101-20. Chernaik contends that 'Milton, Winstanley and such Leveller pamphleteers as Walwyn, Overton, and Lilburne ... share in a common project: the creation of a public sphere of discourse which, by its very existence, challenged the hegemony of ruling elites' (p. 101).

4   The sincerity of the Diggers' gender radicalism has been questioned. Elaine Hobby, for example, contextualising Winstanley within a growing tradition of female activism at the time, has argued that 'Although Digger pamphlets are haunted by the possibility that their arguments for equality might be extendable to women, the case is never developed by them' ('Winstanley, Women and the Family', *Prose Studies*, 22 (1999), pp. 61-72 (p. 71)). Davis has also characterised Winstanley as a defender of patriarchal authority (see Davis, *Utopia and the Ideal Society*, chapter 7).

5   *The Case of the Armie Truly Stated*, in D.M. Wolfe (ed.), *Leveller Manifestoes of the Puritan Revolution*, New York, Humanities Press, 1967, pp. 196-222 (p. 212); *A Fiery Flying Roll*, p. 22.

6   *Ibid.*, p. 24.

7   *Ibid.*, p. 27.

8   See Macpherson, *The Political Theory of Possessive Individualism*, chapter 3 for more detail on Leveller franchise proposals. Anti-Macpherson arguments can be found in, for example, Ashcraft, *Revolutionary Politics*; Keith Thomas, 'The Levellers and the Franchise,' (in Aylmer, *The Interregnum*, pp. 57-78); and Ian Hampsher-Monk, 'The Political Theory of the Levellers: Putney, Property and Professor Macpherson' (*Political Studies*, 24 (1976), pp. 397-422). Mark A. Kishlansky plays down the role of the Levellers in the development of political radicalism within the New Model

Army in the lead-up to Putney (see *The Rise of the New Model Army*, New York and Cambridge, Cambridge University Press, 1979).

9   'The Putney Debates', in A.S.P. Woodhouse (ed.), *Puritanism and Liberty: Being the Army Debates (1647-9) from the Clark Manuscripts, with Supplementary Documents*, London, J.M.Dent and Sons, 1938, pp. 1-124 (p. 53). For a contextualisation of the Putney Debates within the wider history of the New Model Army, see Austin Woolrych, *Soldiers and Statesmen: The General Council of the Army and its Debates, 1647-1648*, Oxford, Clarendon Press, 1987.

10   'Putney Debates', p. 57.

11   Hampsher-Monk, however, has argued that 'property' was a less precise concept in the seventeenth century than now, and that it could just as easily refer to having 'rights' in a general sense as having material possessions (see 'The Political Theory of the Levellers').

12   'Putney Debates', p. 58.

13   *Ibid.*, p. 59.

14   *Ibid.*, p. 26.

15   For a vigorous defence of Winstanley's communist credentials, see James Holstun, 'Communism, George Hill and the *Mir*: Was Marx a Nineteenth-Century Winstanleyan?', *Prose Studies*, 22 (1999), pp. 121-48. Other commentators have played down the communist aspect, with Davis, for example, seeing instead a movement from millenarianism to utopianism in Winstanley's thought (see *Utopia and the Ideal Society*, chapter 7).

16   John Lilburne, William Walwyn, Thomas Prince, and Richard Overton, *A Manifestation*, in Wolfe (ed.), *Leveller Manifestoes*, pp. 384-99 (p. 388).

17   *Ibid.*, pp. 388, 391.

18   *Ibid.*, p. 391.

19   Richard Overton, *A Remonstrance of Many Thousand Citizens and Other Free-borne People of England, to their owne House of Commons*, in Wolfe (ed.), *Leveller Manifestoes*, pp. 109-30 (pp. 113-4).

20   *Ibid.*, p. 116.

21   *Ibid.*, p. 122.

22   'From the Grievances of Regiments, Presented at Saffron Walden, 13th-14th May', in Woodhouse (ed.), *Puritanism and Liberty*, p. 399.

23   *True Levellers Standard*, p. 258.

24   Hill, Introduction to *The Law of Freedom and Other Writings*, p. 9.

25   *True Levellers Standard*, pp. 252, 257.

26   *Ibid.*, p. 86. Nigel Smith, 'Gerrard Winstanley and the Literature of Revolution', *Prose Studies*, 22 (1999), pp. 47-60 (p. 48).

27   Winstanley, *A Declaration from the Poor Oppressed People of England*, in *Works*, pp. 267-77.

28   *True Levellers Standard*, p. 265.

29   *Poor Oppressed People*, p. 269.

30   *Ibid.*, p. 270.

31   Winstanley, *Fire in the Bush*, in *Works*, pp. 443-97 (p. 448).

32   *Ibid.*, p. 452.

33   *Ibid.*, p. 458.

34   *Ibid.*, pp. 471-2.

35   *Ibid.*, pp. 472, 473.

36   *Ibid.*, p. 496.
37   'He was never an anti-authoritarian ... Winstanley was seeking to use, rather than to discard, those existing authorities and powers which he felt could be on the side of righteousness' (Davis, *Utopia and the Ideal Society*, pp. 182, 183).
38   Winstanley, *The Law of Freedom in a Platform, Or, True Magistracy Restored*, in *Works*, pp. 499-602 (p. 519).
39   *Ibid.*, p. 520.
40   *Ibid.*, p. 515.
41   *Ibid.*, p. 520.
42   *Ibid.*, p. 529.
43   *Ibid.*, p. 530.
44   *Ibid.*, p. 534.
45   *Ibid.*, p. 537.
46   *Ibid.*, p. 543.
47   *Ibid.*, p. 542.
48   *Ibid.*, p. 556.
49   Petegorsky, *Left-Wing Democracy*, p. 177.
50   *The Law of Freedom*, p. 569.
51   *Ibid.*, p. 572.
52   Several commentators have argued for an anarchistic strain in Winstanley's thought. See, for example, W. Schenk, *The Concern for Social Justice in the Puritan Revolution*, London, Longmans, Green, 1948, chapter 6.
53   Davis, *Utopia and the Ideal Society*, p. 182.

Chapter 4

Milton and the State of Nature

We turn now to Milton's conception of natural law and man's condition in a state of nature as expressed through a range of his prose and poetry. In *The Tenure of Kings and Magistrates*, *Eikonoclastes*, *A Defence of the English People*, and *A Second Defence of the English People* Milton describes at considerable length the reasons why the republic was created and in the process continually justifies the regicide, arguably its defining moment. *A Defence*, as is well known, is a reply and rebuttal of *Defensio Regia*, written by the noted continental humanist Salmasius to express Europe's horror at the unprecedented act of putting a king on trial for his life and then executing him when he was found guilty of crimes against the state. At the heart of the debate lie widely differing interpretations as to what constitutes the law of nature and the origins of sovereignty. While both writers agree that the welfare of the people lies at the heart of a ruler's responsibilities, their idea of where power resides is entirely incommensurate: for Salmasius natural law dictates that sovereignty is embodied in the king; Milton, on the other hand, argues that ultimate power resides in the people.

Exactly what constitutes 'the people' in Milton's terms, however, is a vexed question. Milton is rarely kind to the 'blockish vulgar', and as Hill relates with reference to *The Readie and Easie Way* (1660), by the end of the 1650s Milton was ready to severely restrict the franchise and place government in the hands of a 'perpetual oligarchy'.[1] Those who are dedicated to the cause of kingship, even if they are in the vast majority, have lost their right to resist the lawful authority of the republic, 'both in reason and the trial of just battel'. According to Milton it is patently unfair and unjust that the majority in favour of subjugation to a monarch should impose their will on an ascendant minority who believe in freedom. 'More just it is doubtless, if it com to force, that a less number compell a greater to retain, which can be no wrong to them, thir libertie, than that a greater number for the pleasure of thir baseness, compell a less most injuriously to be thir fellow slaves'.[2] These are strong words, and uncomfortable ones too for those who happen to be in the unfortunate majority crying out by now for the return of the monarchy and the abolition of an intensely unpopular government. This is an attitude that hardened considerably when *Samson Agonistes* was written, probably in the early 1660s:[3]

> I was no private but a person rais'd
> With strength sufficient and command from Heav'n
> To free my Country; if their servile minds
> Me their deliver sent would not receive,
> But to their masters gave me up for nought,
> Th' unworthier they; whence to this day they serve.[4]

Samson's belief is that the people get no more than they deserve, fitted, as they are 'to love bondage more than liberty'.[5] Had Milton's patience with the rude multitude simply run out over the course of the decade, then his attitude here would have perhaps been understandable. As early as *Eikonoclastes* (1650), however, Milton stands ready to accuse the people of being unfit to make appropriate political judgements. They are 'exorbitant and excessive in all thir motions, are prone ofttimes not to a religious onely, but to a civil kinde of idolatry in idolizing their kings'.[6] In *A Defence* Milton states that what is meant by the people 'we mean all citizens of every degree'. On the same page, however, in response to Salmasius' attack on the people as 'blind and brutish', Milton appears willing to make concessions. The charge 'may be true of the dregs of the populace, but hardly of the middle class, which produces the greatest number of men of good sense and knowledge of affairs'.[7]

The political situation in England in 1651, both domestic and foreign, required that the fledgling republic be nurtured and protected. This meant by cultural as well as political means. Kevin Sharpe has recently argued that the lack of a republican literary culture was instrumental in the failure of the republic ultimately to sustain itself. 'The failure of republican politics was the failure to forge a republican culture that erased or suppressed the images of kingship, images that sustained a monarchical polity, even in the absence of the king'. Paradoxically texts such as Milton's *Tenure of Kings and Magistrates* and *Eikonoclastes* undermine rhetorically their own content. By constantly foregrounding monarchy, even a corrupt one, such texts act effectively as royalist polemic. According to Sharpe it is rare before 1650 to find classical republicanism used as a defence of the commonwealth.[8]

Yet as Sean Kelsey has recently argued, with a nod to Patrick Collinson, there was a residual 'gentry republicanism' present in England in the Elizabethan and Jacobean periods. 'Between 1649 and 1653 the quasi-republicanism implicit in Englishmen's beliefs about the duties of magistracy and virtuous civic responsibility helped fill the gaping hole torn in the fabric of order and authority by revolution'.[9] Civic responsibility and virtue are terms steeped in the humanist recovery of classical texts in the sixteenth and seventeenth centuries. These took on an ideological colour that was fostered in the expansion of the universities during the Tudor regime. This in turn changed the nature of the language of politics in the early modern period. The governing spirit was Machiavelli.[10] Pocock's analysis suggests that the humanist philosophy of education with its shift away from a scholastic syllabus and its emphasis instead on Roman rhetoric, history, poetics and classical literature, provided the intellectual and ideological building blocks of the modern state. Even if Sharpe is entirely correct in his analysis (and this is highly contentious), then the *de facto* existence of the republic 'regardless of the relative lack of theory and practice' speaks volumes in itself. It beggars belief that the republic sprung from nowhere.[11]

With an eye on what he perceived as Presbyterian backsliding, Milton sought in the *Tenure of Kings and Magistrates*, to offer a reasoned and rational explanation for rebellion and regicide with precedents drawn from examples 'which ... shall be all Protestant and chiefly Presbyterian'. Men have a right, indeed an obligation to rebel when they are under the oppression of a tyrant. Such men are 'guided then by the very principles of nature'.[12] Regicide is justified, according to Milton's understanding of natural law, on the basis that Parliament had every right to execute the king. 'If you still demand "By what right or what law"', says Milton to Salmasius in *A Defence*, 'my reply is "By that law of Nature, and of God that whatever is for the safety of the state is right and just"'.[13] From this stark opposition between views we can track many of the debates that arose between not just royalist and republican in the 1650s, but also divisions between writers engaged with questions of political authority in the Restoration and Hanoverian periods. Milton's language in this quotation has Machiavellian echoes in its primary concern with the safety of the state. This is an echo that is elaborated later when Milton states that 'the infection' of a people from a 'diseased king' who 'kills his people and wholly ruins the state', deserves all that the law allows in respect of bringing him to book.[14] What makes it more trenchant, however, is the manner in which Milton marries religion to statecraft arguing that both are natural in that they are based upon expediency and a correct understanding of God's law. This is entirely appropriate given the relationship that is apparent between man, God, and the law in *Christian Doctrine*: 'Man was made in the image of God and the whole law of nature was so implanted and innate in him'. Milton believed absolutely that 'the law of nature ... is itself sufficient to teach whatever is in accord with right reason'.[15] The law of nature 'is the only law of laws truly and properly to mankinde fundamental'.[16] Throughout his prose works Milton draws continually on scriptural evidence in defence of political and spiritual liberty. Indeed, *Christian Doctrine* is built upon Milton's interpretation of natural law.[17] As Arthur Barker long since noted, Milton invariably kept 'the adjective "Christian" ... at his hand to modify, if necessary, the substantive "liberty"'.[18] In *A Defence* Milton argues that 'all things indeed have their source and sanction in God', and if this means that kings are in some sense divine, then the people too have God as their ultimate warrant for political and religious freedom.[19]

Central to Milton's conception of the state of nature then, is its relationship with divine law. Liberty and Christianity are closely enmeshed, indeed inseparable. In this respect Milton is at one with that strain of English radicalism that would not or could not divorce secular from spiritual freedom. Milton explicitly links the two in *A Defence* and in the *Readie and Easie Way*.[20] As Jonathan Scott has argued, radical Protestant intellectuals saw religious and secular liberty in tandem, not just in their own country, but also as part of a drama taking place on a European stage. In his dispute with Salmasius Milton attacks kingship on many fronts, historical and intellectual. Never far from his mind, however, is the correlation between papal absolutism and its secular equivalent. In making comparisons between Charles and Nero, for instance, Milton makes it plain that Charles' tyranny has been adapted from Catholicism: 'he did great violence to the conscience of godly men, and forced on all certain rituals and superstitious practices, which he had brought back into the church from the depths of popery'. This charge is further extended when Milton accuses Charles of betraying those soldiers who died fighting the French at La Rochelle. This was a preparation for domestic tyranny in that it bled the military strength of citizens.[21] Claims to rule by the grace of God, says Milton, are papal in their origin and therefore not to be trusted. Milton's invective against Salmasius denies the latter his status as a good protestant and is steeped in anti-Catholic rhetoric: 'In addition to that Independence you mock, there is another saint canonized by you in all earnest, Royal Tyranny, and so you will become High Priest of the royal Saint Tyranny'.[22] The Thirty Years War, successive conflicts with the Dutch, the French, and the Spanish in the seventeenth century, as well as a myriad of domestic 'popish plots' with a European dimension, stretching from the reign of Elizabeth onwards, all had religion at their core. The seventeenth century in Europe witnessed a return to Catholicism as the Counter-Reformation rolled back the Protestant State. As the seventeenth century progressed, many English Protestants believed themselves to be under siege by the Catholic powers and often called for a war of religion to be prosecuted against those powers. A French Catholic wife and a perception in some quarters that he favoured papists at home and abroad, combined with a refusal to aid European Protestants with arms, were powerful reasons for dissent against Charles I. As far as Milton is concerned the correlation between the Stuarts and popery is endemic. In 1660 in *The Readie and Easie Way* Milton is exhorting the nation to turn its back on Charles II because from 'the cradle', he has been 'traind up and govern'd by *Popish* and *Spanish* counsels, and on such depending hitherto for subsistence'.[23]

Milton's recourse to the law of nature is, however, a complex matter, and not simply a case of opposing divine right and patriarchy with radical libertarian ideas based upon a newly founded republican constitution. As Scott has argued persuasively, contexts of European religion and politics were central to the development of events in England. Milton could not conceive of a secular political system that did not have liberty of conscience at its heart. In this he was consistent. Nor could he fully support the Cromwellian regime once it became apparent that it had failed to measure up to his exacting standards, especially in its religious policy.[24] Milton's great hero and contemporary, Sir Henry Vane, called in 1656 for 'just natural rights in civil things, and true freedom in matters of conscience'. Milton states that it is to Vane that we owe knowledge of the limitations of the civil and spiritual sword.[25] Milton believed emphatically that 'The whole freedom of man consists either in spiritual or civil libertie'. Contentment is impossible when there are restraints placed upon spiritual freedom.[26] Vane was also damning of what he perceived as excessive self-interest, military domination of free institutions, and corruption. These are views that Milton would echo in his *History of Britain*, and again in *Paradise Lost*, where scorn is heaped on flatterers and ambitious courtiers. In the *Second Defence* Milton suggests that men are often weakened by the unfettered and selfish pursuit of their own desires. Unless a vigilant eye is kept open and a guard placed against self-interest, moral and political weakness may well lead to 'factions, hatreds, superstitions, injustices, lusts, and rapine against one another'.[27] We are none too far from the spectre of a Hobbesian state of nature here. In such a state the court is the natural habitat of the vicious, presided over by a king who 'must be ador'd like a Demigod, with a dissolute and haughtie court about him, of vast expense and luxurie, masks and revels, to the debaushing of our prime gentry both male and female'.[28]

The constant themes in Milton's works are the fight against tyranny, the elaboration of sovereignty, its roots and origins and also its possession and dispossession. Moreover, as we go on to discuss *Paradise Lost* we become aware of Milton's division of natural law in its primary and secondary states. Briefly, this refers to nature in its pre-fallen and fallen condition. Before the fall man lived in circumstances of natural equality that was lost upon expulsion from the Garden of Eden. This constituted liberty in its natural state. As William J. Grace has written in his introduction to *A First Defence*, the secondary, in effect, post-fallen state of nature is 'an imperfect expression of the original law of nature'. However, for the regenerate – those who have experienced the workings of the Holy Spirit – a renewal of the law as it applied to Adam is possible. 'The law of nature, therefore sometimes refers to the law as it would apply to the regenerate in a Christian commonwealth'. This is borne out in *Paradise Lost* when God tells his Son that even though salvation is 'Freely vouchsafed', 'through grace', 'Some I have chosen of peculiar grace, / Elect above the rest; so is my will'.[29] It is only the regenerate who can enjoy this '*natural*' liberty; however, the secondary law of nature applies to any people who find themselves living under tyranny.[30]

The regenerate, in the early 1650s at least, consists of the Army and fervent supporters of the republic; they are moved to act according to a higher law of nature as the representatives of the people. Again, one finds Milton making distinctions between those who are fit to appreciate the state of nature they find themselves in and those who are not. 'But now, with a besotted and degenerate baseness of spirit, except some few, who yet retain in them the old English fortitude and love of Freedom, and have testifi'd it by thir matchless deeds, the rest, imbastardiz'd from the ancient nobleness of thir Ancestors, are ready to fall flatt and give adoration to the Image and Memory of [Charles I].' This low and debased feature of the people Milton ascribes 'First, to the Prelats' and secondly to the 'factious inclination' of men driven by self-interest.[31] Both *Eikonoclastes* and *A Defence of the English People* have an air of urgency that sometimes verges on desperation. The regenerate, fit audience though few, are not those who need to be convinced that revolution, regicide, and republicanism are the proper condition of man in a political state of nature. Throughout Milton's prose one sees this constant drive to make distinctions between a politically sophisticated elite and a mass that has no political consciousness and should therefore be led unquestioningly down the road to a republic. The problem is one of education. The majority is unfit to make political judgements. This is all very different in its aspect from Charles I's massively successful and hugely effective, defence of his own actions. In *Eikon Basilike* Charles argues that what Milton refers to as a 'fit audience though few', is in reality far too many. The people are best served by a sovereignty that lies not in the many, Parliament that is, but in the singular person of the king: 'the supreme power can be but in one, the head'.[32]

Milton was also keen to make distinctions within the philosophy of patriarchy. Like Locke later in the century, Milton would have no truck with the notion that kings were God's representatives upon earth.[33] Patriarchy is a social rather than political system, and is treated by Milton in terms that are entirely different from writers such as Salmasius and Filmer. The idea that there is a natural correlation between fathers as heads of households and kings as fathers of their nation is made to look ridiculous. The difference between the two is based on biology and economics rather than politics. 'Our fathers begot us, but our kings did not, and it is we, rather, who created the king. It is nature which gave the people fathers, and the people who gave themselves a king; the people therefore do not exist for the king, but the king for the people'.[34] The comparison made by Salmasius between kingdoms and families is, according to Milton, forced.[35] Fathers, it is true, have a right to rule their families, as it is he who begets and supports them financially. The people, on the other hand, *maintain* kings, in every sense of that word. Later in *A Defence* Milton quotes Aristotle to the effect that kings and fathers are distinct and unlike things, there being differences in 'species' as well as 'number'. Kingly claims to be *pater familias* are therefore fatuous.[36]

Such a view is not unique to *A Defence*. In *Eikonoclastes* Milton makes use of the biological metaphor, but this time to suggest that the people gave birth to the king. Here Parliament is gendered as female, as a mother, 'which, to civil being, created both him [Charles I], and the royalty he wore'. Charles' belief that Parliament, like women, cannot beget but can only receive, is turned on its head by Milton who argues that far from it being the king's 'procreative reason' that 'is necessary to all nature's productions, it is a tyrannous, unnatural, incestuous act. Charles in the end is once again compared to Nero.[37] Charles is similarly like Nero, says Milton, in that he too made frequent threats to do away with the senate and rule tyrannically.[38] It follows from this that if Parliament is generative insofar as power and sovereignty is concerned, then the people are at liberty to choose whatever government suits them best and, if they wish to, change it at their will. Indeed, it would appear that Milton's God has distinct republican sympathies. Glossing Deuteronomy 17:14 Milton states: 'A republican form of government ... [is] ... better adapted to our human circumstances than monarchy'. This 'seemed to God more advantageous for his chosen people; he set up a republic for them and granted their request for a monarchy only after long reluctance'. In *The Readie and Easie Way* this view is again reiterated, with Milton arguing that 'God in much displeasure gave a King to the *Israelites*, and imputes it a sin to them that they sought one'.[39] At all times kings are subject to and not above the law: 'Kings, if they offend, have no privilege to be exempted from the punishments of Law more than any other subject'.[40]

During the course of *A Defence* Milton constructs a formidable argument that draws on a wide range of classical and biblical sources to argue for a people's natural right to rebel against their king. Indeed, kingship itself is seen to be an unnatural political state. With his emphasis on divine and natural law, Milton argues, as Harrington would in 1656, and against Hobbes that it is legality that governs and 'controls the destiny of all that lives'. For Hobbes, the sovereign is not empowered by the people; quite the reverse.[41] Works by Aristotle, Plato, and Cicero are mustered to support the argument that the laws are as far superior to the magistrates as the magistrates are to the people.[42] As the pamphlet develops further Milton goes to the heart of legally constituted authority and the right of rebellion:

> Whoever resists authority, that is lawful authority, resists the ordinance of God. This decree touches kings too, who resist the laws and the senate. But does he who resists an illegitimate authority, or the corrupter and subverter of a legitimate one, resist the ordinance of God?[43]

The short answer to the question is no, and Milton duly cites Romans 13:3-4 to clinch the argument. Even Augustus and other Roman emperors recognised that sovereignty is something that resides in the people and not in the hands of any single individual. The idea that modern kings are anointed by God will not stand up to intellectual scrutiny; kings derive their power from the free consent of the people, or by their soldiers, or by their supporters. Cicero's *On the Agrarian Law*, says Milton, states unequivocally that '"It is agreed that all power, authority, and agency is derived from the whole people, and in particular those offices which were established for the benefit or convenience of the people"'.[44] Even if it were true that God did anoint all kings, he informs Salmasius, 'you could never make me believe that this makes them superior to the law and beyond punishment for any of their crimes'.[45]

Ancient authority and scripture are the basis for much of Milton's argument in the *First Defence*. He continually sees a natural correlation between the law of God and the law of man as delineated by pre-Christian intellectuals. Plato's *Epistles* and Aristotle's *Politics*, says Milton, are explicit on this very point. From Plato: 'Let the royal power be accountable for its actions; let law rule the kings too if they contravene the law in any way'. And from Aristotle: 'In the Spartan state is the best example of monarchy ruled by law'. Milton believes that ultimate sovereignty lies in the gift of the people, and it follows from this that 'whenever the public interest requires it, the people, which has granted power to another for public safety, may for the same reason take it back again without injustice'.[46] The question of sovereignty lies in the law. Because the people and its representatives in Parliament are the source of ultimate political power, then *ipso facto* they have the right to bring the king to account for his crimes against his subjects. The king 'has no power but in, and through, the courts of the realm'. As Parliament is the highest court in the land, it maintains 'a continuous authority and control over all regular courts and officials, even without a king'.

The question of where the origins of power naturally and legally lie is at the heart of the debate between Milton and Salmasius, particularly as it relates to regicide. Salmasius' argument rests on the point that the king is the source of all power; if this is so then the republican court had no jurisdiction over Charles and could not legally execute him. Legally, says Salmasius, a king cannot be tried by his own subjects because he has no peers. This was a factor upon which Charles relied when he was put on trial. In his argument against the unnatural and illegal status of the court, and in his emphatic belief that he was above all earthly law, Charles paradoxically argued that he was standing for the liberty of the people.[47] This forms the central plank of Salmasius' case.

Yet Milton, once again citing biblical and classical precedent, proceeds to demolish such an argument as specious and contradictory. Even though, as Salmasius argues in the *Regia*, the Hebrew judges held power 'one at a time and for their whole lives, [and] the Scripture calls them kings', yet they were tried by the representatives of the people, the Sanhedrin.[48] Like the Sanhedrin, the English Parliament was within its rights in trying Charles: 'Parliament is the supreme council of the nation, established and endowed with full powers by an absolutely free people for the purpose of consulting together on the most vital issues'.[49] So when Salmasius asks in chapter 11 of his *Regia* 'by what authority' do you try the king, Milton's response is brief: 'by the highest authority'.[50] Among the list of charges that were read out at his trial Charles was accused of betraying his trusted mission to rule within limits 'and according to the laws of the land'.[51] In the *Tenure of Kings and Magistrates* Milton is adamant that without the proper application of reason there can be no liberty. Nothing that contradicts the laws of God or right reason can be considered law, says Milton. 'If men within themselves would be govern'd by reason and not generally give up their understanding to a double tyrannie, of Custom from without, and blind affections within, they would discerne better what it is to favour and uphold the Tyrant of a Nation'.[52] Reason, as *Paradise Lost* makes clear, is choice.[53] The law is double-edged in its compulsion to obey and to resist: 'if we must obey a king and a servant of God, for the same reason and by the same law, we must resist a tyrant and a servant of the devil'. The attempt to enslave a freeborn people is the act of a tyrant. Once a king goes down that road he loses his right to the title invested in him by the very people he is trying to subjugate to his will. When that is established then there is no reason why he cannot be tried for 'any man is his peer and fit to act as judge in sentencing him to death'.[54]

Once again, however, we are thrown back upon Milton's very reductive vision of what constitutes the people. For instance, Milton defends as perfectly natural the events of Pride's Purge, the manner in which a greater part of the House of Commons opposed the actions of the army and were denied entrance to the House by Colonel Pride and his soldiers. Such actions were justified on the grounds that it was the 'act of the better, the sound part of the Parliament, in which resides the real power of the people'. The power of the people appears only to refer to and include those who support the actions of revolution.[55] What is more, Milton's continual citation of classical authority, particularly as it refers to the Roman republic, serves to emphasise the narrowness of his view. The Roman republic consisted of a particularly restrictive oligarchy that for the most part confined power to a very small class of people who had dominated its politics since the expulsion of Tarquin.[56] There is something disingenuous about Milton's remarks that even Roman emperors recognised checks upon their power by the senate. More so given his reference to Tacitus, the greatest of Roman historians and the most incisive critic of absolutism.[57]

A Defence of the English People is an epic undertaking and rightly made Milton famous as well as notorious among the European intelligentsia. As David Loewenstein has pointed out, *A Defence* is a literary tour de force with Milton transforming the figure of the rhetor into a poetic warrior for the republic.[58] This is powerfully felt at the work's conclusion when Milton points out once more the relationship between the state of nature and the people in an ideal polity. The English people,

> were born in freedom, they live in independence, and they can make for
> themselves what law they wish; they cherish particularly one law of great age,
> passed by Nature herself, which makes all laws, all rights, all civil govern-

ment depend not on the desire of kings but primarily on the well-being of the better citizens.[59]

Despite sounding egalitarian, Milton qualifies the independence and freedom of English citizens, somewhat. He is keen to separate, as always, the 'better citizens' from what he disparagingly refers to elsewhere as the rabble. Milton's preoccupations with the origins of power and sovereignty in the prose works of the 1640s and 1650s is transferred to the structure and content of *Paradise Lost* in the period of the Restoration when the republic is overwhelmingly rejected by the political nation in 1660. *Paradise Lost* enacts these themes in its intensive analyses of man in a fallen state. Satan's rebellion, the nature of God's political authority, Adam's pre-fallen sovereignty over all living things, the relationship between Adam and Eve in a pre- and postlapsarian condition, are all scrutinised by Milton in his epic. There are also structural implications in that the fall of the republic must have been at the forefront of Milton's mind throughout the composition of later books. Similarly there is the relationship between the worlds of heaven, hell and earth. No stone is left unturned. It follows from this that the political state of nature in a work as vast and as complex as *Paradise Lost* takes many forms. The themes of obedience, secular and religious, are figured through Satan's rejection of God's (as he sees it) arbitrary authority. Milton undoubtedly sees God as the natural fount of all authority, temporal as well as spiritual. This is complicated to an inordinate extent, however, by the charismatic persona of Satan as the leader of a doomed rebellion.

As critics have long since recognised, it is the problem of ascribing heroism to Satan that makes the political content of the poem so hard to fathom. Much of the debate that is still taking place is derived from the manner in which the Romantic period's greatest writers and critics interpreted Satan's role in the poem.[60] The issue of sublimity versus political radicalism and Milton's alleged retreat from political writing are as current now as they have ever been, as critics continue to debate the poem's republican content. Waldock's assertion that Milton is continuously at pains to correct the grandeur of Satan's rhetoric in order to point out its speciousness is to deny the impact of that rhetoric on its readership, particularly if that reader had republican sympathies. Stanley Fish, for one, has pointed out the deficiency in Waldock's analysis regarding Milton's continual attempts to destabilise Satan's emergent charisma and has offered an extremely influential analysis of the manner in which Satan's rhetoric works: 'in the attempt to follow and analyse Satan's soliloquy[s], the larger context [of the poem] in which [they] exist will be forgotten'.[61] In other words, despite their resistance to Satan's rhetoric and their feeling that because it is Satan that is talking then it must be lies, readers of Milton's poem get caught up in Satan's charismatic language against their will. The instances where Milton undercuts the rhetoric and provides the necessary correctives are lost in a work so vast. The picture of Satan that emerges in the first two books is the one that makes the greatest and most abiding impression on the reader. Milton was composing the first two books of *Paradise Lost* at the same time as he was writing *The Readie and Easie Way*, a last-ditch attempt to prevent the restoration of Charles Stuart. 'Milton, it seems, was ready to stake his life on behalf of republicanism at exactly the same time as he was rejecting its values in favour of serene resignation'.[62]

Norbrook is surely correct in locating the poem's gravitational centre in the politics of the 1650s. The debates that take place in the poem between the representatives of good and evil on the nature of the ideal state are extremely complex when one considers them in relation to the various political contexts in which they were written. Those who argue that Milton would hardly put into the mouth of the father of all lies a political ideology in which he himself believed, miss the point. Apart from the rather obvious inference that to do so would be a measure of authorial self-preservation, Satan's revolt from the suzerainty of God raises, even at face value, questions about the nature of authority and consent that were present everywhere in the 1640s and 1650s. When Milton talks about Satan's 'foul revolt' from the 'throne and monarchy of God',[63] this should not be read as an indictment of rebellion as such. Satan's rebellion is foul because it is unnatural; it runs against the grain of the relationship that Milton constructs between divine and natural law in a wide range of the prose works and the major poems. The sovereignty of God presented so favourably in *Paradise Lost* is an entirely different construct from that of the Stuarts.

In book V of *Paradise Lost* Raphael makes clear to Adam that God has 'ordained thy will / by nature free, not over-ruled by fate / Inextricable, or strict necessity. And: 'freely we serve, / Because we freely love, as in our will / To love or not; in this we stand or fall'. It follows from this that the angels and Adam too enter into a contractual agreement with God that is based upon consent governed by reason and choice.[64] Raphael's task is to make Adam aware that his 'nature free, not overruled by fate' places upon him the responsibility of fulfilling his side of the contract. With this in mind Adam is informed about the ascendancy of the Son and the rebellion in heaven led by Satan. In the host assembled in heaven by Satan to foment rebellion Abdiel, a lone voice, who points to the essential justice of God's theocracy and his right to determine the succession, strikes the only chord of dissent. Satan's idea that 'orders and degrees / Jar not with liberty' and that God has no right in reason to 'assume / Monarchy over such as live by right / His equals', is a specious claim if it is not supplemented by obedience. In Abdiel's view Satan's reasoning leads to licence and not liberty.[65]

This is further elaborated in book 6 when Abdiel once again confronts Satan, not in debate, but on the field of battle. In response to Satan's accusation that Abdiel is a 'seditious angel' and servile to boot, Abdiel replies through recourse to the law of nature as Milton sees it:

> Unjustly thou depravs't it with the name
> Of servitude to serve whom God ordains,
> Or nature; God and nature bid the same,
> When he who rules is worthiest, and excels
> Them whom he governs. This is servitude,
> To serve the unwise, or him who hath rebelled
>
> Against his worthier, as thine now serve thee,
> Thy self not free, but to thy self enthralled.[66]

As we can see, Abdiel's position with regard to natural law is perfectly in line with Milton's delineation of the law of nature in the prose works to which we have earlier referred. Abdiel's position is the more legitimate one because he sees that the law of nature is in accord with the law of God. If rebellion against authority is to have any credibility at all then it must be a godly rebellion and not be based upon naked self-interest and over-weaning ambition to usurp power for its own sake. Any accusation of God's absolute authority in *Paradise Lost* and a corresponding defence of Satan's revolt against the nature of that authority needs to be qualified. As David Loewenstein has recently remarked, 'it is one thing to rebel against an earthly monarch – as English saints had done in 1648-49 – and another to resist "Heaven's matchless King"'.[67]

Notes

1   Christopher Hill, *Milton and the English Revolution*, London: Faber, 1977, p. 186. For a trenchant view of Milton's contempt for the people broadly defined see, Hugh Trevor-Roper, *Catholics, Anglicans and Puritans*, London, Fontana, 1989, pp. 231-82. See also, Herman Rapaport, *Milton and the Postmodern*, Lincoln, NA, University of Nebraska Press, 1983.

2   *The Readie and Easie Way* (1660, Second Edition) in Don Wolfe, *et. al.* (eds), *The Complete Prose Works of John Milton*, New Haven, CT and London, Yale University

Press, 1953-1982, I-VIII; VII, p. 455. All further references are to this edition; hereafter abbreviated to *CPW*.

3   Blair Worden, 'Milton, *Samson Agonistes*, and the Restoration', in Gerald MacLean (ed.), *Culture and Society in the Restoration*, Cambridge, Cambridge University Press, 1995, pp. 111-36.

4   *Samson Agonistes*, in John Carey, ed., *Milton: Complete Shorter Poems*, Harlow: Longman, 1971, ll. pp. 328-400, 12-16.

5   *Ibid.*, l. 270.

6   *Eikonoclastes, CPW*, III, p. 343.

7   *CPW*, IV.i, p. 471.

8   Kevin Sharpe, 'An image doting rabble', in Sharpe and Zwicker, eds, *Refiguring Revolutions: Aesthetics and Politics from the English Revolution to the Romantic Revolution*, Berkeley, Los Angeles, CA and London, University of California Press, 1998, pp. 25-56; pp. 26-7. For an entirely opposite view, see David Norbrook, *Writing the English Republic: Poetry, Rhetoric and Politics, 1627-1660*, Cambridge, Cambridge University Press, 1999.

9   Sean Kelsey, *Inventing a Republic: The Political Culture of the English Commonwealth, 1649-1653*, Manchester, Manchester University Press, 1997, p. 2. Patrick Collinson, 'The Monarchical Republic of Elizabeth I', in *Bulletin of the John Rylands Library* 69 (1986), pp. 394-424.

10   The seminal work here is Pocock, *The Machiavellian Moment: Florentine Republican Thought and the Atlantic Republican Tradition*, Princeton, NJ and London, Princeton University Press, 1976.

11   Kelsey, *Inventing a Republic*, p. 5.

12   *The Tenure of Kings and Magistrates* (1649), *CPW*, III, p. 212; p. 222.

13   *A Defence of the People of England* (1651), IV.i, pp. 317-8.

14   *Ibid.*, p. 359.

15   *CPW*, VI, p. 353.

16   *The Readie and Easie Way* (1660, 2nd ed.), *CPW*, VII, p. 413.

17   See R.S. White, *Natural Law in English Renaissance Literature*, Cambridge, Cambridge University Press, 1996, pp. 216-42. White sees a diminished role for Calvinist theories of man's reprobate nature. See n.1, pp. 267-8.

18   Arthur Barker, *Milton and the Puritan Dilemma, 1641-1660*, Toronto, University of Toronto Press, 1940, p. 138.

19   *CPW*, IV.i, p. 369.

20   *Ibid.*, p. 535; *CPW*, VII, p. 456.

21   *CPW*, IV.i, p. 522, pp. 528-9.

22   *CPW*, IV.i, p. 481, p. 484. See also *Ibid.*, p. 489.

23   Scott, *England's Trouble, passim. CPW*, VII, p. 457.

24   See Blair Worden, 'John Milton and Oliver Cromwell', in Ian Gentles, John Morrill and Blair Worden (eds.), *Soldiers, Writers and Statesmen*, pp. 243-64; Austin Woolrych, 'Milton and Cromwell: "A Short but Scandalous Night of Interruption"?', in Michael Lieb and John T. Shawcross (eds), *Achievements of the Left Hand: Essays on the Prose of John Milton*, Amherst, MA, University of Massachusetts Press, 1974, pp. 185-218.

25 Sir Henry Vane, *A Healing Question Propounded and Resolved* (London, 1656), cited by Austin Woolrych in his 'Historical Introduction' to *CPW*, VII, pp. 19-20. Sonnet XVII, 'To Sir Henry Vane the Younger'. See Worden, 'Milton and Cromwell', pp. 251-2.

26 *CPW*, VII, p. 456.

27 *CPW*, V, p. 257; in *Paradise Lost* Belial is the ultimate courtier: 'suave, dilettante, dissolute and lacking in courage', Balachandra Rajan, ed., *Paradise Lost Books I and II* (1964), p. 35. *Second Defence*, *CPW*, IV.i, p. 684.

28 *The Readie and Easie Way* (2nd ed. 1660), *CPW*, VII, p. 425.

29 *Paradise Lost*, Alastair Fowler, ed., Harlow, Longman, 1971, III: pp. 174-5, 183-4. All further references to *Paradise Lost* are to this edition.

30 *CPW*, IV.i, p. 291; Barker, *Milton and the Puritan Dilemma*, p. 190.

31 *Eikonoclastes*, *CPW*, III, p. 344.

32 Philip A. Knatchel (ed.), *Eikon Basilike: The Portraiture of His Sacred Majesty in His Solitudes and Sufferings*, Ithaca, NY, Cornell University Press, 1966, p. 49. The popularity of this book can hardly be overstated. For the context of its publication, see Steven N. Zwicker, *Lines of Authority: Politics and English Literary Culture, 1649-1689*, Ithaca, NY, Cornell University Press, 1993, pp. 37-59, and Sharon Achinstein, *Milton and the Revolutionary Reader*, Princeton, NJ,: Princeton University Press, 1994, chapter 4. Both Achinstein and Zwicker are keen to emphasise the aesthetic dimension of Milton's battle with the king's book, bringing out in the process the cultural warfare that occurred in the 1640s and 1650s.

33 For a vigorous reading of common ground between Milton and Locke in relation to liberal humanism see Mathew Jordan, *Milton and Modernity: Politics, Masculinity and Paradise Lost*, London, Palgrave, 2001, chapter 1.

34 *CPW*, IV.i, p. 327; see also, *Ibid.*, n. 9.

35 In his 'Introduction' to *Milton: Political Writings*, Cambridge, Cambridge University Press, 1991, Martin Dzelzainis has argued that comparisons between Salmasius and Salmacis, Circe, and a Terentian eunuch, along with references to Salmasius as henpecked husband, creates a picture of 'domestic servitude' that 'undermines Salmasius' credibility as a spokesman for patriarchalism' (p. xx).

36 *CPW*, IV.i, p. 428, p. 472.

37 *CPW*, III, p. 467. See Lana Cable, 'Milton's Iconoclastic Truth', in David Loewenstein and James Grantham Turner (eds.), *Politics, Poetics and Hermeneutics in Milton's Prose*, Cambridge, Cambridge University Press, 1990, pp. 135-51; p. 140.

38 *CPW*, IV.i, p. 522.

39 *CPW*, VII, p. 424.

40 *CPW*, IV.i, p. 344, 345; *CPW*, III, p. 224.

41 Gimelli Martin, 'The Phoenix and the Crocodile', pp. 242-70; p. 246.

42 *CPW*, IV.i, p. 383.

43 *Ibid.*, p. 385.

44 *Ibid.*, pp. 485-6.

45 *Ibid.*, p. 402.

46 *Ibid*, p. 402; pp. 455-6, p. 460.

47 The classic account is C.V. Wedgewood, *The Trial of Charles I*, Harmondsworth, Penguin, 1983; first published, 1964, pp. 119-45; pp. 131, 137-8. *CPW*, IV.i, p. 508.

48   *CPW*, IV.i, pp. 464-5.

49   *Ibid.*, p. 497.

50   *Ibid.*, p. 516.

51   Cited by Wedgewood, *The Trial of Charles I*, p. 130.

52   *CPW*, III, p. 190. On the differences between Milton and Hobbes on the use of 'right reason', both of whom draw on Cicero, see: Gimelli Martin, 'The Phoenix and the Crocodile', pp. 249-50; Jean Hampton, *Hobbes and the Social Contract Tradition* Cambridge: Cambridge University Press, 1986.

53   *Paradise Lost*, III: 108.

54   *CPW*, IV.i, pp. 492, 494. Law and reason proved to be vexed terms in Charles' trial. See Wedgewood, *Trial of Charles I*, p. 138.

55   *CPW*, IV.i, pp. 457-8. The definitive account of Pride's Purge is David Underdown, *Pride's Purge*, Oxford, Clarendon Press, 1971. See also Blair Worden, *The Rump Parliament*, Cambridge, Cambridge University Press, 1971.

56   See Ronald Syme, *The Roman Revolution*, Oxford, Oxford University Press, 1939; pbk edn., 1960, chapter 2.

57   *CPW*, IV.i, p. 460. Tacitus makes it brutally apparent in the *Annals* that Tiberius, for one, recognised no such checks to his power.

58   David Loewenstein, 'Milton and the Poetics of Defence' in Loewenstein and Turner, (eds), *Politics, Poetics and Hermeneutics*, Cambridge, Cambridge University Press, 1990, pp. 171-93.

59   *CPW*, IV.i, p. 533.

60   The *locus classicus* for these widely divergent readings are, of course, Blake and Coleridge. See Joseph Wittreich, *The Romantics on Milton: Formal Essays and Critical Asides*, Cleveland, Case Western Reserve University, 1970. The classic study of Milton's influence on the Romantics is Harold Bloom, *The Anxiety of Influence: A Theory of Poetry*, Oxford, Oxford University Press, 1973. For a more recent interpretation that takes issue with Bloom see, Lucy Newlyn, *Milton and the Romantic Reader*, Oxford, Clarendon Press, 1993.

61   Waldock, *Paradise Lost and its Critics*, Cambridge, Cambridge University Press, 1947, pp. 77-8; Stanley Fish, *Surprised by Sin: The Reader in Paradise Lost*, London, Macmillan, 1967, 2nd edition, 1997), p. 10. In turn Fish's reading of *Paradise Lost* has been recently described by David Norbrook as 'placing the poem in a quietist framework', *Writing the English Republic*, p. 337.

62   The best treatment of this is David Norbrook, *Writing the English Republic*, p. 433.

63   *Paradise Lost*, I, 33, 42.

64   *Paradise Lost*, V. 526-8, 538-40.

65   *Paradise Lost*, V. 792-6. As Fowler's note glossing these lines states: 'Satan omits altogether the value of obedience or discipline, which Milton regards as the essential condition of republican freedom'.

66   *Paradise Lost*, VI. 174-81.

67   David Loewenstein, *Representing Revolution in Milton and his Contemporaries: Religion, Politics and Polemics in Radical Puritanism*, Cambridge: Cambridge University Press, 2001, p. 229. Loewenstein is quoting from book IV. 41.

PART II

RESTORATION TO REVOLUTION

Chapter 5

Locke, Sidney, and the Whig State of Nature

The absolutist position on sovereignty that created the most stir in the later seventeenth century was that of Filmer rather than Hobbes ('politically the least important of all the absolutist writers', for Peter Laslett[1]). Hobbes' unremitting pragmatism proved too much for even the most absolutist-minded of royalists – including Filmer himself, who went on to remark of his notorious contemporary: 'I consent with him about the rights of exercising government, but I cannot agree to his means of acquiring it'.[2] The lack of any really significant spiritual dimension in Hobbes proves to be the sticking point for Filmer – and for so many others, for whom Hobbes was little better than an atheist in consequence. Certainly, there is no mystique about kingship in *Leviathan* of the kind that Filmer wished to foster; Hobbes having, as J.P. Kenyon has summed it up, 'divorced political obligation from the supernatural altogether'.[3] Although written much earlier (parts as early as 1628 according to some commentators[4]), Filmer's *Patriarcha* was not published until 1680, and immediately drew the ire of the emerging Whig movement, prompting replies from several figures, most notably John Locke and Algernon Sidney.[5] Peter Laslett has noted that 'the Tories, champions of the Monarchy against Shaftesbury and the Whig Exclusionists, scored a notable propaganda victory', with the publication of *Patriarcha*.[6] The Whigs certainly took Filmer's defence of the divine right of kings very seriously indeed, as Sidney's introductory remarks to his *Discourses Concerning Government* (written between 1681 and 1683, although not published until 1698) make clear:

> Having lately seen a book entitled *Patriarcha*, written by Sir Robert Filmer, concerning the universal and undistinguished right of all kings, I thought a time of leisure might be well employed in examining his doctrine, and the questions arising from it; which seem so far to concern all mankind, that, besides the influence upon our future life, they may be said to comprehend all that in this world deserves to be cared for.[7]

Such 'universal and undistinguished right' was anathema to Whig theorists, especially to an unrepentant republican like Sidney, who had served as one of the commissioners at the trial of Charles I and had described the latter's execution as, 'the justest and bravest action that ever was done in England, or anywhere'.[8]

Both Sidney and Locke (in the *First Treatise of Government*) provided vigorous, closely-argued refutations of Filmer's doctrine of divine right, positing very different conceptions of human nature and mankind's natural state from those espoused by Filmer. Even more to the point for our purposes in this study, Locke went on to write a *Second Treatise of Government*, where the state of nature was sketched out in more detail: a state that was taken to entail a very different kind of government and notion of political obligation from those to be found in Hobbes. Collectively, Locke and Sidney give us what might be called a 'Whig state of nature' to pose against the absolutist forms that so appealed to the royalist mentality (bearing in mind Ashcraft's reservation that Sidney and Locke were at the radical end of the Whig spectrum[9]). Encoded in this Whig state are republican sympathies (it is no accident that both Locke and Sidney found such favour amongst the North American colonists in the later eighteenth century[10]) as well as an implicit commitment to personal sovereignty, with the latter building on the nonconformist tradition in this respect.[11] Filmer's broadside in *Patriarcha* against reformist divines ('favourers of the Geneva discipline' being picked out for special mention[12]), indicates how sensitive the old order was to the political implications of such notions as personal conscience – presciently so if Filmer was indeed writing well before 1640.

Filmer's doctrines had immense symbolic significance in terms of the absolutist leanings of the restored Stuart monarchy, with its known admiration for the French 'sun king' model of government then coming into fashion on the continent. *Patriarcha* had the great virtue of providing biblical justification for the monarchy's real, if not always publicly acknowledged, long-term political objectives; hence the detailed, not to say long-winded, responses that Sidney and Locke felt compelled to offer in reply (far longer in each case than Filmer's fairly slender treatise). For Laslett, Filmer's appeal to the royalist movement lay in his talent as 'the codifier of conscious and unconscious prejudice'.[13] Filmer's idea is quite a simple one: all kings are descended from Adam, the first king, and they are fathers of their people:

> It is true, all kings be not the natural parents of their subjects, yet they all either are, or are to be reputed as the next heirs to those progenitors who were at first the natural parents of the whole people, and in their right succeed to

the exercise of supreme jurisdiction. And such heirs are not only lords of their own children, but also of their brethren, and all others that were subject to their fathers.[14]

Given this lineage, continued even through the dispersal of the tribes in the aftermath of Babel, Filmer feels justified in claiming the principle of absolute monarchy: 'As the father over one family, so the king, as father over many families, extends his care to preserve, feed, clothe, instruct and defend the whole commonwealth'.[15] Repeatedly, scripture is appealed to for evidence of kingly authority and the subjection of the individual this entails, with Filmer rejecting the notion that the people can have any right to choose in matters of government. God has given us kings, and we have no option but to obey his will in this respect: 'God did always govern His own people by monarchy only', and scripture, according to Filmer, sanctions no other kind of government *but* monarchy.[16] To reject this natural order of things is to court heresy.

Filmer is adamant that there is no such thing as a 'natural' liberty that the individual can be said to enjoy, observing, with yet another careful eye on scripture, 'that the desire of liberty was the cause of the fall of Adam'.[17] Any desire we might have for liberty can only be regarded, as *Patriarcha*'s subtitle informs us, as 'unnatural'.[18] Catholic and reform divines are roundly criticised for encouraging such beliefs, with Filmer showing himself well aware of the threat that is posed to the established order by such a conception of sovereignty. The full title of one of his pamphlets, 'The Necessity of the Absolute Power of all Kings: And in particular, of the King of England', published anonymously in what for royalist supporters were the dark days of 1648 (and republished, significantly enough, in 1680), indicates just how passionately he adhered to his beliefs in the face of growing political crisis.[19] For Filmer, it is enough to declare that the doctrine of man's natural liberty 'is not to be found in the ancient Fathers and doctors of the primitive church' for it to be dismissed – tradition firmly rules his politics, and rebellion in any form can never be countenanced.[20] Kings are held to be above the law: 'as kingly power is by the law of God, so it hath no inferior law to limit it'. Parliament exists only by the grace and favour of the king, and can have no pretensions to sovereignty on behalf of the people, since kings are to be considered to have 'unlimited jurisdiction' over their nation and its subjects.[21] If we are to speak of natural rights, then it must be the 'natural right of regal power' – by which we are bound, it would seem, unto eternity.[22] Natural right is yet another issue on which Filmer disagrees with Hobbes, who assumes that each individual does have that right but that it is best curbed for the benefit of humanity at large.[23]

Sidney's reply to Filmer is openly contemptuous of his rigid conception of monarchical succession, whereby,

> We are not to examine, whether he or she be young or old, virtuous or vicious, sober minded or stark mad; the right and power is the same in all. Whether virtue be exalted or suppressed; whether he that bears the sword be a praise to those that do well, and a terror to those that do evil; or a praise to those that do evil, and a terror to such as do well, it concerns us not; for the king must not lose his right, nor have his power diminished on any account.[24]

Against this blind acceptance of tradition, Sidney preaches the right to rebellion, based on a belief that natural merit, rather than mere accident of birth, should determine who ought to govern a nation: 'He only is fit to conduct a ship, who understands the art of pilot'.[25] No governor should assume that he or she is in possession of a sinecure either; although we give up some of our natural liberty by entering into a state of government, Sidney insists that,

> we ourselves are judges how far 'tis good for us to recede from our natural liberty; which is of so great importance, that from thence only we can know whether we are freemen or slaves; and the difference between the best government and the worst, doth wholly depend upon a right or wrong exercise of that power.[26]

We retain this right to decide whether or not the government is exercising its power in the common good, and no government can consider itself above such judgement (or can only at its own risk, as Charles I found to his cost). Sidney even believes that God leaves the decision as to form of government up to us: 'the whole is forever left to the will and discretion of man. We may enter into, form, and continue in greater or lesser societies, as best pleases ourselves'.[27] God is a notably less doctrinaire entity in this reading of mankind's history than in Filmer's.

Sidney raises historical, sociological, and ontological objections to Filmer's defence of the principle of divinely-ordained absolute monarchy. Overall, Sidney's argument is based on the premise that 'every man is originally free', and that is an ontological condition that no action of monarchy can materially affect.[28] No matter how much we may be tyrannised that natural freedom always remains, to be accessed by us when possible. Given that, and given a natural equality that means all of us have the right to lead our lives as we see fit (as long as this involves no encroachment on the liberties of others), then no-one has the right to claim special status. Even kings are subject to the law, and when they fail to respect the law we have the right as citizens to remove them from office. Neither is such an act to be considered rebellion in the stricter sense of the term:

> The whole body therefore of a nation cannot be tied to any other obedience than is consistent with the common good, according to their own judgment: and having never been subdued or brought to terms of peace with their magistrates, they cannot be said to revolt or rebel against them to whom they owe no more than seems good to themselves, and who are nothing of or by themselves, more than other men.[29]

The message is clear that sovereign power lies in the body of the people not the body of the king, and that kings are, at best, temporary expedients that nations can cast off when it suits them, without having to worry themselves about any spiritual implications: 'the whole is forever left to the will and discretion of man'. The events of 1688-9 will see such quintessentially Whig principles put into actual practice. Even later Tory theorists such as Bolingbroke can be found appealing to the 'common good' (see chapter 11).

While he does not deny that some men may be fitter to rule than others, Sidney finds the notion grotesque that such 'fitness' can be genetically transmitted down the generations as Filmer is claiming is the case from Adam onwards. The historical record furnishes Sidney with a host of instances to the contrary:

> The Assyrian valour was irresistible under Nebuchadnezzar, but was brought to nothing under his base and luxurious grandson Belshazzar. ... The fruit of all the victories gained by Edward the first and third, or Henry the fifth of England, perished by the baseness of their successors: the glory of arms was turned into shame; and we, by the loss of treasure, blood and territory, suffer'd the punishment of their vices.

Sidney espouses the very modern view that it is the principles and institutions of the state that are of greatest importance in any political settlement: if these are well designed then the holders of public office can be changed on a regular basis, with no risk to the state's innate stability – 'good constitutions remain, tho the authors of them perish'.[30] If, on the other hand, the principle of patriarchalism is adhered to as strictly as Filmer proposes, then the state *is* at risk every time succession occurs – with the inevitability that, sooner or later, a weak child will follow a strong parent. Against the 'baseness' of successors, Filmer's discourse of sovereignty can offer us no protection. In such cases, the 'natural right of regal power' manifestly fails us, and, having reverted to the state of nature, we have no option, according to Sidney, but to take matters into our own hands and reconstruct the state.

Sidney believes that power is 'arbitrary' and that such arbitrariness is a good thing, since it enables us to adapt to changing socio-historical circumstances. What might have suited the Israelites, on whom Filmer, inveterate scriptural scholar that he is, lays so much weight as a source of examples, might equally be disastrous when applied to a seventeenth-century society such as England. Yet again, the spiritual dimension of politics is played down, with Sidney noting that, *'Magna Charta*, which comprehends our ancient laws, and all the subsequent statutes were not sent from heaven, but made according to the will of men'.[31] Furthermore, Parliament, not the King, is where legal authority really lies; with Sidney impishly pointing out that this is even the case in France, the pretensions of the 'sun king' party, and their English admirers, notwithstanding. For the French king to act otherwise, is for him to sink to the level of being a mere 'pirate' stealing parliament's right.[32]

Sidney offers a disruptive reading of Filmer, which emphasises historical discontinuity and social change. Where Filmer sees an unbroken linear narrative of monarchical sovereignty stretching from the time of Adam to the present, and binding us in the process, Sidney sees gaps and ruptures that render the Filmerian position untenable. Where Hobbes draws back in horror from a civil war, Sidney sees it instead as a source of social progress. Social change is a powerful factor in Sidney's argument, and one almost totally missing from Filmer, for whom the divine right of kings applies in all times and all places, irrespective of local socio-political circumstances. For Sidney, on the other hand, those local circumstances dictate what form the government of a nation should take, and that form is always to be considered open to change and negotiation. What fits one society and one historical period may not fit another, and certainly has no right to be considered to set a precedent for future generations (a point to be made particularly forcefully a century later by Thomas Paine, to justify yet another assault on traditional conceptions of power[33]). Times change and so do men's ideas (as Sidney's did on regicide); equally, men sometimes make mistakes, as in their choice of form of government, and must be allowed the opportunity to correct those mistakes: 'All human constitutions are subject to corruption, and must perish, unless they are timely renewed'.[34] Neither should we assume that such changes go against God's will: 'God helps those who help themselves', as Sidney puts it, all but authorising rebellion as long as it is undertaken with a sincere belief in one's cause.[35] One can see why traditionalists would be so worried at this appeal to the individual's self-interest – especially after the events of the 1640s and 1650s.

Sidney also offers an incommensurable reading of Aristotle to that of Filmer, arguing that the latter is guilty of taking things out of context or of generalising from particular circumstances. Where Filmer had taken Aristotle to be recommending governmental absolutism founded on a belief in patriarchy, Sidney merely finds an argument for a magistracy based on those most fitted to rule:

> Aristotle ... seems to think, that those who believed it not to be natural for one man to be lord of all the citizens, since a city consists of equals, had not observed that inequality of endowments, virtues and abilities in men, which render some more fit than others, for the performance of their duties, and the work intended; but it will not be found, as I suppose, that he did ever dream of a natural superiority, that any man could ever have in a civil society, unless it be such a superiority in virtue, as most conduces to the publick good.[36]

Greek classical philosophy in general provides no support for the Filmerian cause. Neither Aristotle nor Plato can be considered to argue the case for patriarchalism, but rather for fitness for the task in hand; the concern being to ensure that only those best qualified, intellectually and morally, attain public office. What Sidney extracts from Greek classical political theory is a commitment to meritocracy: a concept that Filmer and the traditionalists could only regard with horror. There is little doubt that Sidney regards meritocracy as in the state's best long-term interests, and a clear suggestion that a republic is this condition's natural home.[37] Indeed, Jonathan Scott has described the *Discourses* as 'a series of increasingly strident republican diatribes' of unmistakable insurrectionary intent.[38]

Sidney concludes that *Patriarcha* is 'a heap of contradictions and frauds', and cannot be taken seriously.[39] Locke's *First Treatise* takes a similarly dim view of the worth of Filmer's arguments:

> And truly, I should have taken Sr. Rt: Filmer's *Patriarcha* as any other Treatise, which would perswade all Men, that they are Slaves, and ought to be so, for such another exercise of Wit, as was his who writ the Encomium of *Nero*, rather than for a serious Discourse meant in earnest, had not the Gravity of the Title and Epistle, the Picture in the Front of the Book, and the Applause that followed it, required me to believe, that the Author and Publisher were both in earnest.[40]

Locke goes on to express an unequivocal commitment to individual freedom, arguing that Filmer's belief in our bound condition is based on nothing more substantial than 'a bare supposition of *Adam's Authority*, without offering any Proof for that Authority'.[41] Given that Filmer is, in effect, advocating slavery as man's natural condition, Locke will demand a level of philosophical sophistication that Filmer is not capable of in order to back this up: 'bare supposition', and even 'bare *Creation*' in Adam's case, will not suffice. If 'bare *Creation*' by God were enough to confer monarchical authority, then, as Locke tartly notes, a lion would 'have as good a Title to it' as Adam.[42]

Locke picks apart Filmer's argument with practised philosophical skill, querying his assumptions and disputing his definitions to reveal the generally threadbare quality of Filmer's reasoning.[43] Phrases such as '*by the Appointment of God*' are subjected to close scrutiny, as is the term 'Monarch' itself.[44] When it comes to the circumstances of Adam's creation, Locke concludes that all Filmer manages to prove is that Adam '*was Governor by Right of Nature*, because he was *Governor by Right of Nature*'. He objects further that if such authority is grounded in being a father, then at the point of creation Adam fails to meet that crucial specification; which leaves Filmer in the awkward position of assuming Adam 'to be a Father before he was a Father, and to have a Title before he had it'.[45] Filmer stands guilty of assuming as fact what he should be required to prove, and his argument does not bear very close examination at this critical point. In the absence of unconditional proof that Adam has the status of a monarch from the moment of creation onwards, then Filmer has no case whatsoever for a lineage-based patriarchalism extending down to the current king of England.

Locke demolishes any claims that Adam is invested with absolute sovereignty by God, arguing instead, in what is becoming prototypically Whig fashion, that Adam has no more than 'right in common with all Mankind'.[46] The argument turns on whether being awarded dominion over '*every moving thing, that moveth upon the Earth*' (1 Gen. 28), can be considered to include the rest of mankind or not: for Filmer it does, for Locke categorically it does not. Close reading can reveal to Locke no more than a reference to those creatures created *before* Adam came onto the scene, in which case there is no question of 'Monarchical Power over those of his own Species'. Filmer stands guilty yet again of the sin of superficial textual interpretation. Adam has no '*Private Dominion*', therefore, 'but a Dominion in common with the rest of Mankind'.[47] The most we can infer from *Genesis* is that Adam stands for the whole species of mankind, who, collectively, can be said to have dominion over the lesser species – with women, too, from Eve onwards, sharing in this dominion. Sovereignty stubbornly refuses to allow itself to be detached from the individual member of the human species: 'this Grant spoken to *Adam* was made to him, and the whole Species of Man'.[48] Adam proves to have largely symbolic status in Locke's reading, with his status as the first man conferring no particular privileges upon him.

Locke is very careful to separate property, and the benefits accruing to the owner from this, from sovereignty. To be in possession of property is not to gain rights over the bodies of others, since all of us have the right to survival and the disposal of our own persons as we see fit: 'And how will it appear, that *Property* in Land gives a Man Power over the Life of another? ... we know God hath not left one Man so to the Mercy of another, that he may starve him if he please'.[49] The nature of property and ownership will be explored in more detail in the *Second Treatise*, but it is already clear that as far as Locke is concerned they fall far short of providing a basis for absolute power over others. Whether or not Adam can be said to be the owner of the earth (and Locke contends that he cannot) is irrelevant, given that property does not entail political subjection.

Neither does the subordinate social position of women entail absolute sovereignty: 'if this be the *Original Grant of Government* and the *Foundation of Monarchical Power*, there will be as many Monarchs as there are Husbands'. As was noted earlier, Locke is also careful to detach 'Conjugal Power' from 'Political Power', with Filmer standing accused, yet again, of inaccurate definition.[50] The former grants certain rights within the family, but cannot be treated as equivalent to political sovereignty, which trades in matters of life and death. Even fatherhood fails to justify the assumption of absolute power over the person of others: that would be for the individual to 'Arrogate to himself the Incomprehensible Works of the Almighty'.[51] Another discrimination is being insisted upon: this time between human creation and divine creation, the former being much more circumscribed than the latter, and indeed, being contingent upon the latter. Such contingency means that it can never attain to the condition of absolutism, which remains forever a preserve of the divine. Ultimately, God, not man, is the source of life. Locke also shifts the emphasis from fatherhood to parenthood, on the grounds that the mother is as much the source of human creation as the father – an argument which further undermines the cause of patriarchalism. And he also makes it quite clear that honouring one's parents, as the commandments require of us, is by no means the same thing as being in subjection to them.

Locke concludes that paternal power can neither be inherited nor transferred, which leaves no basis whatsoever for patriarchalism. Any powers that Adam had are to be presumed to have died with him, and there are no grounds at all for constructing a line of political succession from him. As in Sidney's case, the notion of authority being genetically transmitted is dismissed out of hand – even if it were possible to determine who was the true heir, which Locke, who rejects the principle of primogeniture anyway, vehemently denies. The minute we move past Adam and his immediate descendants, the more problematical succession becomes, with Locke teasing Filmer quite mercilessly on the issue:

> I go on then to ask whether in the inheriting of this *Paternal Power*, this *Supreme Fatherhood*, The Grand-Son by a Daughter, hath a Right before a Nephew by a Brother? Whether the Grand-Son by the Eldest Son, being an Infant, before the Younger Son a Man and able? Whether the Daughter before the Uncle? or any other Man, descended by a Male Line? Whether a Grand-Son by a Younger Daughter, before a Grand-Daughter by an Elder Daughter? Whether the Elder Son by a Concubine, before a Younger Son by a Wife?[52]

Patriarchalism is made to seem foolish by such manoeuvres, and once Locke has pointed out all the ruptures and discontinuities of world history since Adam, the patriarchal project lies in ruins. In Locke's eyes, the nature of the state must still be assumed open to negotiation.

The Second Treatise makes explicit the link between the state of nature and the nature of the state, and becomes something of a blueprint for the Whig political project.[53] Locke's state of nature is a significantly less hostile environment than Hobbes' ('in the beginning all the World was *America*, and more so than it is now', in Locke's poetic phrase[54]); although that has led some critics to dismiss it as unrealistic, with one referring slightingly to Locke's conception as 'a benign *political* condition having all the idealized marks of a political society and none of its drawbacks'.[55] The state of nature is 'a *State of perfect Freedom*' and 'also *of Equality*', which no-one can be removed from 'without his own *Consent*'.[56] That we retain the right as individuals to withdraw that consent is precisely what Filmer consistently denies is possible.

The Second Treatise takes it as its brief to outline the nature of political power, defined by Locke as,

> a *Right* of making Laws with Penalties of Death, and consequently all less Penalties, for the Regulating and Preserving of Property, and of employing the force of the Community, in the Execution of such Laws, and in the

defence of the Common-wealth from Foreign Injury, and all this only for the Publick Good.[57]

In order to understand the basis of political power we need to go back and examine our original 'State of perfect Freedom'; that is, existence in the state of nature. Although a state of freedom, this is not, Locke warns us, to be regarded as 'a State of Licence'; in fact, in that state we stand under a 'Law of Nature' (also dubbed a 'Law of Reason'), which dictates that we ought not to inflict harm either on ourselves or others.[58] To that end, all of us possess the right to enforce that law of nature, and to punish those who transgress it. Transgressors are held to be guilty of 'a trespass against the whole Species', and become fair game for the rest of humanity – even to the extent of each of us having the right to kill a murderer for the benefit of all humankind.[59] Furthermore, if anyone makes war upon us, we may summarily 'destroy' such an individual as we would a wolf or lion – they no longer merit treatment as human beings, having reverted by their actions to the status of mere beasts of prey (or, put another way, to extreme versions of Hobbesian self-interest). Tellingly enough, Locke believes that striving to put someone under our absolute power is to be in a state of war with them.

It is to avoid such problems that we quit the state of nature and enter into civil society, which provides us with greater personal security against the advent of the state of war or abuses of executive power. Civil society assumes consent, and where this does not exist we are deemed to be in a state of slavery, which, in effect, 'is nothing else, but the State of War continued'.[60] Locke goes on to contend that absolute monarchy is 'inconsistent with Civil Society', since in combining the legislative and executive power absolute rulers allow of no independent appeal against their judgements, hence our natural liberties are not being properly safeguarded.[61] We cannot be said to have consent in such cases, and without consent we have no proper civil society guaranteeing our natural freedoms. When those freedoms are abused in this way, we have the right to dissolve the government: at which point 'the People are at liberty to provide for themselves, by erecting a new Legislative, differing from the other, by the change of Persons, or Form, or both as they shall find it most for their safety and good'.[62] It is a similar conclusion to that drawn by Sidney: that in certain circumstances open revolt is not simply justified but morally correct, and that, ultimately and inalienably, sovereignty resides in the individual not the ruler. Again, 1688-9 will be a practical demonstration of this principle in action, although we must always remember that the Whig conception of the political class is still not a very extended one at this point: as noted earlier, Sidney's natural sympathies incline towards the aristocracy. Its repercussions may go much wider, but the 'Glorious Revolution' is largely a case of two political elites struggling for control. For all their references to the 'people', we are not yet in the era of mass politics (although Ashcraft is willing to make a case for Locke being more radical than most on this issue[63]).

One of the things that we are most concerned to provide protection for in civil society is property, and Locke is at pains to provide a theory for this that links it to personal sovereignty: 'every Man has a *Property* in his own *Person*. This no Body has any Right to but himself'.[64] Property comes about originally through the act of 'mixing' one's labour with nature. Once that has occurred the objects acted upon become my sole property, even if the 'mixing' in question is done by someone else working under my direction – for example, someone who has agreed to 'sell' his labour power to me for an agreed time for an agreed fee:

> Thus the Grass my Horse has bit; the Turfs my Servant has cut; and the Ore I have digg'd in any place where I have a right to them in common with others, become my *Property*, without the assignation or consent of any body. The *labour* that was mine, removing them out of that common state they were in, hath *fixed* my *Property* in them.[65]

The point of the whole exercise is to make the best use of nature that we can in order to improve the human lot; Locke regarded this as an invitation extended to us by God in the state of nature. It is one of the great virtues of civil society that it makes such divinely-sanctioned industry easier to prosecute – as well as securing the fruits of it in a way impossible to ensure in the state of nature. As Ashcraft has summarised it: 'In Locke's view, God has a wider purpose in mind than simply providing for the individual's self-preservation; rather, individual labour is seen as a contributory action to the improvement and benefit of life, taken in a collective sense'.[66]

The critical point to emerge from the work of Sidney and Locke is that sovereignty is in the individual. Collectively we may have decided to accept restrictions on this natural trait in order to gain greater protection for our persons, but it can never be ceded on a permanent basis: our consent must always be considered to be contingent. We retain the power, as Andrew Norris has neatly put it, 'to judge that judge' appointed over us.[67] In effect, we carry that state of nature within us, and can choose to access it when circumstances – as in the case of a tyrannical government – put our person under threat. Like the notion of conscience, it can be suppressed but never eradicated, and there are clear parallels to be noted with the non-conformist outlook on this matter of personal sovereignty. In a very real sense that sovereignty stands above the state, regardless of what the state or its representatives may say or do; with John Bunyan's refusal to give up lay preaching, to conform with the law of the Restoration regime, constituting a highly symbolic act in this respect. No amount of rhetoric can turn subjection to an absolute monarch into mankind's natural condition.

Overall, the Whig state of nature presents a much more optimistic picture of the human condition than that of the Hobbesians or the patriarchalists. We are free beings, and most of us respect each other's right to be so; we may be tyrannised on occasion, but we retain both the desire and the ability to correct that situation. The human condition is perceived as one capable of improvement, and one in which most of us are well disposed towards others; only in exceptional circumstances does it decline into a 'warre of every man against every man', and even then it can contribute positively to social change. Human nature is less something to be curbed and policed, more something to be trusted and encouraged to develop; with conscience and reason to the fore in this process. The state is less a repressive mechanism to keep ruthless, self-seeking individuals in check by inhibiting social change, than an enabling device to help us realise our potential for the common good; and there are at least implicit sympathies for such a state being republican in form (although this will not necessarily remain the case throughout the party struggles of the later part of our period). Ideally, national sovereignty should express personal sovereignty, with the latter constituting the foundation of any just society. Between the libertarian and authoritarian visions of the state and human nature, however, there is still much conflict to be enacted.

Notes

1   Introduction to John Locke, *Two Treatises of Government*, Peter Laslett (ed.), Cambridge, Cambridge University Press (rev ed.), 1988, p. 67. Ashcraft, on the other hand, makes greater claims for Hobbes' influence on Tory thinking in the 1680s (see *Revolutionary Politics*, pp. 293-4).

2   Sir Robert Filmer, 'Observations Concerning the Originall of Government, Upon Mr Hobs *Leviathan*, Mr Milton against *Salmasius*, H. Grotius *De Jure Belli*', in Filmer, *Patriarcha and Other Writings*, Johann P. Sommerville (ed.), Cambridge, Cambridge University Press, 1991, pp. 184-234.

3   J.P. Kenyon, *Revolution Principles: The Politics of Party 1689-1720*, Cambridge, Cambridge University Press, p. 17.

4   For a discussion of the dating of *Patriarcha*, see Johann P. Sommerville's introduction to Filmer, *Patriarcha*, pp. xxxii-xxxiv.

5   For another important contemporary contribution to this debate, see James Tyrrell's *Patriarcha non Monarcha* (1681).

6   Introduction to *Two Treatises*, p. 51.

7   Algernon Sidney, *Discourses Concerning Government*, Thomas G. West (ed.), Indianapolis, IN, Liberty Fund, 1996, p. 5.

8   Quoted in Thomas G. West, Foreword to *Ibid.*, p. xxix. Interestingly enough, Sidney had been opposed to regicide in 1649.

9   For Ashcraft, neither Locke nor Sidney are entirely typical Whigs, but he agrees that their work grows out of, and shares many of the assumptions of the general Whig movement of the time. Whig ideology is considered in detail in chapter 5 of Ashcraft's *Revolutionary Politics*. Another commentator to treat Sidney as a radical Whig is James Conniff ('Reason and History in Early Whig Thought: The Case of Algernon Sidney', *Journal of the History of Ideas*, 43 (1982), pp. 397-416. For Jonathan Scott, on the other hand, Sidney's radicalism takes him beyond the boundaries of Whiggism: 'In fact he had never been a whig; he was the product of a previous age; a violent civil war era insurrectionary of an entirely different order' (*Algernon Sidney and the English Republic, 1623-1677*, Cambridge, Cambridge University Press, 1988, p. 2). Exactly what Whiggism involved in this period is still a matter of some debate, but Scott's exclusionist position seems extreme and we shall follow Ashcraft and Conniff in regarding Sidney as a radical Whig. For the development of Whiggism in the immediate post-1689 period, see Kenyon *Revolution Principles*.

10   For a detailed analysis of Sidney's impact on American thought, see Houston, *Algernon Sidney and the Republican Heritage*. Blair Worden also notes that 'French revolutionaries carried busts of Sidney on demonstrations' ('The Commonwealth Kidney of Algernon Sidney', *Journal of British Studies*, 24 (1985), pp. 1-40 (p. 33).

11   Some commentators have identified Calvinist influences in Locke's thought; see, for example, John Dunn, *The Political Thought of John Locke*, Cambridge, Cambridge University Press, 1969. Ashcraft sees yet another possible source of influence, placing 'Locke in much closer proximity to the Levellers and to the radical political theory they developed than has previously been supposed' (*Revolutionary Politics*, p. 165).

12   *Patriarcha*, p. 3.

13   Peter Laslett, Introduction to *Patriarcha and Other Political Works of Sir Robert Filmer*, Oxford, Blackwell, 1949, p. 41.

14   *Patriarcha*, p. 10.

15   *Ibid.*, p. 12.

16   *Ibid.*, p. 23.

17   *Ibid.*, p. 2.

18   'The *Naturall* Power of Kings Defended against the Unnatural Liberty of the People', *Ibid.*, p. 1.

19   In Filmer, *Patriarcha and Other Writings*, pp. 172-83.

20   *Patriarcha*, p. 3.

21   *Ibid.*, p. 35.

22   *Ibid.*, p. 11.

23   See Filmer, 'The Originall of Government'.

24   *Discourses*, p. 7.

25   *Ibid.*, p. 51.

26   *Ibid.*, p. 31.

27   *Ibid.*, p. 56.

28   *Ibid.*, p. 529.

29   *Ibid.*, p. 519.

30   *Ibid.*, p. 211.
31   *Ibid.*, p. 569.
32   *Ibid.*, p. 574.
33   'There never did, there never will, and there never can exist ... any generation of men, in any country, possessed of the right or the power of binding and controlling posterity to the *"end of time,"* or of commanding for ever how the world shall be governed, or who shall govern it' (Thomas Paine, *The Rights of Man*, Henry Collins (ed.), Harmondsworth, Penguin, 1969, p. 63).
34   *Discourses*, p. 150.
35   *Ibid.*, p. 210.
36   *Ibid.*, pp. 80-81.
37   For an argument emphasising the aristocratic bias to Sidney's thought, however, see Zera S. Fink, *The Classical Republicans: An Essay in the Recovery of a Pattern of Thought in Seventeenth-Century England* (2nd ed.), Evanston IL, Northwestern University Press, 1962.
38   Scott, *Algernon Sidney and the Restoration Crisis, 1677-1683*, p. 207.
39   *Discourses*, p. 502.
40   *Two Treatises*, p. 141.
41   *Ibid.*, p. 149.
42   *Ibid.*, p. 151.
43   For a reading which emphasises the wider context of Locke's critique (particularly the ecclesiological), see Mark Goldie, 'John Locke and Restoration Anglicanism', *Political Studies*, 31 (1983), pp. 61-85, where it is argued that 'Locke's target was not only Filmer', but 'all the agents of Anglican authoritarianism' (p. 61).
44   *Two Treatises*, p. 151.
45   *Ibid.*, p. 153.
46   *Ibid.*, p. 157.
47   *Ibid.*, p. 161.
48   *Ibid.*, p. 162.
49   *Ibid.*, pp. 169, 170.
50   *Ibid.*, p. 174.
51   *Ibid.*, p. 179.
52   *Ibid.*, pp. 230-31.
53   Ashcraft emphasises this link: 'That England in 1688 had been returned to a state of nature was a fundamental premise of the radicals' argument ... [and] ... Locke's assessment of the Glorious Revolution and the condition of England in 1689 exactly expresses the radicals' position' (*Revolutionary Politics*, pp. 569, 577).
54   *Two Treatises*, p. 301.
55   Sheldon S. Wolin, *Politics and Vision: Continuity and Change in Western Political Thought*, Boston, Little, Brown, 1960, p. 305. For Andrew Norris, however, this reading underestimates the problems Locke himself identifies in the state of nature (see 'Locke Reading the Law of Nature: Lockeian Hermeneutics and Political Judgment', in Kevin L. Cope (ed.), *1650-1850: Ideas, Aesthetics, and Inquiries in the Early Modern Period*, vol. 5, New York, AMS Press, 2000, pp. 37-62 (pp. 45-7)).
56   *Two Treatises*, pp. 269, 330.
57   *Ibid.*, p. 268.
58   *Ibid.*, pp. 270, 305. For an argument that the law of nature and the law of reason remain unreconciled in Locke, see Norris, 'Locke Reading'.

59   *Two Treatises*, p. 272.
60   *Ibid.*, p. 284.
61   *Ibid.*, p. 326.
62   *Ibid.*, p. 411.
63   'Locke goes to some lengths to defend the people taken broadly and in a literal sense' (Ashcraft, *Revolutionary Politics*, p. 305). Ashcraft is to be contrasted with earlier commentators on Locke, such as J.P. Kenyon, for whom the *Treatises* 'are to be regarded as an essentially conservative, bourgeois interpretation of the Revolution' (*Stuart England* (2nd ed.), Harmondsworth, Penguin, 1985, p. 271).
64   *Two Treatises*, p. 287.
65   *Ibid.*, p. 289.
66   Ashcraft, *Revolutionary Politics*, p. 264.
67   Norris, 'Locke Reading', p. 38.

Chapter 6

Neville: The Utopian State of Nature Revisited

Henry Neville and Aphra Behn provide us with two utopian fictions written during the Restoration period that are startling in their similarities and differences. Both texts create a world in which libertinism and political order are intertwined, seemingly inextricably. Similarly, both the *Isle of Pines* (1668) and *Oroonoko* (1688) present fictional worlds and the events that take place in them, that are easily translated into the fraught political context of late Stuart history. Rebellion against authority and its justification is central to the content of both novellas and provides the modern reader with a state of nature that is vividly drawn from political theories that are diametrically opposed. *Oroonoko*, along with *Love Letters from a Nobleman to his Sister* by Aphra Behn, is the subject of the chapter following, where we shall see that Behn is no advocate of rebellion against one's legitimate ruler, except in unusual circumstances. For the moment, however, we turn in detail to Henry Neville's controversial utopian text, *The Isle of Pines*.

Henry Neville was one of the most prominent republicans in seventeenth-century England. His influence upon, and his debt to, the thought of James Harrington, and his defence of it in the years following the restoration of the monarchy, is well known.[1] As well as translating Machiavelli's works, Neville was the author of a significant republican treatise entitled *Plato Redivivus*, first published in 1681 when the Exclusion crisis was raging.[2] Neville's republican credentials were, therefore, unimpeachable. He stood out against Cromwell during the Protectorate and would have no truck with placing the protectorate on a monarchical footing, believing that if there was to be a king then that king should be Charles Stuart, whose entitlement to the post was much greater than either Oliver or Richard Cromwell. Neville is constantly seen during the upheavals of the 1650s acting in defence of parliament's privileges against arbitrary rule, wherever this may originate.[3] Although he was not against the principle of a 'chief magistrate' he believed that this magistrate's powers should be limited and not arbitrary. In this respect, as in many others he is close to Harrington. Ideas regarding the limitation of sovereignty formulated in the 1640s and 1650s did not simply disappear at the return of the Stuarts, but proved adaptable in the Restoration period when what became known as Whig political theory emerged.[4] Neville did not believe in the arbitrary changing of one monarch for another and did not indulge recklessly in the many plots that were apparent during the Exclusion crisis. He was dismissive of attempts to exclude the Duke of York in favour of Monmouth as successor to the throne upon the death of Charles II. Only a republic was worth the dangers of a conspiracy. In a pamphlet written in 1659 entitled *The Armie's Dutie: or, Faithful Advice to the Souldiers*, in which Neville may well have had a hand, support for Richard Cromwell was not forthcoming. Instead a 'popular assembly' was proposed 'to set up a government determined by the "immutable laws of nature"'.[5] As we have seen in chapter two, Harrington was a determined advocate of the rule of law, and in *The Isle of Pines* Neville adopts Harringtonian principles on the subordination of every individual to the law and on the natural leadership qualities of the gentry.

Neville's political writings and beliefs have not lacked attention from, in particular, historians of political thought. As a writer of fiction, however, Neville has fared less well. The *Isle of Pines*, as its latest editor has remarked, has not received much in the way of critical attention, and with one notable exception critics treat the text as little more than masculine fantasy.[6] Caroline Robbins describes it as no more than an example of high spirits and Rabelasian humour', with Neville writing merely for his own amusement. Susan Bruce offers briefly a number of more interesting and suggestive contexts in which *The Isle of Pines* has, and may be read: as a treatise on patriarchy; as a colonialist text, and more intriguingly, within a political context intimately related to Anglo-Dutch relations in the mid- and later seventeenth century. Neville's republicanism and the proto-Whig politics that simmered beneath the surface of Restoration political life are further contexts that need to be addressed. Neville significantly charts the development of social and political relations on the island over three generations, a development that sees the eventual demise of a free-wheeling form of sexual libertinism, replaced on the Isle of Pines by a democratic form of republicanism that is accountable to emerging political institutions. Accordingly, 'The Isle of Pines is a fiction of the origins of a nation in patriarchal dominance and draws on patriarchal political theory'. This results in the eventual forced transition from a patriarchy to 'a state based on law'.[7] William Pine's position as chief magistrate referred to above is consistent with Neville's views as they were expressed in the 1650s.

The Isle of Pines posits a narrative of events based on the following premise. George Pine, along with four women, consisting of his master's daughter, two maidservants, and a black woman, are the sole survivors of a shipwreck and are washed up on an uninhabited island. The island itself is extremely fecund and blessed with a temperate climate. After a period of some four months Pine begins sexual relations with the maidservants, then his former master's daughter, Sarah English, and finally the black slave. All five seem happy with the arrangement and by this means the island is populated. In its lack of embarrassment about Edenic sexual relations, Neville's text has affinities with Behn's poem, 'The Golden Age' and the pre-fallen sexuality and fecund topography of *Paradise Lost*. The children born of George's 'wives' are formed into tribes, identified by the matriarch's surname. In this manner a social structure develops and a process of colonisation takes place as the clans gradually spread across the island.

The narrative opens with a framing device. Cornelius Van Sloetten, a Dutch merchant, happens on the island during the rule of William Pine, the grandson of the original patriarch. At this stage the island is populated by a considerable number of people, and is verging on the edge of anarchy. The libertinism that lies at the heart of the colony's foundation has now become a liability and rebellion against William's rule is imminent. This, such as it is, is a bare exposition of the events that make up the first part of the framing narrative. Van Sloetten's first encounter with authority on the island is William Pine, its current leader. The manner in which this takes place and the description he offers of William is instructive:

> The Prince himself (whose name was William Pine, the grandchild of George Pine, that was first on this island) came to his palace door and saluted us very courteously, for though he had nothing of majesty in him, yet he had a courteous, noble and debonair spirit, wherewith your English nation (especially those of the gentry) are very much endued.

The Dutchman carefully describes William as having the demeanour of a member of the English upper class. The fact that he has no air of royalty about him does not detract from his abilities. William has the qualities of that class of person that republicans seem to most admire. He is rational, courteous, and has an innate nobility that becomes immediately apparent in the manner that he treats his guest. Food and drink on the island is the same for everyone, and despite the fact that William lives in a palace, 'prince and peasant' eat and drink exactly the same.[8] Immediately, therefore, we are faced with a society that is infinitely more egalitarian than any that is current in Europe. If anything William resembles the ideal 'chief magistrate' to which we have already referred in previous chapters. Nevertheless, as we shall see, there is trouble in paradise.

Van Sloetten is presented with a narrative by William, written by his grandfather as a relation of events explaining how the island came to be settled. This document is held in great reverence by William and his father before him and represents the history of settlement. It serves also as a document legitimising the right of succession to rule the island by George Pine's descendants. As a history of government, such as it is, the document represents loosely the island's constitution and gives the air of legitimacy to the Pines' right to rule. George rapidly impregnates the women and soon begins to look upon them as property. As he grows older he assumes the role of patriarch: 'Thus having lived to the sixtieth year of my age and the fortieth of my coming thither, at which time I sent for all of them to bring their children, and they were in number descended from me by these four women, of my children, grand-children and great-grandchildren, five hundred and sixty of both sorts'. In his eightieth year George observes the rule of primogeniture and passes on to his eldest son the reins of power on the island, naming him 'both King and Governor of all the rest'. Equipped with the manners of Europe and instructed to observe the Christian religion, George musters the clans for the last time in his eightieth year, discovering that the island's populace is now figured at 'one thousand seven hundred eighty, and nine'.[9]

George's tenure on the island has been accredited by him as the gift of providence. Like Crusoe, it is God's will that George has survived the horrors of shipwreck, along with four women destined to fulfil his patriarchal vision on a domestic and political level.[10] Unlike Milton's Adam whose work in Eden is to tend the garden in all its fruitfulness, thereby preventing idleness and wantonness, George positively thrives on the lack of toil. 'Idleness and a fullness of everything begot in me a desire for enjoying the women'. A deficiency of labour is therefore the route cause of libertinism. There are echoes here of Charles II's widely perceived preference for sexual pleasure over the necessity of taking care of the state. An undisciplined monarch in a political state of nature that is underpinned by patriarchal principles is bound inevitably to lead to conditions of unrest. After George's death, and under the regime of his son, there appears a falling away from the Edenic ideal. This is directly attributed by William, who has now resumed the narrative, to be caused by a growing population unwilling to accept the rule of patriarchy laid down by his grandfather.

But as it is impossible, but that in multitudes disorders will grow, the stronger seeking to oppress the weaker, no tie of religion being strong enough to chain up the depraved nature of mankind, even so amongst them mischief began to rise, and they soon fell from those good orders prescribed them by my grandfather. The source from whence those mischiefs spring, was at first, I conceive, the neglect of hearing the Bible read, which according to my grandfather's prescription, was once a month at a general meeting, but now many of then wandering far up into the country, they quite neglected the coming to it, with all other means of Christian instruction, whereby the sense of sin being quite lost in them, they fell to whoredoms, incests and adultery; so that what my grandfather was forced to do for necessity, they did for wantonness.[11]

According to William's reading of man in a political state of nature, disobedience of authority is instinctual. William's view is based on a conventionally Calvinist view of man's innate depravity allied to his almost Hobbesian reading of the natural compunction of the strong to govern the weak. Sexual libertinism, practised during George's times as a necessity (albeit highly pleasurable), has now been embraced for its own sake. Without an emphasis on biblical reading, whereby moral lessons are learnt, liberty has led to licence, and rape becomes a regular occurrence. The lack of discipline alluded to earlier – there is no creed of public virtue and service to the greater good on the island – has seen what passed for a loosely constructed patriarchal order break down under the pressure of unrestricted hedonism and the wilfully destructive pursuit of self-interest. Idleness, a virtue in itself to George, is the root cause of potential chaos when practised in what has now become a state, and not simply a small gathering thrown together by necessity. The roots of discontent are built into the system from the beginning. With no work ethic and no notion of the collective good binding them together, unchecked self-satisfaction is leading to a state where every man's hand is turned against his fellow.

The reaction of William's father to this state of affairs is revealing. In a public assembly the culprits are identified and an armed force is organised to bring order where there is chaos. The leading culprit is executed and William's father, in consultation with an executive council, inaugurates a rule of law that must be observed. In many ways this is quite draconian and has affinities with agendas proposed by the rule of the saints during the Commonwealth and Protectorate. Blasphemy is punishable by death, as is rape. Any man caught in the act of adultery risks castration; any woman, partial blinding. If a woman is guilty of a second offence, then capital punishment follows. Disobedience towards, or defamation of, the Governor is punishable by whipping and banishment. In essence what we have here is a condensation of the Mosaic Law with its source in Exodus 21. 23-5. Puritan law emerges as a backlash against the Bacchanalian excesses practised previously. This in itself, however, maps merely a transitional phase. Neville, as we have seen above, was anything but puritan in his religious beliefs. Nevertheless, republicans often had a severe moral code derived from their admiration for Sparta and Rome, an attitude that sometimes made their social philosophy appear puritan in its aspect. Neville's belief in the classical republican idea of Ciceronian *virtu*, roughly translated by Worden as the pursuit of ethical values demonstrated in public life and public action – was mixed with Machiavelli's confrontational conception of *virtu*, which puts courage and resolution before ethical scruples, seemingly without 'any sense of contradiction'.[12] Neville's political radicalism, not unlike Milton's, is supported by a classical republican heritage that emphasises practical morality and militates against excess when it disrupts social order.[13] It was far from unusual in the 1650s to see common cause made between classical republican values such as the commonwealthmen adhered to, and the more austere forms of puritan thought on morals. Ciceronian moral philosophy lacked nothing in severity. As Steven Pincus has argued, 'apocalyptic republicanism was anything but rare in the period.[14] This accounts in large part for the gravity of the backlash against those who advocate self-interest above social responsibility on the island, and also for the austere and unforgiving laws designed to prevent such an event happening again. As Neville later puts it in *Plato Redivivus*, austerity and virtue equals strength: 'Breach of rules and order causes division; and division, when it comes to be incurable, exposes a nation, almost as much as a tyrannical government does'. Neville's example here is derived from Roman history, with Machiavelli drawn on for support.[15] From here on in, morality and its lack on the Isle of Pines, is closely policed.

William's status as the island's chief magistrate begins to take on the trappings of royalty as the visit by the Dutch comes to a close. Van Sloetten refers to him as 'Prince William Pines', and the Dutch help to build him a palace. William by now has servants, 'And now was he attended after a more royal manner than ever we saw him before'. Balanced crucially against this quasi-monarchical depiction of William, however, is his austerity. This is evidenced in the text by his refusal of strong European liquor and his preference for water; his 'very sparing' diet, and his brisk attention to affairs of state throughout Van Sloetten's stay on the island. The last example of this is an insurrection against William's rule on the point of Van Sloetten's departure from the island. Rebellion breaks out as Henry, a leading descendant of the 'black tribe' of Phipps, begotten by George on the Negro slave in the original shipwreck, rapes the wife of one of the principal members of the Trevors family. The Trevors' resultant action precipitates a 'great hurly-burly' as the island is thrown into chaos and civil war looks to be a real possibility, 'they being two great potent factions, the bandying of which against each other threatened a general ruin to the whole state'.[16] We have come a long way since George landed on the island. The outbreak that is about to take place is not based upon generally riotous or libertine behaviour, but a feud between powerful factions. This is a structural fissure, rather than the excesses of unchecked individualism. Rape is the means that justifies the end: open revolt against legally instituted authority.

William can only put down this revolt by asking for aid from the Dutch. His initial attempt to reconstitute order fails. As Van Sloetten states, 'where the hedge of government is once broken down, the most vile bear the greatest rule'.[17] The Dutch deploy their superior weaponry and the conclusion is inevitable; after a minor fracas, order is restored. Henry Phill is then executed for inciting insurrection. The message here is clear: the rule of law can only be upheld by force. These are Van Sloetten's last direct observations on the island's history and politics; the question of the afterlife of government there once the Dutch have left, is left open to question. William's authority on the island has been upheld by force, without the threat of which there can be no foundation for order. The blurred status of the chief magistrate, variously referred to as a prince and as a sterling example of the gentry, is perhaps deliberate. Republican discourse, as we have argued earlier, was during the Restoration period modified to suit the prevailing political situation. As a form of government republican ideas were adapted to account for a monarch as head of state. Given the restored monarchical context in which *The Isle of Pines* is written and published, the ambiguity of William's representation is hardly surprising. This is not an advertisement for monarchy as such, nor can it be given Neville's politics. Rather, what we have here is an example of what can occur when liberty is mistaken for licence.

The rule of law cannot be upheld on William's island without the presence of two crucial factors: a socially and politically virtuous gentry class, the majority of whom prove willing to support propriety in the public sphere, and the existence of an executive arm to enforce action when the law is broken. This is represented in the text by three of the four families that inhabit the island, the Trevors, Englishs, and Sparks in the first instance, and by the Dutch in the second. The two are mutually supportive. Without these two conditions William's rule is always going to be precarious. It is no accident that William's saviours are the Dutch, and not the Spanish or the French. As an aggressive protestant republic, they are the ideal commentators to provide value judgements on the positive and negative aspects of rule on the island. In another sense it matters little if William appears to carry the trappings of royalty with him as events on the island prove that these are no more than ephemera and carry with them no intrinsic power. Of the four clans that are formed as a result of George Pine's sexual activities when he lands on the island, it is only the Phills that do not obey the law as it is laid out by George's son. It follows from this that true to contract theory the people place themselves willingly under a ruler who is meant to safeguard their interests. When he cannot do so all pretensions to order necessarily break down. To reiterate a point, law must be upheld in the final analysis by the terror it is able to impose upon those who defy its strictures. This rule is extended to all of the island's inhabitants. It is the laws that safeguard the freedom of the subject, without which 'neither lives, liberties, or estates' could be maintained or flourish.[18] Accordingly in *The Isle of Pines*, it is the maintenance of enforceable law and not the presence of a prince that guarantees liberty. Complete freedom of the type that we see at the beginning of Neville's text, is an unsustainable fantasy. As another seventeenth-century political theorist would write, "'the end of all government is (or ought to be) the good and ease of the people, in a secure enjoyment of their rights, without pressure or oppression" from rulers or fellow citizens'.[19] The crucial point to be drawn from this quote is that tyranny can come from more than one source. On the Isle of Pines, oppression derives from those who refuse to obey the law, and not from a prince or chief magistrate who has not the means to enforce it. As Mark Goldie has written in terms that can just as easily be applied to this depiction of William in *The Isle of Pines*, royal power 'after 1660 was, for Neville, chimerical, for it no longer had natural foundations'.[20] This is just as true of the Stuart monarchy in the later seventeenth century as it is of Neville's utopian paradise.

Notes

1   Neville was thought by contemporaries such as Hobbes, Aubrey and Hartlib, to have had a hand in the composition of Harrington's *Oceana*; see Blair Worden, 'Part 1, Chapters, 2, 3 and 4', in David Wooton, (ed.), *Republicanism, Liberty and Commercial Society, 1649-1776*, Stanford, CA, Stanford University Press, 1994, pp. 82-193, especially pp. 116-17. Pocock, (ed.), *The Political Works of James Harrington*, pp.

100-4, 125-9. Caroline Robbins, (ed.), *Two English Republican Tracts: Plato Redivivus or, A Dialogue Concerning Government by Henry Neville, An Essay upon the Constitution of the Roman Government by Walter Moyle*, Cambridge, Cambridge University Press, 1969, pp. 7, 11-12.

2   Worden has described the Machiavelli translation as 'elegant', and a major contributing factor to the emerging Whig political discourse of the later seventeenth century ('English Republicanism', p.458).

3   Ludlow describes Neville as 'a person of singular affection to the Commonwealth', *The Memoirs of Edmund Ludlow*, C.H. Firth, (ed.), Oxford, Clarendon Press, 1894, I-II; II, p. 98.

4   Worden, 'Oceana: Origins and Aftermath', in Wooton, (ed.), *Republicanism, Liberty and Commercial Society*, p. 131.

5   Robbins, (ed.), *Two English Republican Pamphlets*, pp. 9-10. Robbins believes that Neville may well have put his name to this work. Given its 'appeals to Christ and more than a touch of unctuousness', however, he is unlikely to have written any of it, 'even if he shared its fundamental principles' (p. 10). This seems credible given Neville's alleged preference for Cicero over the Bible.

6   Susan Bruce, (ed.), *Three Early Modern Utopias: Utopia, New Atlantis, The Isle of Pines*, Oxford, Oxford University Press, 1999, p. xlix. All further references to *The Isle of Pines* are to this edition. Neville was also the author of a particularly scurrilous pamphlet entitled *The Parliament of Ladies* written in two parts and published in 1647. *The Isle of Pines* as male fantasy is the view of James Holstun, *A Rational Millennium: Puritan Utopias of Seventeenth-Century England and America*, Oxford, Clarendon Press, 1987, pp. 109, 244. Bruce is surely correct in her assessment that the best work to date on *The Isle of Pines* has been written by Susan Wiseman, '"Adam the Father of All Flesh:" Porno-Political Rhetoric and Political Theory in and After the Civil War', in James Holstun (ed.), *Pamphlet Wars: Prose in the English Revolution*, London, Frank Cass, 1992, pp. 134-54. Wiseman's analysis is sophisticated and suggestive; however, it is all too brief and does not make the specific claims made in this chapter.

7   Wiseman, 'Adam the Father of all Flesh', p. 153.

8   Neville, *The Isle of Pines*, p. 192.

9   *Ibid.*, pp. 199-200.

10   *Ibid.*, pp. 195, 196.

11   *Ibid.*, p. 201.

12   Worden, 'Marchamont Nedham and English Republicanism', p. 47; 'Republicanism and Restoration', pp. 144-5, in Wooton, (ed.), *Republicanism, Liberty and Commercial Society*.

13   Jonathan Scott, *England's Troubles*, pp. 231-2. Scott is not referring to Neville directly here; rather, he is referring to shared traits among English classical republicans.

14   Steven C.A. Pincus, *Protestantism and Patriotism: Ideologies and the Making of Foreign Policy, 1650-1668*, Cambridge, Cambridge University Press, 1996, p. 19.

15   Neville, *Plato Redivivus*, p. 97.

16   Neville, *Isle of Pines*, pp. 206-7.

17   *Ibid.*, pp. 207-8.

18   Neville, *Plato Redivivus*, p. 122.

19   Marchamont Nedham, *The Excellency of a Free State* (1656), cited by Quentin Skinner, *Liberty Before Liberalism*, Cambridge, Cambridge University Press, 1998, p. 20.
20   Mark Goldie, 'Restoration Political Thought', in Lionel K.J. Glassey (ed.), *The Reigns of Charles II and James VII & II*, London, Macmillan, 1997, pp. 12-35; p. 34.

Chapter 7

Behn and the
Paternal State of Nature

Aphra Behn stands in a problematical relation to the predominantly patriarchal attitudes that govern the Tory state of nature as read through Filmer
and Hobbes. The major problem perhaps, lies in relation to gender. Behn at
once supports and deconstructs the very politics that are associated with the
Tory vision of church and state: 'Behn's treatment of gender often seems to
complicate and refract, if not indeed to contradict, her party politics, creating in her work the sense of multiple and incommensurate ideological
agenda'.[1] Yet as Janet Todd has argued, for seventeenth-century female
writers such as Behn and Margaret Cavendish, the court provides a more
enabling atmosphere in which to work than 'the masculine institutions of an
emerging bourgeois democracy'. One explanation for this in the works of
royalist women writers in the later seventeenth century, is the unqualified
loyalty accorded to the monarch as a result of the betrayal of the 1640s and
1650s, when republicanism was viewed by many such writers as a scourge
inflicted upon this nation by God. The people, said Anne, Lady Halkett,
'paid nott that subjection that was due to theire lawful King'. Keeble points
to the unequivocal support for patriarchy royalist women displayed in their
memoirs. By the same token, however, he points to the liberating effect that
the war had upon aristocratic and upper class women, who up until then
had never been expected to act upon their own initiative. The experience of
exile and the necessity of movement 'are a measure' for royalist women of
their 'cultural journey': 'as they come out of their houses, so they come out
of their houswifely roles'.[2] Belief in patriarchy need not necessarily, therefore, result in total subjection.

This is particularly the case for women like Behn who must earn their
living. Given Behn's profession as playwright and 'staunch apologist for
the Stuart kings, there was the added advantage that the commercial theatre
was dominated by the court whatever the shifting components of its audience'.[3] In texts such as *Love Letters from a Nobleman to his Sister*, *The
Fair Jilt*, *Oroonoko*, *The Rover*, and a wide range of Behn's poetry, one is
faced with a Tory ideology that is scrutinised, found wanting, and then

ultimately upheld by a reactionary politics that subordinates gender to the prevailing and dominant patriarchal ideology. In *The Rover* and *The Fair Jilt*, for instance, the male representatives of patriarchal power are often seen to be inadequate to the task at hand. Willmore is a bumbling and intellectually deficient would-be rapist, and Miranda continually manipulates Prince Tarquin in her attempts to control the power structures by which she is governed. In *Love Letters to a Nobleman from his Sister*, Sylvia is by turns protagonist and victim, yet never loses sight of her desire to wield power by indirect means. In Behn's works this most usually takes the form of controlling men through sex; manipulating their desire in order to bring about some form of autonomy. This has been addressed by Donald R. Wehrs who argues that 'In *Love Letters*, Behn attempts to demonstrate how, through surrendering "received" positions within the symbolic order, both men and women come to act under the sway of interest and pleasure and so deprive themselves of selfhood in the very act of aggrandizing the self'. In her movement from Philander's sister-in-law to his lover, and eventually to whore – a downward moral spiral that sees her ultimate fate as an outcast from all respectable society – 'Sylvia transforms herself into the sexual, feminine equivalent of a deligitimated throne that every fool may aim at'.[4] Wehrs' reading of the novel combines a poststructural analysis of language blended with Hobbesian self-interest theory. His point that 'royalist principles' do not restrain Sylvia is only partially correct, however, as the constant reiteration of Tory, particularly Filmerian patriarchal theory is ever-present in the text. To argue rather one-sidedly that both Philander and Sylvia surrender uncritically to Hobbesian libertinism is to negate the text's function as a broader elucidation of politics and ideas in the 1680s. Wehrs never successfully accounts for the manner in which Sylvia offers a running critique of Whig politics and remains true to these principles throughout.[5] There is therefore an uneasy tension in the novel between Hobbesian individualism and Filmerian paternalism.

A telling example of Sylvia's attitude towards Philander's politics is made early in the novel:

> It is not enough, oh *Philander*, for my eternal unquiet and undoing to know you are Married, and cannot therefore be entirely mine? is not this enough, oh cruel *Philander*? but must you espouse a fatal cause too, more pernicious than that of Matrimony and more destructive to my repose.[6]

Clearly, for Sylvia, at least, Philander's political treachery is more reprehensible than his adulterous, and in the context of the times, incestuous love for his sister-in-law.[7] Nor should this be surprising given the reverence and awe with which Behn looked upon Charles II. Consider the following lines of poetry composed to eulogise Charles upon his death in 1685:

No *Show'rs* of blood, no Temples *Vale* is rent,
But all is *Calm*, and all is *Innocent*.
When *Nature* in *Convulsions* should be hurled,
And *Fate* should shake the Fabrick of the World;
Impossible! Impossible! I Cry.
So great a King! So much a God! So silently should die!

In this poem Behn perceives the nature of the monarchy as being explicitly Filmerian. As she goes on to describe the death of Charles it is made apparent that the link between king and God, especially as it governs the succession, is one that is based on the former's quasi-divinity. On its route to heaven Charles' soul is 'of the divinest dress' making '*CHARLES a God*! and *JAMES a Monarch* too!'.[8] These lines are not the expression of a conventional and opportunistic poetic response to the death of a king, but are instead indicative of a loyalty that Behn felt towards the Stuarts throughout her life. An indication of this is the poem praising Queen Mary and deliberately omitting William, written early in 1689, and her refusal to take on a commission offered by the Whig apologist and cleric, Gilbert Burnet. Although she acknowledges the compliment that Burnet has paid her, Behn states that her muse is not up to the task: 'but Loyalty Commands with Pious Force / That stops me in the thriving Course'. Once again one notes that as far as Behn is concerned, loyalty is connected with piety: how can man put asunder what God has decreed? Behn seems to be saying that she cannot write panegyric in support of a throne that has been irreligiously usurped. She believes that she stands, 'like the Excluded Prophet'. Not particularly known in her writing for an excessive preoccupation with religious zeal, Behn nevertheless appears to view writing in defence of the Glorious Revolution as an act of blasphemy.[9]

Love Letters is an intensely political work of fiction. Commentators have recognised that it is a thinly veiled account of the politics of the 1680s illustrated by means of reference to the scandalous love affair and elopement of Ford Lord Grey with his sister-in-law, Lady Henrietta, rendered fictionally in the novel as Philander and Sylvia. Published in three parts between 1684 and 1687, *Love Letters* maps political crises such as the Rye House Plot of 1683 and Monmouth's rebellion upon the death of Charles in 1685. As much a novel of political ideas as a love story, in the figures of its central protagonists we see Behn's defence of Filmerian patriarchy against the libertinism popularly associated with Hobbes and also with Whig political theory, tainted irredeemably in Behn's eyes by its association with the good old cause.[10] This is particularly the case in Part Three where Robert Ferguson, the Whig radical nonconformist and refugee from the Rye House Plot, figures prominently in the narrative.

In the realm of concrete political behaviour as well as the world of abstract political thought, the years between the end of the Exclusion crisis and the successful invasion of William of Orange, mark a victory for Tory political management and witness the triumph of Filmerian paternalism. This is the battleground on which the sexual and secular politics of *Love Letters* is fought. The year 1681 proved to be a political watershed in Charles' reign, with Charles and the Tories being in the ascendant until the crisis that precipitated the Glorious Revolution occurred in 1688. According to Mark Kishlansky fear of rebellion rather than popery had induced an energised Anglican ministry to label 'Exclusion a ploy' instigated by nonconformists determined to ruin church and state. 'In the spring of 1681 Tory mobs replaced Whig ones as the dominant force in London', and increasingly parallels between the current crisis and the 1640s and 1650s were being drawn. Shaftesbury was equated with Pym, and the Duke of Monmouth with Cromwell', the latter having his illegitimacy reasserted twice.[11] At the end of March 1681 the storm of exclusion had been weathered successfully and 'for the first time in his reign' Charles enjoyed 'a conclusive victory over his opponents'. Monmouth was widely perceived to be Shaftesbury's puppet; moreover, he lacked support even from the majority of Whigs: 'Because of Charles' indulgent affection for him he was a useful political tool, but no one of any weight regarded him as a serious candidate for the throne'.[12] According to David Ogg, it was Monmouth's illegitimacy that made him attractive to Whig radicals on the grounds that it would ensure his subservience to Parliament.[13] This, however, as Hutton argues, is a position applied retrospectively by modern historians.[14] To contemporaries such as Aphra Behn the prospects of a Whig revival in fortunes had to be continually guarded against. This was particularly the case when one considers that both Lord Grey and James Scott, Duke of Monmouth, the Philander and Cesario respectively of Behn's *Love Letters*, play such prominent parts in the novel. Even more so as Monmouth continued from 1679-85, and especially after 1682, to provide a charismatic focal point for those who wished to see the eventual accession of the king's Catholic brother denied. As J.R. Jones has remarked, 'Monmouth possessed charisma'. He was 'affable, handsome, athletic [and] popular'. Accordingly, he 'was indispensable to provide a focus for feelings that were otherwise diffuse'.[15] It is the involvement of Monmouth and Grey in the Rye House Plot of 1683 that provides the immediate political context of the first part of *Love Letters* published in 1684.

Behn's antipathy to Monmouth/Cesario is pronounced; she can see no reason for his pretensions or the participation of Grey/Philander in his plots and schemes. This is clearly flagged in Part One of *Love Letters* when Sylvia is adamant that Philander can have no legitimate reason for plotting to rebel against his rightful king:

> Is it to make *Cesario* King? oh what is *Cesario* to my *Philander*? If a Monarchy you design; then why not this King, this great, this good, this Royal Forgiver? – This who was born a King; and born your King; and holds his Crown by right of Nature, by right of Law; by right of Heav'n itself; Heav'n who has preserv'd him, and confirm'd him ours, by a Thousand miraculous escapes and sufferings, and indulg'd him ours by Ten Thousand acts of mercy and indear'd him to us by his wondrous care and conduct, by securing of Peace, plenty, ease and luxurious happiness, o're all the fortunate limits of his Blessed Kingdoms; and will you, wou'd you destroy this wondrous gift of Heaven: this Godlike King ... [for one who is] ... unfortunate in his Principles and Morals: and whose single Ingratitude to his Majesty, for so many Royal Bounties, Honours and Glories heap'd upon him, is of itself enough to set any honest generous heart against him.[16]

The Filmerian rhetoric in this passage is pronounced: the 'right of Heav'n itself' immediately reinforces the 'right of Nature'. Hobbesian self-interest, of which both Philander and Cesario stand accused, is seen to be diametrically opposed to the paternal and patriarchal position adopted by Sylvia throughout this text when the discussion turns to high politics. Sylvia's pursuit of Hobbesian self-interest in her private life is carefully divorced by Behn from her staunchly held support for patriarchy in the public sphere. The iniquity of Cesario's position is emphasised to a greater extent when one takes into account the fact that Monmouth is Charles' illegitimate (and favourite) son. The largess with which he has been endowed from the public purse diminishes rather than enhances his stature. His ingratitude is therefore unnatural on a number of levels, as Behn goes on to remark: 'he that can cabal and contrive to dethrone a father, will find it easie to discard the wicked and hated Instruments that assisted him to mount it'.[17] A false son will surely prove to be a false friend. The break with paternal authority by Philander and Sylvia, as well as Cesario, leads, as Rosalind Ballaster has argued, to 'a steady decline into vice and manipulation'.[18]

Despite their partisan point of view, Behn's remarks on Cesario/ Monmouth's character prove to be astute. Even by Shaftesbury, Monmouth was felt to be a weak and intellectually deficient prospect for king. Charles' indulgence towards him is well known and is remarked upon to telling effect by Dryden in *Absalom and Achitophel*. The aftermath of the Rye House Plot was a bloody affair. Sidney and Russell were the most prominent aristocratic victims, though the Whig movement generally was temporarily killed off and nonconformists suffered appalling persecution as a result of its misguided intentions: 'with exclusion lost, the Whigs crumbled, and the nonconformists, as the most readily identifiable of their supporters, bore the brunt of the "Tory revenge"of 1681-6 in the most severe and sustained period of persecution they were called on to endure'.[19] Monmouth's involvement was suspected and alleged rather than proven. Nevertheless, modern biographers of Charles testify to the extent to which he was upset by Monmouth's assumed patricidal intentions. Charles' relations with his illegitimate son had been fraught since 1680. These feelings of antipathy were exacerbated by Monmouth's congratulation of Shaftesbury upon his acquittal on treason charges in 1681. Monmouth's refusal to succumb to James when he returned merely ensured Charles' anger towards him, and as a result he was banned from court, 'And yet, through all this bickering Charles' paternal affection remained patent. He ensured that his son received regular payments from the Treasury to help him subsist, and when a play was written in July 1682, satirising Monmouth, the King forbade its performance'.[20]

In his political biography of Charles II Hutton points to a politically volatile context of personal allegiances that were in a constant process of redefinition between 1678 and 1681, when the tide finally turned in favour of the King and his brother. Monmouth's position within this context became fraught. Unable to accept that James was the 'natural' successor to his father he was continually associated throughout these years, as we have seen, with Whig opposition to popery and arbitrary rule. As a consequence, and through his links to Shaftesbury, Monmouth was the figurehead of Whig anti-papal rhetoric aimed against both Charles and James Stuart from the Popish Plot to the Western Rising of 1685. The latter is the focus of Part Three of *Love Letters*, published in 1687.

Lack of belief in a Filmerian patriarchal political theory and advocacy of Hobbesian self-interest in the public sphere is further attacked in *Love Letters* when Philander expresses ambitions that lie well outside the pale, at least as Behn understands it. In response to Sylvia's charge that he is being led astray by Cesario's political pretensions Philander makes the following statement:

Oh *Sylvia!*, when Three Kingdoms shall ly unpossesst, and be expos'd, as it were, amongst the Raffling Crowd, who knows but the chance may be mine, as well as any others, who has but the same hazard and throws for't; if the strongest Sword must do't (as that must do't) why not mine still? Why may not mine be that fortunate one? *Cesario* has no more right to it than *Philander*; 'tis true, a few of the Rabble will pretend he has a better title to it, but they are a sort of easy Fools, lavish in nothing but in noise and nonsense, true to change and inconstancy, and will abandon him to their own fury for ... Neither is there one part of fifty (of the Fools that cry him up) for his Interest, though they use him for a Tool to work with, he being the only great Man that wants sense enough to find out the cheat, which they dare impose upon.[21]

The construction of this passage serves several purposes. In the first instance Philander demonstrates the extent to which self-interest, rather than political probity or real disaffection with the prevailing order, is dictating the agenda. Taken to its extreme Hobbesian individualism treats the crown as no more than a prize that can be won by those strong and unscrupulous enough to reach for it. Philander's cynical reasoning argues that outside of patriarchy there is no bar to the crown if one has the wit and daring to seize it. The 'strongest Sword', or those who can inspire the greatest fear, throws open the door to fortune. Behn also draws our attention to the popular Tory refrain (not without merit) that Cesario/Monmouth is being used as a stalking horse by someone of infinitely superior political intellect. Philander alludes to this in no uncertain terms when he refers to Cesario as having political ideas that 'are as shallow as his Parts'. Self-interest and self-promotion define Philander's actions in every respect. In his comments that Cesario would have done better to stay at court, where 'his Interest might have carry'd on better'; and in his observation that as it stands Cesario is 'so opposite to all Laws of Nature, Religion, Humanity and Common gratitude, the politics of the text become tangled. One sees the curious sight of a Whig political radical mouthing Filmerian platitudes about the proper course of duty. The strength of Behn's Tory belief is so strong that it disrupts the logic of Philander's position.

Overall, however, Philander's ruthless Hobbesian individualism is naked in Part One and exposes him for the opportunist that he is. This aspect of his character is pointed out by Sylvia's sister, Mertilla. Slightly later in Part One, she (prophetically, as it turns out) advises her sibling to return to the patriarchal fold before 'this faithless man, this cause of all, will leave thee too, grow weary of thee, nauseated by use'.[22] The personal and the political are closely allied in Philander's thoughts and actions, making him a character of considerably less sophistication than Sylvia, whose Hobbesian pursuit of personal self-gratification lies in almost continuous conflict with her staunchly paternal and patriarchal views about the political state of nature. Nor should this surprise us, as it is Behn's belief that such a view is natural to the human condition. Personal and political liberty measured by their standards, even when duty is defied, is not possible in real terms. In the case of the former both parties become prisoners of the flesh; in the latter both parties are striving after a type of freedom to which they have no right. As Filmer argues, and as Behn makes clear in this novel, true freedom to rebel against one's natural condition is bound to fail. The option to choose the kind of political condition one lives under is not a legitimate course of action.[23] The plots of Philander and Cesario against their heaven-sent king can never be realised in practical terms because they have no intellectual validity. It is a common misconception, says Filmer, that one man's authority over others was 'bestowed according to the discretion of the multitude'. Such a view 'contradicts the doctrine and history of the Holy Scriptures, the constant practice of all ancient monarchies, and the very principles of the law of nature'.[24]

Melinda Zook maintains that Filmer was hardly an influence on Behn as she pays little or no attention to religion, unless it is to satirise it. Behn believed instead in 'an idealized aristocratic ethos' and 'she asserted divine right tenets', but her devotion to monarchy did not rest on patriarchal theories'.[25] This may well be true insofar as Behn continually satirised *dissenting* religious figures in her city comedies, and is similarly true in relation to social or domestic patriarchy. In the realm of high political discussion as it is elaborated in *Love Letters*, however, Behn borrows from a common rhetorical register among Tories that owes its vocabulary considerably to Filmer. With regard to Tory political theory in the later seventeenth century, it is primarily Filmer's idea that the patriarchal state of nature originates in Adam's sovereignty over his children; this is extended to a monarch's natural right to rule over his people. This is the intellectual glue that binds *Love Letters* together. It follows that civil power in general is not only by divine institution, but even the assignment of it specifically to the eldest parent, 'which quite takes away that new and common distinction which refers only power universal as absolute to God, but power respective in regard of the special form of government to the choice of the people. Nor leaves it any place for such imaginary pactions between kings and their peoples as many dream of'.[26] In itself this reduces the plotting of Grey/ Philander and Cesario/ Monmouth to unjustifiable treason. If the premises of their right to rebel are shown to be spurious, then their actions can be motivated by nothing more than ambition.

The abject failure of escaping from a state of nature as Filmer lays it out is explicitly addressed in Part Three of *Love Letters*. Despite her clear abhorrence for Cesario/Monmouth's actions Behn tends to see him as a victim in *Love Letters* and continually excuses his behaviour. The blame falls on the nonconformists and those aristocrats who gravely and fatally misled him. The clearest representatives of these figures in the novel are Fergusano/Robert Ferguson, and the Chivilier Tomaso, a conflation of Sir Thomas Armstrong and the Earl of Shaftesbury.[27] It is Tomaso who relates to Philander Cesario/Monmouth's fate in a thinly veiled account of the aftermath of the Rye House plot. This includes Monmouth's affair with Henrietta Wentworth (Hermione in the novel), and Tomaso's urging of Cesario to seek a pardon from the king, playing on the latter's well known indulgence towards his favourite son. Once a pardon is secured then Cesario will be able freely to move about the court and the country and the plotting against the king will start afresh. Behn accords to Tomaso a central role in the manipulation of a prince who is intellectually out of his depth. The manner of Cesario's pardon is achieved through the mediation of his wife, who pleads with the king by appealing to his divinity: 'She told him his Majesty had more peculiarly the Attributes of a God than any other Monarch upon Earth, and never heard the Wretched or the Innocent plead in vain'.[28] Cesario's pardon by a benevolent and God-like king is an important explication of the novel's politics. In her juxtaposition of a range of opportunists with an essentially merciful king aware of his responsibilities both political and familial, Behn creates in this personification of Charles II the ideal patriarchal monarch. Justice, mercy and benevolence are seen to be ideal monarchical qualities. Tomaso and Cesario are exposed as small-minded, self-interested speculators looking to seize power for their own benefit. Cesario/Monmouth's obsequious behaviour as he throws himself on his knees to beg forgiveness, sees him betray everyone associated with the plot in order to save his own life. Moreover, he reveals himself a rebel not just against his king, but also against his natural condition: 'He own'd himself the greatest Criminal in Nature; that he was drawn from his Allegiance by the most subtile Artifices of his enemies, who under false Friendships had allur'd his Hopes with gilded Promises; and which he now too plainly saw were Designs to propagate their own private Interests, and not his Glory'.[29] Insofar as Behn's own views are concerned this is no more than the simple truth; the fact that this is yet another ruse to ease the pressure from Cesario, is merely a further indication of his perfidy against family and state.

As the narrative heads towards its conclusion we find Cesario and Philander once again plotting, this time in Brussels as they prepare for their invasion of France/England. Characteristically, Cesario/Monmouth is portrayed as a puppet, this time of Fergusano/Robert Ferguson, a one-time secretary to Shaftesbury, ex-Presbyterian and currently an Independent preacher. Fergusano is seen to have direct influence over Cesario's mistress, and through her, over Cesario himself: '*Hermione* undertakes nothing without his Advice; and as he is absolutely her Creature, so his art governs her; and she the prince'. Fergusano 'is the great Engin, that sets the great Work a turning'. In line with her loyalist principles, when Sylvia is informed by Brilljard as to the extent of Cesario's manipulation by Ferguson, she states that she is 'amaz'd, as to hear the Prince could suffer so gross a thing [as invasion] to pass in his name'. Fergusano demonstrates markedly Machiavellian morals in *Love Letters*. True to the spirit of opportunism that is the defining characteristic of the Whig/nonconformist alliance, Fergusano is happy to state that 'No matter, Sir, what Tools you work withal, so the finisht piece be fine at last. Look forward to the Goal, a Crown attend it! And never mind the dirty Road that leads to't'. And so Cesario is rendered in the text as being the plaything of an ambitious woman and a practitioner of the black art of nonconformity.[30] Interestingly enough, in his description of the 'dirty road' that leads to the crown, even Fergusano is acknowledging that their rebellion has no ethical or moral imperative.

As the invasion is on the point of taking place Philander begins to have qualms about the legitimacy of the rebels' actions and to regret his participation in what has been a whistle-stop tour of political events in the 1680s. This is figured in terms that again rest upon the overall justice of Filmerian political theory, although this is qualified in the first instance by a typical recourse to Hobbesian self-interest. Philander reasons that 'since Self-Preservation was the first principle to Nature, he had resolved to make that his aim, and rather be false to a party who had no Justice and Honour on their Side, than to a King who all the Laws of Heaven and Earth obliged him to serve'. This is no doubt a qualification excusing the cowardice that Grey displayed in the battle with King James' army in 1685, which Behn carefully glosses over in the text. The novel concludes, as Monmouth's rebellion concluded, with the abject defeat of an unjust and ungodly rebellion against a monarch anointed by Heaven. Cesario/Monmouth is a broken man as he is led into the capital; 'nor was his mean surrender all, but he showed a dejection all the way they were bringing him to *Paris*'. Once there, again like Monmouth, Cesario writes the most servile letters to the king in an attempt to mitigate his treason and plead for forgiveness. Burnet testifies to the distance Monmouth had fallen: 'and his mind was now so low that he begged his life in a manner that agreed ill with the courage of the former parts of it'.[31] The words of another contemporary, however, are on the whole less charitable. 'Thus ended this quondam Duke ... debauched by lust, seduc'd by crafty knaves', a *'Perkin'*, who like his famous predecessor went one step too far. Evelyn even casts doubt on his status as Charles' son, aligning him with Robert Sidney, brother of the notorious republican Algernon, executed for his alleged involvement in the Rye House Plot.[32] Behn uses similar language of one who was brought low by the 'Ambition and the Inspiration of Knaves and Fools'. Cesario dies a 'Shameful Death' on the scaffold, a victim of aspiration, Whig political rhetoric and nonconformist mumbo-jumbo.[33]

Of the three main protagonists in *Love Letters*, it is Philander who fares best. For her expression of self-fulfilment and individual wilfulness Sylvia becomes little more than a highly paid prostitute, fleecing naïve young aristocrats before moving restlessly on to pastures new. Cesario, as we have seen, dies ignominiously, while Philander is ultimately welcomed back into the fold. Each of these three characters rebel against the paternal and patriarchal political theory most closely associated with the Tories. In *Romulus* (1682), Behn satirises Monmouth in the epilogue in terms that might have been lifted straight out of *Patriarcha* or the writings of Charles' grandfather, James I: 'And of all Treasons mine was most accurst; / Rebelling gainst a *King* and *Father* first. / A Sin which Heav'n nor Man can e'er forgive'.[34] Domestic rebellion against one's family is mirrored in the political domain by rebellion against one's sovereign, and for this a price must be paid. The seeds of Philander's repentance referred to earlier in this chapter serve to pave the way for his eventual re-assimilation into the natural order.[35] Disillusioned with the political theory of contract and the relentless pursuit of Hobbesian individualism, Philander returns to the public sphere in his proper capacity, 'in as much Splendour as ever, being very well understood by all good Men'.[36] As one historian has recently argued, this may be a reflection of Behn's spirit of compromise, progressively evident as the 1680s wore on. Accordingly, '*Love Letters* charts a transformation in Behn's politics from a strident royalism to an increasingly tolerant view of the opposition'.[37] In the spirit of the argument posited here, however, it is more likely to reflect Philander's growing disillusion with the Whig/ nonconformist cause and his return to the ways of patriarchal righteousness. The short time he spends in prison, his increasingly independent cast of mind, and the apparently genuine tenor of his conversion, stand in vivid contrast with Monmouth's amenability to manipulation and insincerity when forgiven by a benevolent king in an episode referred to earlier. The end of *Love Letters* is therefore a triumph of patriarchy over the forces of unnatural usurpation. Hobbesian theories in the private and public domain are observed in this text to profit no one. They lead only to viciousness and moral turpitude. Rebellion against one's monarch is continually figured in terms of a rebellion against God, with man in a paternal state of nature rendered in the most positive terms possible.

As we can see from *Love Letters*, and other works, Behn is no advocate of rebellion against one's legitimate ruler. *Oroonoko*, however, is an exception in that rebellion is justified when it means a return to a Filmerian state of nature. Oroonoko's 'Cesario-like' rebellion against the natural suzerainty of his grandfather constitutes the first half of the novella. *Oroonoko* is made particularly interesting through its structure regarding the fate of man in a pre- and post fallen condition. Even here, however, it is sexual desire that precipitates a fall from grace. A utopian beginning is rapidly superseded by the kind of intrigue associated with the late seventeenth-century French and English courts. In the narrative of Oroonoko's life and death, his movement from the idyllic almost edenic condition of his pre-slavery existence, we can trace a state of nature governed by few rules. According to Behn, Oroonoko exists in circumstances that are nearly perfect, a place where 'Adam and Eve' would seem at home, where bashfulness and nakedness are natural and where 'indecency' is unknown:

> And these people represented to me an absolute idea of the first state of innocence, before Man knew how to sin, and 'tis most evident and plain that simple Nature is the most harmless, inoffensive and virtuous mistress. 'Tis she alone, if she were permitted, that better instructs the world than all the inventions of Man. Religion would here but destroy that tranquillity they possess, by ignorance, and laws would but teach 'em to know offence, of which now they have no notion.[38]

Interestingly enough Behn here appears to be advocating a society stripped down to its essentials. Unlike Harrington, Milton and Neville law and religion are seen as unnecessary structural restraints upon man in a state of nature. Whereas Milton in *Paradise Lost* advocates an edenic existence that comes complete with laws that must be obeyed, work that must be done on a daily basis, and a God to whom absolute deference must be given, Behn suggests that the trappings of order that must exist if society is to function, are pointless in a state of nature where virtue is intrinsic to the human condition. Unlike Neville whose utopian fantasy, the *Isle of Pines*, sees ignorance and innocence degenerate to the extent that they must be policed in order to maintain peace and order, Behn advocates a state of nature that requires no modes of surveillance to preserve its innocence. Indeed, knowledge corrupts innocence and leads to a degenerate condition. Predictably, however, the serpent in this particular garden proves to be the spectre of sexual desire leading ultimately to a fall as Oroonoko himself becomes transposed from the Garden of Eden to the fallen condition of slave in a European colony.

The seeds of this transposition are sown at the outset of Behn's narrative. Despite being the member of a race that is seemingly blissful when in a state of ignorance, Oroonoko has qualities that separate him significantly from the rest of his people. Not the least of these is his innate nobility, his physical beauty, and his education. Ignorance may well be bliss for the vast majority of those who live in Behn's ideal community; amongst its elite, however, such ignorance is a sin in itself. Of those qualities that define Oroonoko – his martial excellence, education, and virtue – it is his physical beauty to which Behn most fully draws our attention. It is this particular characteristic that is the well-spring of all others: 'Besides, he was adorned with a native beauty so transcending all those of his gloomy race, that he struck an awe and reverence even in those that knew not his quality, as he did in me, who beheld him in surprise and wonder when afterwards he arrived in our world'.[39] Coming from, and writing for, a court society that placed inordinate emphasis upon birth and nobility – 'quality' as it is described here – Behn invests the world that Oroonoko inhabits with the court mores of the Restoration. Despite her positive remarks about the innocence and ignorance that characterise Oroonoko's subjects, Behn endows Oroonoko himself with all the attributes of the complete Restoration courtier: 'He had nothing of barbarity in his nature, but in all points addressed himself as if his education had been in some European court'.[40] The lack of knowledge that Behn prizes so highly in the mass of the Coromantien people would seem ideal given the Restoration period's continual scenario of plotting against the sovereign, ideological divisions amongst the elite, and the civil disobedience of those determined to follow their conscience in religion. The sub-strata of this society are quickly passed by, however, in favour of a detailed look at the lives of those who occupy its most senior positions. The more one looks at Behn's construction of Oroonoko's world, the more recognisable it is as a thinly veiled substitute for court life under Charles II. Her reference to the majority of Oroonoko's people as 'gloomy' is reminiscent of Dryden's use of the term 'moody' to describe the English in *Absalom and Achitophel*,[41] and the affinities between the hierarchical point of view in both texts stretches further to include the sexual athleticism of both David and Oroonoko figured as the natural consequence of their innate royalty. Like David in relation to Absalom, Oroonoko's grandfather, the king of the Coromantiens, finally forgives Oroonoko for his all-consuming love for Imoinda. A description that begins in the abstract and extends to include the race to which Oroonoko belongs, rapidly gives way in the text to the specific elaboration of the Coromantien court and Oroonoko's place within it.

Oroonoko's education is, significantly, French in its origins. Through the agency of a French tutor and the natural abilities with which he is endowed, Oroonoko's 'greatness of soul', is perfected by 'a Frenchman of wit and learning' who instructs him in 'morals, language and science'. Behn goes to considerable lengths to separate Oroonoko from any association with African or Negro characteristics. Alongside his 'European' education, Oroonoko's physical appearance perfects his characterisation as a man of the highest quality:

> His face was not of that brown, rusty black which most of that nation are, but a perfect ebony, or polished jet. His eyes were the most aweful that could be seen and very piercing, the white of 'em being like snow, as were his teeth. His nose was rising and Roman, instead of African and flat. His mouth, the finest shaped that could be seen, far from those great turned lips, which are so natural to the rest of the Negroes. The whole proportion and air of his face was so noble and exactly formed that, bating his colour, there could be nothing in nature more beautiful, agreeable and handsome.[42]

What we have here is the complete European courtier ready to embark on a love affair that will shake to its core the foundation of a recognisably European patriarchal order. Behn carefully endows Oroonoko with all the ideological weaponry at the disposal of a Tory-educated prince, all of which is manifest in his appearance. The 'Roman' nose and other non-Negroid facial characteristics are indicative of the ruling order, the Coromantien aristocracy. The premium placed upon physical attractiveness and French manners at the court of Oroonoko's grandfather is indicative of its similarity with its European, particularly English counterpart.

This is similarly the case when one considers the political implications of an unrestrained sexual desire mixed with competitive acquisition. We move from an idyllic opening of the perfect courtier in an edenic environment, to one that more closely represents a Hobbesian state of nature at court when Oroonoko's bodily wants and needs conflict directly with those of his grandfather, the king and absolutist head of state. The route to achieving one's aims in the Coromantien court is through sexual intrigue. Behn rather cynically reminds us of this when it becomes apparent that it is possible for Oroonoko to achieve Imoinda if only he can rescue her from his grandfather's harem. The legal basis for this is the 'contract' of betrothal that exists between them.[43] The agent employed to facilitate this event is Aboan, a young man who is not only 'one of the best quality', but also 'a man extremely well made and beautiful'. *His modus operandi* is to seduce the harem's middle-aged keeper and therefore make it possible for Oroonoko to visit Imoinda with a view to removing her from his grandfather's clutches.[44]

An unmitigated pursuit of love drives the plot. When Oroonoko rebels against the authorities in Surinam and leads a slave insurrection, Behn excuses his revolt against English sovereignty on the basis of those quali- ties that have defined him throughout the novella. His proud spirit, his innate majesty and his physical beauty make him a natural leader amongst a disaffected slave population. The English end the slave rebellion by falsely assuring Oroonoko – re-named Caesar – that they will free him, his wife Imoinda, and his child, once it is born. A contract drawn up in writing is immediately broken and Oroonoko is whipped savagely. This is too much for the proud spirit with which Behn has carefully endowed Oroonoko, and the result is that he takes his wife into the woods and kills her. When he is found barely alive, he takes his own life. Rather than fall victim once more to the 'shameful whip' Oroonoko, 'ripped up his own belly, and took his bowels and pulled 'em out with what strength he could'.[45]

The manner of Oroonoko's death befits the Roman construction of his character and ameliorates the stigma of suicide attached to this act by Christian society. Behn makes every possible attempt in the narrative to excuse his rebellion against authority. This is achieved by carefully con- structing Oroonoko's pre-slave existence and idealising it as a perfect state of nature. Unlike Philander from *Love Letters*, Oroonoko does not take the politic or coward's way out. Instead he remains true to an idea of freedom based upon a patriarchal state of nature of which he is a genuine exponent. His downfall comes at the hands of men who have no honour and who are willing to commit any act in order to further their own demonstrably base economic self-interest. In such a world there is no place for the values espoused by Oroonoko. Rather than accommodate himself to a set of values that are palpably Whig in their orientation, and exiled from his natural environment he takes the only honourable course left available to him.

Notes

1   Ellen Pollack, 'Beyond Incest: Gender and the Politics of Transgression in Aphra
     Behn's *Love-Letters Between a Nobleman and his Sister*', in Heidi Hutner, (ed.), *Re-
     reading Aphra Behn: History, Theory and Criticism*, Charlottesville, VA, and London,
     University of Virginia Press, 1993, pp. 151-86 (p. 155).

2   *The Memoirs of Anne, Lady Halkett and Ann, Lady Fanshawe*, John Loftis, (ed.),
     Oxford, Oxford University Press, 1979, cited by N.H. Keeble, 'Obedient Subjects?
     The Loyal Self in Some Later Seventeenth-Century Royalist Women's Memoirs', in
     MacLean, (ed.), *Culture and Society in the Stuart Restoration*, pp. 201-18 (p.202,
     213).

3   Janet Todd, (ed.), *The Works of Aphra Behn*, I-V, London, Pickering and Chatto,
     1992; I, pp. xxiv-xxv.

4   Donald R. Wehrs, '*Eros*, Ethics, Identity: Royalist Feminism and the Politics of Desire
     in Aphra Behn's *Love Letters*', *Studies in English Literature* 32 (1992), pp. 461-78
     (pp. 468, 470).

5   In an otherwise engaging argument Wehrs makes only a scant attempt to place this
     text within its broader historical context. For a more convincing, albeit more discur-
     sive account, see Janet Todd's introduction to *Love Letters Between a Nobleman and
     his Sister*, Harmondsworth, Penguin, 1996, pp. ix-xxxii. All references to *Love Letters*
     in this chapter are to Todd's edition.

6   *Love Letters*, p. 39.

7   For a reading that places incest at the centre of the novel, see Ellen Pollack, 'Beyond
     Incest', in Hutner, (ed.), *Rereading Aphra Behn*. Janet Todd, on the other hand, sees
     incest in the novel as being no more than a commercial device designed to ensure the
     book sells well. See *The Sign of Angellica: Women, Writing and Fiction, 1660-1800*,
     London, Virago, 1989.

8   Aphra Behn, 'A Pindaric Ode on the Death of Our Late Sovereign: With an Ancient
     Prophecy on His Present Majesty', in Todd, (ed.), *Works*, I, ll. 29-34, 137. All further
     references to Behn's poetry are to this edition. In *Oroonoko* Behn refers to Charles as
     'his late Majesty of sacred memory' (p. 47).

9   Aphra Behn, 'A Pindaric Poem to the Reverend Doctor Burnet on the Honour he did
     me of Enquiring after me and my Muse', *Works*, I, pp. 307-10, ll. 51-2, 62.

10   The term 'libertinism' in the seventeenth century was used to refer to freethinking as
     well as 'loose' sexual behaviour. In this sense, Rochester, Hobbes, Sidney, Neville and
     Locke can be referred to as libertines.

11   Mark Kishlansky, *A Monarchy Transformed: Britain 1603-1714*, London, Penguin,
     1996, p. 259.

12   Geoffrey Holmes, *The Making of a Great Power: Late Stuart and Early Georgian
     Britain, 1660-1722*, Harlow, Longman, 1993, p. 131. Kenyon, *Stuart England*,
     pp. 229-30. Tim Harris, *Politics under the Later Stuarts: Party Conflict in a Divided
     Society*, Harlow, Longman, 1993, pp. 86-7.

13   David Ogg, *England in the Reign of Charles II*, Oxford, Oxford University Press, (2nd
     ed.), 1956, p. 607.

14   Ronald Hutton, *Charles II: King of England, Scotland and Ireland*, Oxford, Oxford
     University Press, 1989, p. 404.

15   J.R. Jones, *Country and Court: England, 1658-1714*, London: Arnold, 1978, p. 228.

16   *Love Letters*, pp. 41-2.

17   *Ibid.*, pp. 42-3.

18   Rosalind Ballaster, '"Pretences of State": Aphra Behn and the Female Plot', in Hutner, (ed.), *Rereading Aphra Behn*, pp. 187-211; p. 195. See also, Idem, *Seductive Forms*, chapter 3.

19   See Keeble, *The Literary Culture of Nonconformity*, p. 61. The fullest historical treatment has been written by Greaves, *Secrets of the Kingdom*.

20   Hutton, *Charles II*, pp. 421-422. See also, Antonia Fraser, *King Charles II*, London, Weidenfeld and Nicholson, 1979, pp. 426-7. The play to which Hutton refers is *The Duke of Guise* (1682), by John Dryden and Nathaniel Lee. The fullest contextual commentary can be found in Vinton A. Dearing and John Roper, (eds), *The Works of John Dryden*, Berkeley, Los Angeles, CA, and London: University of California Press, 1992, XIV, pp. 476-512.

21   *Love Letters*, pp. 44-5.

22   *Ibid.*, p. 75.

23   Filmer, *Patriarcha and Other Writings*, pp. 7-8.

24   *Ibid.*, pp. 2-3.

25   Melinda Zook, 'Contextualizing Aphra Behn: plays, politics and party', in Hilda L. Smith (ed.), *Women Writers and the Early Modern British Political Tradition*, Cambridge, Cambridge University Press, 1998, pp. 75-93; p. 77.

26   Filmer, *Patriarcha and Other Writings*, p. 7.

27   *Love Letters*, note b, p. 319.

28   *Ibid.*, p. 329.

29   *Ibid.*, pp. 330-31.

30   *Ibid.*, pp. 398, 408, 410.

31   Gilbert Burnet, *History of His Own Time*, I-VI, Oxford, Clarendon Press, 1823, III, pp. 48-9.

32   *The Diary of John Evelyn*, E.S. De Beer (ed.), Oxford, Oxford University Press, 1959, pp. 815-16. In referring to Monmouth Tories often used the name 'Perkin'. Behn does so in her poem 'A Letter to Mr. *Creech* at *Oxford*, Written in the last great Frost', *Works*, I, pp.166-8, l. 59.

33   *Love Letters*, pp. 435, 436, 438.

34   'Epilogue to *Romulus*', *Works*, I, p. 24, 11. pp. 7-9.

35   In the world of the novel this holds true. In actual fact Lord Grey went over to William of Orange where 'he quickly established a political career, becoming Earl of Tankerville in 1695, the Lord Treasurer in 1699, and Lord Privy Seal in 1700', *Love Letters*, p. 439, note c.

36   *Ibid.*, p. 439.

37   Zook, 'Contextualizing Aphra Behn', pp. 75-93 (p. 88).

38   *Oroonoko, the Royal Slave*, in *Aphra Behn: Oroonoko and Other Writings*, Paul Salzman (ed.), Oxford, Oxford University Press, 1998, pp. 3-73 (pp.7-8). All further references to *Oroonoko* are to this edition.

39   *Ibid.*, p. 10.

40   *Ibid.*, p. 11.

41   *Works*, II, line 45.

42   *Oroonoko*, p. 12.
43   *Ibid.*, p. 17.
44   *Ibid.*, p. 21.
45   *Ibid.*, p. 70.

Chapter 8

Dryden: *Don Sebastian* and the Ideal Ruler

John Dryden is customarily perceived by critics as an apologist for the Stuart regime. His views on politics and religion are most often read as being supportive of the prevailing Stuart ideology of benevolent patriarchy. Poems such as *The Medal, The Hind and the Panther*, and of course, *Absalom and Achitophel*, are partisan documents intended to participate actively in a debate about party. As a result of his unequivocal support for the late Stuart monarchy and the continual charges of turncoat levelled against him during his lifetime, Dryden's reputation has suffered. Born into a prominent puritan family and a civil servant under Cromwell, indeed the author of a fulsome elegy upon Cromwell's death and present in his funeral entourage, Dryden was felt by contemporaries opportunistically to have cut his cloth to suit the prevailing political situation. The following is representative:

> Great truckling soul, whose stubborn honesty
> Does with all revolutions still comply!
> Thy useful muse gilt an usurper's bays
> And for kin-killing smoothly sang his praise,
> Nay, valiantly and wisely fawn'd on's hearse
> And strove to embalm his name in loyal verse

and

> Thou mercenary renegade, thou slave,
> Thou ever changeling, still to be a knave;
> What sect, what error will thou next disgrace?
> Thou art so lewd, so scandalously base,
> That anti-Christian Popery may be
> Asham'd of such a proselyte as thee…
> 'Twas int'rest reconcil'd thee to the cheat,
> And vain ambition tempted thee to eat.[1]

Dryden quickly moved to support the restored monarchy and Episcopal Church government in 1660, satirised ruthlessly the puritan class to which he belonged, and to put the cap on it converted to Catholicism when the Duke of York succeeded to the throne in 1685. Yet Dryden deserves better treatment than many have accorded him. The critical orthodoxy on Dryden's lack of principles first published in the nineteenth century, and continually reiterated since have only recently been rigorously challenged.[2]

We shall be considering Dryden's view of the state of nature in the last two decades of his life, by drawing attention to political ideas referred to in a selection of Dryden's writing in the years between the Exclusion crisis and the Glorious Revolution. In *Don Sebastian* (1689) in particular Dryden's political beliefs can be most clearly felt. This text demonstrates a mature consideration of belief in political ideas that had been formed across a forty-year period. Moreover, by analysing Dryden's works against the politics of 1688-9, it becomes possible to see how he elaborated a state of nature that was a development from the Tory paternalism that he was associated with before William and Mary were 'invited' into the country in 1688. To be sure, the paternalism with which Tory ideologies of the state were so closely associated were to the fore in Dryden's work after 1688. However, in a context that was for the first time hostile to his personal beliefs, both political and religious, the political state of nature in *Don Sebastian* is recognisable as something that would quickly be identified as Jacobite. Such a reading serves to investigate Dryden's part in the creation of a Jacobite literary culture.[3] Dryden had little time for those Tories who had reneged on the doctrine of passive obedience. As the leading writer in the literary representation of late Stuart divine right theory, Dryden's late works provide a point of entry into political ideas that were to rage in the first half of the eighteenth century.

Absalom and Achitophel is a masterpiece of political satire that demonises the Earl of Shaftesbury in particular and the Whig cause in general. Even as he falls under the magic spell of Achitophel's compelling political rhetoric, Absalom elaborates a paternal state of nature that provides the abiding political message of the play. Like *Don Sebastian* at the end of the decade, *Absalom and Achitophel* is concerned as much with family loyalty as it is with its political correlative. Under siege from Achitophel to rebel against his natural ruler, Absalom states that 'My Father Governs with unquestion'd Right; / The Faiths Defender, and Mankinds Delight'. 'And Heaven by wonders has Espous'd his Cause'. The Filmerian equation between father, king and God, is at the heart of Dryden's defence of David/Charles' actions. Despite his natural temptation to rebel against both parent and monarch, Absalom is tied ultimately by 'Natures Holy Bands', that 'Curb my Spirits, and Restrain my Hands'. Moreover, Absalom recognises that the crown upon his father's death is 'Justly Destin'd for a Worthier Head'.[4]

Achitophel's rejoinder slightly later in the poem that 'the People have a Right Supreme / To make their Kings; for Kings are made for them' is the classic Whig statement of where sovereignty ultimately lies and can be found in Milton, Locke, Neville and Sidney. In *Plato Redivivus* published in the same year as *Absalom and Achitophel*, Neville makes this startlingly apparent: 'I believe if we could trace all foundations of polities since the world began[,] we shall find none of them to be descended from paternal power'. The Bible, says Neville, provides us with no textual evidence to support paternal power in the political sphere.[5] Such rhetoric, however, is never allowed to stand unchallenged and the major attack on it comes not from Absalom, who is intellectually unfitted to make it, but from the narrator/poet himself. In an extended passage of some eighty-seven lines, Dryden makes it crystal clear that the best defence of property and political rights is not contract theory, central to Whig ideology, but lies in the hands of the incumbent monarch and his prerogative to settle the succession. According to Dryden it is the king and not the crowd that is best suited to govern, make and uphold the law. If Charles' entitlement to nominate his successor according to the laws of hereditary right is to be superseded by a committee then no private property is safe from the hands of those who would unnaturally usurp it.[6]

> Add, that the Pow'r for property allow'd,
> Is mischievously seated in the Crowd:
> For who can be sure of private Right,
> If Sovereign sway may be dissolv'd by might?
> Nor is the Peoples Judgment always true:
> The most may err as grossly as the few.[7]

In effect Dryden was echoing the speech made by Charles to the Oxford Parliament, 21 March 1681, in which Charles declared that an attack against his prerogative was an attack against the principle of property itself. Dryden hammers home this point in *The Medal* (1682), a poem written to satirise the medal struck to commemorate Shaftesbury's release from prison on the back of a verdict of 'ignoramus' returned by a London grand jury against the charge of treason. *The Medal* similarly inverts the premise of Whig arguments about sovereignty by pointing to the people's representatives inciting mob rule.

The surly Commons shall respect deny;
And justle Peerage out with Property.

Their Gen'ral either shall his Trust betray,
And force the Crowd to Arbitrary sway.[8]

Charles warned the Commons that 'neither Your Liberties nor Properties can subsist long, when the just Rights and Prerogatives of the Crown are invaded, or the Honour of the Government brought low and into Disreputation'.[9] Philip Harth informs us that this form of rhetoric from the king is an example of a new and confident assertiveness, a much-needed requirement if Tory propagandists who were champing at the bit were ever to realise their full potential. Typically, Charles had been following a policy of 'dissimulation' since 1678, with good will to parliament being no more than a 'posture'. Such delaying tactics, however, were at best a short-term expedient. The bull, as it were, needed to be grabbed firmly by the horns.[10] In effect, Harth argues that *Absalom and Achitophel* is the culmination of Tory propaganda that had been gathering momentum from March 1681 and that was accelerated by the discovery of a so-called 'Protestant Plot' which involved the intention to seize the king. This plot allegedly involved not only Shaftesbury, but also the rest of the Whig leadership.[11]

As the logic of his argument progresses in *Absalom and Achitophel*, Dryden makes it clear that if the king is to be deprived of his sovereign sway, then the spectre of a Hobbesian state of nature is not far away: 'Government it self at length must fall / To Natures state; where all have right to all'.[12] *Absalom and Achitophel* marks the apex of Tory propaganda in satirical and allegorical form and is the most powerfully realised public poem of the seventeenth century. The poem's concluding couplet resounds with the reestablishment of royal prerogative and a return to the political status quo: 'Once more the Godlike *David* was restor'd, / And willing Nations knew their Lawfull Lord'. Dryden manages significantly to contribute to the Tory propaganda triumph that helped to achieve the seemingly certain political victory that duly appeared within six months of the poem's publication in November 1681. The eagerness with which Dryden participated in such debates is important when attempting to assess the strength of his commitment to the Stuart cause.

Steven Zwicker argues that Dryden was desperate to enter into the debate regarding the events of 1688-9. The immediate result was the creation of the decade's literary masterpiece, *Don Sebastian*. Zwicker goes on to state that, 'The popular success of the play in 1689 is particularly puzzling, for the fall of that year was a time when both former laureate and his former master were under savage attack'. The open Catholicism at James' court, the birth of a male heir during the reign and the strength of feeling generated by courtiers excluded from political power, led quickly to revolution.[13] The play itself exposes the shallow and hypocritical nature of the political nation.[14] Like *Absalom and Achitophel* and *The Duke of Guise*, *Don Sebastian* points to the ingratitude of a country that does not know how best to appreciate the benevolence of Stuart and Tory rule. The Dedication to *Don Sebastian* reveals the key philosophical ideas at work in the play, as well as referring to what is now an extremely delicate and complex political situation. In it Dryden praises Philip Sidney, the incumbent Earl of Leicester and scion of the aristocratic family most closely linked with Restoration republicanism and Whig politics. Dryden praises Sidney for his stoic attitude, and catches at the same time the atmosphere of a world on the cusp of political change:

> Every man in all changes of Government, which have been, or may possibly arrive, will agree, that I cou'd not have offer'd my Incense, where it coul'd be so well deserv'd. For you, My Lord, are secure in your own merit; and all Parties, as they rise uppermost, are sure to court you in their turns; 'tis a tribute which has ever been paid your vertue.[15]

Sidney's stoicism and political dignity is something that Dryden extends to himself in the Preface to the play, where he states flatly that he writes without 'any expectation to be pitied'.[16]

The lines to Sidney and his reflections on his own fall from grace, are a self-presentation of dignity and integrity from Dryden in the face of a radically changed political situation which may bring with it victimisation. Paul Hammond has recently drawn attention to this aspect of Dryden's dedicatory plea to Leicester, describing it as an elaboration of the 'centred self': 'In thus complimenting Leicester, Dryden describes his own mode of freedom'. Similarly, David Bywaters points to the affinities between Sidney and Dryden, in that they both have had to suffer the indignity of being on the wrong side at the wrong time. The implicit correlation being made is that Dryden must now do as Sidney did. Once a powerful politician under Cromwell, when the tide turned against him Sidney withdrew from public affairs and embraced political passivity on his estate. Both Paul Hammond and David Bywaters point to the affinities that Dryden sees in his Dedication and Prologue between himself and Cicero, both of whom had been on the losing side in a revolution.[17] This extends to more than just a plea to be left alone under a new and friendly regime. In *Don Sebastian* Dryden draws on Ciceronian doctrines of appropriate public service personified in

Sebastian and later in Dorax, and contrasts them with the Hobbesian and Machiavellian doctrines of self-interest and *realpolitik* that characterise Muley-Moluch, Benducar and Mufti.

The Prologue to *Don Sebastian*, also picks up the stoic theme and makes a plea for toleration:

> *The British Nation is too brave to show*
> *Ignoble vengeance, on a vanquished foe.*
> *At least be civil to the Wretch imploring;*
> *And lay your Paws upon him without roaring:*
> *Suppose our Poet was your foe before;*
> *Yet now the bus'ness of the Field is o'er;*
> *'Tis time to let your Civil Wars alone,*
> *When Troops are into Winter-quarters gone.*[18]

The tone of the Dedication, Preface and Prologue to *Don Sebastain* is filled with foreboding and reflective of Dryden's vulnerability in the immediate aftermath of the revolution. These preambles to the text proper demonstrate that a cagey dialogue is apparent elsewhere with a newly evolving political establishment that is hostile to Dryden's religious and political position. The plea is for peace and goodwill. Yet this hardly sits well with a play that has as its hero a king who voluntarily embraces exile after first successfully repelling an attempt to wrest power from him by armed force. The villains of the piece in *Don Sebastian* are a fickle rabble that changes its mind constantly, a nobility that is treacherous, and a religious leader primarily concerned with accruing wealth and secular power. These structural and institutional constituents of the play – nobility, church and people – are in a continual state of conflict with one another as they jostle for position and scheme for power. They are reinforced by an emperor who has illegally usurped the throne, killing members of his own family in order to do so.

One is immediately confronted in *Don Sebastian* with the question of political legitimacy, and indeed this is the central political theme in the play, complementing the ethical stoicism associated with the play's morally upright characters. On hearing of the death by drowning of Mahomet, a pretender to the throne, Muley Zeydan, exclaims: 'Thus, then, a doubtful title is extinguished'.[19] The ironies here rapidly become manifest. Muley Zeydan is plotting with the chief minister, Benducar, against the rule of his brother, the Emperor, Muley Moluch, himself the usurping incumbent of a throne to which he has no right. Into this sink of political corruption steps Sebastian, King of Portugal, and now prisoner of the Emperor. In a work written immediately after a revolution that sees a good king sent into exile only to be replaced by members of his own family, Dryden puts under intense scrutiny the iniquities of family betrayal and the political virtue of what will be at the play's end, a displaced monarch.

In a play that abounds with treachery and plotting, pretenders and legitimate rulers, the arbitrary and tyrannical Moluch and his henchman Benducar set the tone. As with most seventeenth-century tragedies, the locus of power is the court. As Webster's Antonio has it in *The Duchess of Malfi*, the court is the common fountain from which all must drink.[20] Benducar proves true to the spirit of the disaffected courtier desperate to effect a coup, and uses the emperor's brother Muley Zeydan as a stalking horse for his own political pretensions. To cool the essentially good Muley Zeydan and prevent him from rushing precipitately into a confrontation with his tyrannical brother, Benducar urges caution and counsels the rash pretender to proceed through the arts of the court, the tone of which has been set by Moluch:

> Be still, and learn the soothing arts of Court;
> And when they praise him most, be you the loudest;
> Your brother is luxurious, close and cruel,
> Generous by fits, but permanent in mischief.
> The shadow of a discontent would ruin us;
> We must be safe before we can be great:
> These things observed, leave me to shape the rest.[21]

Rebellion in this play is constantly figured against the family. Domestic politics are therefore intimately related to national politics in a manner that makes it impossible to see anything but strong correspondence between the two. Political incest is the wider corollary of the literal incest unknowingly committed between Sebastian and Almeyda, and which provides the pretext for their voluntary exile at the play's conclusion. This in itself participates in the debate that raged at the time as to whether James had voluntarily abdicated the throne or whether he had been usurped. Despite the rectitude of Muley Zeydan's objections against his brother's tyranny, the rebellion that is being effected is one that militates against the Tory and patriarchal state of nature with which Dryden is closely associated. Intrigue against one's ruler is an unforgivable sin. The similarity between Moluch's closest advisers and those whom Dryden believed consistently let down both Charles and James Stuart, is evident in the manner by which they proceed in the play.

Of the two plotters it is Benducar who is by far the most dangerous. In this respect he has close affinities with an earlier incarnation of the gifted genius well practised in the black arts of political subversion, Shaftesbury/ Achitophel. Achitophel, like Benducar, is the ultimate court animal, a creature of its environment and a past master in its ways. Both Achitophel and Benducar share the dubious distinction of trying to subvert what Dryden perceives to be an appropriate government by driving a wedge between blood relations. The route to revolution is through domestic as well as national politics. Despite the fact that Moluch does not deserve to rule, Dryden makes it apparent, as we shall see, that Benducar in particular has no right to rebel. From this point on the play exposes the iniquities of Moluch's rule but offers no creditable alternative to it until Dorax and Sebastian enter the action. Like Benducar, Dorax is a disaffected malcontent; he is also a renegade. Once a leading member of Sebastian's court, and its best soldier, Dorax has gone over to Moluch's empire and is merely awaiting the opportunity to revenge himself on Sebastian for what he regards as the latter's ingratitude.

The hatred that Dorax feels for Sebastian is continually on view in the play. His animus derives from Sebastian's displacement of him as court favourite, and also the manner in which Violante, the woman he loves, is given to a court rival. As always in Stuart court literature, sexual politics play an important role. When Benducar is trying to recruit Dorax into the plot against Moluch, he refers to Sebastian as Dorax's 'master', to which the latter responds: 'By what title / Because I happen'd to be born where he / Happen'd to be a King?' These lines are immediately undercut, however, by the ones that quickly follow, describing Sebastian, albeit grudgingly, as one 'ev'n towering to *Divinity*. / Brave, pious, generous, great, and liberal'.[22] In a description of Sebastian close in many ways to Aphra Behn's description of Oroonoko's 'natural' beauty and majesty, Dorax cannot help but define Sebastian in positive terms. Nor can he escape the strong residual ideology of patriarchy that defines the Tory position during the late seventeenth century. This is evident even to the tyrant Moluch. At the point that Sebastian, hitherto unrecognised by any but Dorax, steps forward to draw lots for his life, Moluch casts an admiring glance at the once and future king:

> Mark him who now approaches to the Lottery,
> He looks secure of Death, superior greatness,
> Like *Jove* when he made Fate, and said *thou art*
> *The slave of my Creation;* I admire him.[23]

At the point when Sebastian looks doomed to die, Moluch having reduced the number of those who must be executed to one in order to save the still disguised Sebastian, the latter draws the black marble and must face death alone. Only at this point does Sebastian throw off his disguise and declare himself to be King of Portugal. The nobility of Sebastian's soul proves to be his saviour, in this instance at least. Moluch's remarks are instructive and laden with descriptive terms for kings of the period:

> Ha! It must be he; no other
> Could represent such suff'ring Majesty:
> I saw him, as he terms himself a Sun,
> Struggling in dark Eclipse, and shooting day
> On either side of the black Orb that veil'd him.

Sebastian responds to Moluch by stating that his subjects' safety is his first consideration, 'Kings who are Fathers, live but in their People'.[24] From this exchange we can gather that Sebastian is the play's true personification of patriarchal rule. Imbued with a sense of self-sacrifice, physical beauty, and greatness of soul, Sebastian inspires fanatical loyalty amongst his supporters and proves to be the charismatic centre of the play and the only true representative of monarchy in it. Moreover, the stoic sufferance of majesty creates an association with the deposed James Stuart that must have struck a chord with an audience that was confused as to the fate of their absent king. The only dissenting voice willing to critique this view is Dorax whose views are mistakenly held, as his climactic confrontation with Sebastian later in the play reveals. This is a point to which we will return. It is through Dorax and his acerbic comments on the current political situation, his ever more visible Tory ideology, that the play damns those who have no adherence to a code of ethics that transcends individualism and property.

The question of legitimacy is further confused when Almeyda similarly throws off her disguise and points us to the means by which Moluch achieved power.

> Thy Father was not more than mine, the Heir
> Of this large Empire; but with arms united
> They fought their way, and seiz'd the Crown by force:
> And equal as their danger was their share:
> For where was Eldership, where none had right,
> But that which Conquest gave? 'Twas thy ambition
> Pull'd from my peaceful Father what his Sword
> Help'd thine to gain: Surpriz'd him and his Kingdom,
> No provocation given, no War declar'd.[25]

Almeyda's outrage here raises several issues germane to political legitimacy. The events that led to her current situation are never contradicted in the play. Her depiction of rapacious individualism founded upon duplicity and political violence are the means by which her family has risen, and also the means by which they fall. Neither Almeyda's father, nor Moluch's, had any right to the throne they captured and seized by force. This is a world where 'Eldership' has no meaning and where expediency is all that matters. The implication is strong that the empire has been gained illegally merely through conquest: the natural order has been usurped and hereditary right has been broken asunder by the ambition of unscrupulous men. With neither father having the 'natural' right to succeed, the laws of ambition triumph and the strongest brother prevails. By now the waters have been truly muddied. There is a world of ideological difference between the natural sovereignty of a prince such as Sebastian based upon a patriarchal theory of the state of nature, and the empire of the Moors, the legitimacy of which is underpinned by nothing more substantial than conquest through might.

Hobbesian self-interest and a crude form of Machiavellian statecraft are continually exposed in the play as iniquitous. Moluch is the ultimate Hobbesian sovereign, one who sees himself as being above the law. As he declaims: 'What's Royalty but pow'r to please my self? / And if I dare not, then am I the Slave, / And my own Slaves the Sovereigns'.[26] One can usefully compare Almeyda's critique of Moloch's route to power with Dryden's relation of the transfer of sovereignty in *Threnadis Augustalis*, his elegy upon the death of Charles II. Here James has power passed on to him by a king who recognises that his brother is the legitimate heir to the throne:

> He took and prest that ever loyal hand,
> Which cou'd in Peace secure his Reign,
> Which cou'd in Wars his Pow'r maintain,
> That hand on which no plighted vows were ever vain.
> Well for so great a trust, he chose
> A Prince who never disobey'd.[27]

Not only is the transfer smooth, it is also deemed to be natural – James' power is vested in a legitimate right of lineal succession. Dryden describes the terms in which this occurs in terms of James' filial love and sorrow at the loss of so dear a brother and so great a king. In *Threnodia Augustalis* Dryden depicts a brother waiting patiently in line for the throne. His descriptions of James are filled with sympathy. Unlike Moluch who would have Mufti rewrite the Koran for the sake of sexual and political expediency, James is continually referred to in this poem as being pious in the extreme.[28] Like Sebastian, James recognises that his first duty is to the people; unlike Moloch, Sebastian 'With broken Oaths his fame he will not stain; / With Conquest basely bought, and with Inglorious gain'.[29] As Derek Hughes has written, Dryden constructs Muley-Moluch as 'Unregenerate Man personified'.[30] The knock-on effect of this from Dryden's point of view is that Moluch appears also as the personification of an alien Protestant religion being forced on an unwilling nation. Unlike James, he is completely lacking in piety. With her references to undeclared war, family treachery, and the acquisition of power by 'surprize', Almeyda in her references points to uncomfortable affinities with the events of the Glorious Revolution.

Moluch's empire is run along ideological lines that are recognisably Whig. The agent for exposing and highlighting this is the renegade Tory, Dorax, whose conversations with the ruthlessly self-serving Mufti and Benducar, respectively the personification of religious and secular political structures in the play, exposes the extent to which this is a fallen political world. Act 2, scene 1 sees Dorax roundly berate Mufti for continually meddling in secular politics. Defined by his 'zeal', Mufti resembles the worldly clerics who were felt by many to be exercising undue political influence in late seventeenth-century England. Topically, Mufti is a strange amalgam of nonconforming dissenter and the defiance demonstrated by Anglican bishops with Whig sympathies:

> Now his zeal yearns,
> To see me burnt; he damns me from his Church,
> Because I would restrain him to his Duty;
> Is not the care of Souls a load sufficient?
> Are not your holy stipends paid for this?
> Were you not bred apart from worldly noise,
> To study Souls, their Cures and Diseases?...
> Bloated with Pride, Ambition, Avarice,
> You swell to counsel Kings and govern Kingdoms.[31]

Mufti's only response to this is further to show his hypocrisy, naming Dorax for a 'Foul, loud-mouth'd Renegade', and promising to pray for his soul. Mufti's 'holy jugglings' that 'startle faith' and make 'all Religions false' bar his own, is a further indication that he has dissenting credentials.[32] Such rhetoric was a common feature of the period and is carried over from the 1640s and 1650s as a standard criticism of Dissent. Too much juggling with religion, wrenching words out of their meaning, makes religion no more than sophistry. This is demonstrated clearly enough in the text when the Emperor puts pressure upon Mufti to change the law so that he can marry Almeyda, an uncomfortable reminder of not only Henry VIII's political genesis of the English Reformation, but also to the marriage of the first cousins William and Mary.[33]

Moreover, Dorax's response to Benducar when the latter tries to induce him to betray Moluch, is laden with the Tory rhetoric of obedience. Dorax is appalled that Benducar, supposedly Moluch's 'Creature, nay his Friend' offers to betray him.

> Why then no bond is left on human kind:
> Distrusts, debates, immortal strifes ensue;
> Children may murder Parents; Wives their Husbands;
> All must be Rapine, Wars, and Desolation,
> When trust and gratitude no longer bind.

Here we have in a nutshell the Tory state of nature ideologically displayed to its most powerful effect. Dorax is an outsider in this world and, with a strong sense of moral rectitude and no desire to benefit from its corruption, can therefore comment upon the court authoritatively. Highlighted here are the Stuart and Filmerian rhetoric of passive obedience to one's ruler, the correlation between domestic and state hierarchies, and the consequence of trying to usurp the natural order. The price for doing so is chaos and anarchy. Benducar, quite naturally in the circumstances, points to Dorax's hypocrisy, and in the exchange that follows we go to the heart of Dorax's differences with Sebastian. Dorax draws a distinction between rebellion and betrayal, the former being a public and unforgivable crime, while the latter is personal. Sebastian, says Dorax, 'with disdainful Language dar'd my worst. / I but accepted War, which he denounced'.[34]

The extent to which Dorax chastises both Mufti and Benducar, serves to accentuate the differences between himself and Sebastian. These are not ideological, but personal. As the pair meet at the play's climax to settle their differences Sebastian manages to make Dorax see the error of his ways:

> Spare my confusion:
> For pitty spare, and say not, first, you err'd.
> For yet I have not dar'd through guilt and shame,
> To throw myself beneath your Royall feet.
> Now spurn this Rebell, this proud Renegade:
> 'Tis just you should, nor will I more complain.

In an argument that has raged between the two regarding compulsion, duty, service and the reciprocal nature of obligation and reward, Dorax admits his guilt and is welcomed back into the paternal fold. He is 'in one moment' 'reconcil'd / To Heaven, and to my King, and to my love'. The proper chain of honour, obligation and duty is therefore reconstituted in both the political and domestic spheres. Bywaters rightly glosses Dorax's regret at the desertion of Sebastian in his hour of need as symptomatic of the manner in which the Tories similarly deserted James during the crisis of 1688-9.[35] Dryden's critique of recent events takes place not just at the level of an allegorical representation of leading political players during the Glorious Revolution, he also makes a trenchant critique of the political ideas that are associated with both sides in the conflict. This takes place through the transformation of Dorax into a moral and ethical being and provides the reader with a counterweight to those values represented by Muley-Moluch, Benducar and Mufti.

The reformed Dorax personifies to a significant extent the correct ethical and political code of public service that Cicero elaborates in *De Officiis*. Cicero argues that 'if greatness of spirit were detached from sociability, and from the bonding between humans it would become a kind of brutal savagery'. Sociability, according to Cicero, conforms to nature.[36] As is well known, Cicero advocates active participation in public life for those best suited by their birth and education to fulfil their duty to the state. This extends to the performance of duties that are unpleasant in the extreme, leading if necessary to actions that appear on the face of it to be detrimental to the state: 'For some things are so disgraceful, or so outrageous, that a wise man would not do them even to protect his country'.[37] When the play begins Dorax is alienated from his natural condition by a mistaken interpretation of Sebastian's actions. Although he is allied to the cause of Muley-Moluch, he is detached from the rampant individualism and self-aggrandisement that defines the emperor's court. The inhabitants of the court are themselves personifications of ideas regarding imperialism and the pursuit of glory for its own sake that Cicero condemned. The reformed Dorax, on the other hand, urges self-exile on Sebastian when Alonzo proves the veracity of his incest in the play's final act. In this regard Dorax is acting perfectly in accord with Cicero's philosophy.

According to Cicero, man in a state of nature has obligations that transcend the pursuit of self-interest:

> Now then: for one man to take something from another and to increase his own advantage at the cost of another's disadvantage is more contrary to nature than to death, than poverty, than pain, and than anything else that may

happen to his body or his external possessions. In the first place, it destroys the common life and fellowship of men: for if we are so minded that anyone will use theft or violence against another for his own profit, then necessarily the thing that is most of all in accordance with nature will be shattered, that is the fellowship of the human race. ... However, nature does not allow us to increase our means, our resources and our wealth by despoiling others.[38]

Within the ellipsis in this quotation Cicero uses the familiar trope of the body politic to illustrate his point. Unrestrained individualism is seen to be the high road to chaos and anarchy: more than any other act, this is seen to be unnatural. The content of this passage is crucial to a proper understanding of the differences that lie between Sebastian and Dorax early in the play, and the manner in which they are resolved when the two finally confront one another in the fourth act. At the outset Dorax sees Sebastian's supposed ingratitude for his bravery and his giving of Violante, Dorax's intended, to his chief rival Enriquez, as acting against nature. Dorax has been a leading figure at Sebastian's court, and like all courts this is an extremely competitive environment. The pride that Dorax feels for his accomplishments is driven by his own self-interest, and not consideration for the greater public good. This leads to a misunderstanding or misrecognition of Sebastian's need to balance preferment at court in a manner that is conducive to internal peace. The ironies here are manifest, and Dorax is not slow to recognise these deficiencies in the men that create and execute policy at the court of Muley-Moluch.

In his position as Sebastian's chief general Dorax falls within that category of men that 'are led most of all to being overwhelmed by forgetfulness of justice when they slip into desiring positions of command or honour or glory'. Cicero goes on to state that in any environment in which competition is intense, and where it is impossible that many will be outstanding, 'it is extremely difficult to maintain a "sacred fellowship"'[39] Only at the point when Sebastian has satisfactorily explained his own situation in acting fairly with both Dorax and Enriquez, can the two be reconciled. Sebastian, it is revealed, is an exemplar of public service dedicated not to honour and glory for its own sake, but the greater good of his subjects. A return in kind for services rendered is considered by Cicero to be fundamental, especially with regard to rulers. 'A good man, however, is not permitted to fail to return [a kind service] (provided, of course, that he can do so without injustice)'. The qualification in parenthesis is a crucial one. In the world of the play, as Sebastian demonstrates clearly to Dorax, his responsibilities as ruler dictate that he cannot serve one man badly in order to gratify another. When Dorax comprehends the justice of Sebastian's actions, the stage is set for a reconstitution of the natural order. Once again Sebastian is an example of Ciceronian good practice.

At first it seems that *Don Sebastian* will end on a positive note. Sebastian, the only true exemplar of royalty in the play, overcomes the tyrannical Muley-Moluch and his henchman and is reconciled to the disaffected courtier Dorax without in any sense compromising his own position. This, however, merely sets us up for the sensational revelation of incest revealed by the elderly retainer Don Alvarez in the final scene. Sebastian embraces voluntary exile on the grounds that to return to Portugal 'and reign, that were to show / Triumphant Incest and pollute the Throne'.[40] In his refusal to taint the throne with scandal, regardless of his innocence in committing incest, Sebastian demonstrates his capacity for self-sacrifice and his willingness to suffer for the common good. Although he is the rightful king his abdication is a necessary act. The topical relevance of such an act must have resounded strongly with an audience witnessing in reality events that often run parallel to the play.

Notes

1   'To Mr Dryden', ll. 1-6; 'To Mr. Bays', in George deF. Lord (Gen. Ed.), *Poems on Affairs of State*, I-VII, New Haven, CT, and London, Yale University Press, 1968, IV, Galbraith M. Crump (ed.), pp. 75, 79, 80.

2   For a corrective, see most recently Zwicker, *Lines of Authority*, chapter 6; James Anderson Winn, *John Dryden and his World*, New Haven, CT and London, Yale University Press, 1987, pp. 428-513; David Bywaters, *Dryden in Revolutionary England*, Berkeley, Los Angeles and London, University of California Press, 1991; Paul Hammond, *Dryden and the Traces of Classical Rome*, Oxford, Clarendon Press, 1999.

3   The leading exponent of this view is perhaps Howard Erskine-Hill. See particularly his *Poetry of Opposition and Revolution: Dryden to Wordsworth*, Oxford, Clarendon Press, 1996, particularly chapter 1.

4   *Absalom and Achitophel*, in *The Works of John Dryden*, H.T. Swedenberg Jnr. (Gen. Ed.), I-XX, Berkeley, Los Angeles, London, University of California Press, 1956- in progress, II, ll. pp. 317-8, 320, 339-40, 348. All further references to Dryden's writing are to this edition and are abbreviated to *Works*, followed by the relevant volume number.

5   Neville, *Plato Redivivus*, p. 86.

6   'Commentary', *Works*, II, pp. 272-73.

7   *Absalom and Achitophel*, *Works*, II, ll. 777-82.

8   *The Medal*, in Ibid. ll. 311-14.

9   Cited by Philip Harth, *Pen for a Party: Dryden's Tory Propaganda and its Contexts*, Princeton, NJ, Princeton University Press, 1993, p. 66.

10   *Ibid.*, p. 64. Mark Knights, on the other hand, sees Charles' actions both before and during March 1681 as an attempt to play both ends against the middle: 'The King was always unwilling to follow a single clear-cut policy' (*Policy and Opinion in Crisis*, Cambridge: Cambridge University Press, 1994, p. 96).

11   Harth, *Pen for a Party*, pp. 86, 88.

12   *Absalom and Achitophel*, *Works*, II, ll. pp. 793-4.

13   One of the most significant of those courtiers frustrated by their lack of access to power was the younger brother of Dryden's dedicatee. Henry Sidney 'had known disappointment at court', was denied preferment 'and was thus taken much into Williams confidence' in the period immediately preceding the latter's invasion (Alan Marshall, *The Age of Faction: Court Politics, 1660-1702*, Harlow, Longman, 1999, pp. 147, 148).

14   Zwicker, *Lines of Authority*, p. 182.

15   *Don Sebastian*, *Works*, XV, Earl Miner (ed.), p. 59.

16   *Ibid.*, p. 65.

17   Hammond, *Dryden and the Traces of Classical Rome*, p. 67. Bywaters, *Dryden in Revolutionary England*, pp. 35-6.

18   'Prologue to *Don Sebastian*', *Works*, XV, ll. 7-14.

19   *Ibid.*, XV, 1.1.15.

20   John Webster, *The Duchess of Malfi*, John Russell Brown, (ed.) Manchester, Manchester University Press, 1988, 1.1.4-22.

21   *Works*, XV, 1.1.22-28.

22   *Ibid.*, 1.1.66-8; 102-3.

23   *Ibid.*, 1.i.310-13.

24   *Ibid.*, 1.1.342-6; 419.

25   *Ibid.*, 1.1.451-59.

26   *Ibid.*, 2.1. 46-7.

27   *Works*, III, ll. 229-34.

28   *Ibid.*, III, ll. 36, 71.

29   *Ibid*, III, ll. 489-90.

30   Derek Hughes, *Dryden's Heroic Plays*, London, Macmillan, 1981, pp. 154-5.

31   *Ibid*, 2.i.171-7, 197-8. In *Dryden in Revolutionary England* (pp. 49-52), Bywaters argues persuasively that Mufti is a thinly disguised version of Gilbert Burnet, while Benducar strongly resembles Sunderland. For a brief character sketch of Sunderland and his utter cynicism in pursuit of power, see Alan Marshall, *The Age of Faction*, pp. 138-39. The most fulsome and definitive account of Sunderland's political career is J.P. Kenyon, *Robert Spencer, Earl of Sunderland, 1641-1702*, London, Longmans Green, 1958.

32   *Works*, XV, 2.1.215-6; 218-20.

33   3.1.60-99.

34   2.1.320-21.

35   Bywaters, *Dryden in Revolutionary England*, p. 48. See also, John M. Wallace, 'John Dryden's Plays and the Conception of a Heroic Society', in Perez Zagorin (ed.), *Culture and Politics from Puritanism to the Enlightenment*, Berkeley, Los Angeles CA and London, University of California Press, 1980, pp. 113-34.

36   Cicero, *On Duties*, M.T. Griffin and E.M. Atkins (eds), Cambridge: Cambridge University Press, 1991, p. 61.
37   *Ibid.*, p. 61.
38   *Ibid.*, p. 108.
39   *Ibid.*, p. 11.
40   *Don Sebastian*, 5.1.537-8.

PART III

POST-RESTORATION AND THE HANOVERIAN SETTLEMENT

Chapter 9

Calvinism and the State of Nature:
Robinson Crusoe

Robinson Crusoe is one of the great myths of the state of nature, incorporating elements of both the Lockean and Hobbesian versions of the concept along the way in what turns out to be a fascinating dialogue between the respective theories.[1] Crusoe is returned to the state of nature on his island Despair, forced to create a new society with 'Savage Wretches', as he perceives them to be, lurking on the boundaries of his living space.[2] He must rediscover the process of constructing a society through his interaction with his environment, and, in effect, test Locke's model as he goes (Manuel Schonhorn's somewhat iconoclastic anti-Lockean reading of the narrative will be considered in due course). By the narrative's conclusion he has also arguably shown some Hobbesian propensities in establishing control over, first, the ertswhile 'Savage Wretch' Friday (to whom he appears an absolute sovereign), and then the assorted Spanish and Portuguese sailors similarly marooned on his island: thus Sara Soncini's claim that 'Crusoe's island might therefore be interpreted as an attempt to test the validity of Hobbes' picture of natural and social man', no less than Locke's.[3] A state has been formed, and property rights asserted, in such a manner as to preclude any reversion to the insecurities of the state of nature that Crusoe had experienced at first hand while on his own. There is no suggestion that the island is to be treated as a common treasury for allcomers to share. By 'mixing' his labour with the virgin soil, Crusoe, in approved Lockean 'industrious' fashion, claims the right to ownership of the land.[4] Even spending several years away from the island does not alter this 'right', Crusoe describing how on his return to visit the remaining inhabitants, 'I shar'd the Island into Parts with 'em', but, 'reserv'd to myself the Property of the whole'.[5] Once 'mixed', always 'mixed', it would appear, as long as it leads to the common good.

The state that results is one based on contract, where social relations proceed from that fact. Thus the emissary from the sailors agrees on behalf of his colleagues:

> That he would make Conditions with them upon their solemn Oath, That they should be absolutely under my Leading, as their Commander and Captain; and that they should swear upon the Holy Sacraments and the Gospel, to be true to me, and no other; and to be directed wholly and absolutely by my Orders, 'till they were landed safely in such Country, as I intended; and that he would bring a Contract from them under their Hands for that Purpose.[6]

It is a condition one of us has described elsewhere as amounting to 'no contact without contract' as far as Crusoe is concerned.[7] Yet having said that, something more fundamental than contract law is involved in establishing power and authority over the person of Friday. The latter's fear of being returned to the state of nature effectively prevailing in his own culture, leads him to submit to an absolute sovereignty which Crusoe's Western imperialist character quite naturally disposes him to assume: 'I made him know his Name should be *Friday*, which was the Day I sav'd his Life ... I likewise taught him to say *Master*, and then let him know, that was to be my Name'.[8] From then onwards Friday has ceded his personal sovereignty to the greater power that is Crusoe, transforming himself, willingly enough it would seem, into a Hobbesian subject.

Crusoe's debt to the tradition of spiritual autobiography has been well documented in the critical literature, and Defoe maintains an interesting dialogue with that tradition over the course of his fictional output.[9] From *Crusoe* through to *Roxana* his protagonists operate within a framework largely dictated by the conventions of spiritual autobiography (if somewhat more problematically in the case of the latter narrative, as we shall discover in the next chapter), vividly illustrating that genre's obsessive concern with the individual's destiny. Spiritual autobiography often has a Calvinist cast to it, as we note in the case of John Bunyan's *Grace Abounding to the Chief of Sinners*, although the extent of Defoe's Calvinist sympathies is still a matter of debate amongst the critical community.[10] In the reading that follows, however, the Calvinist aspect of *Crusoe* will be emphasised, as a basis for claiming certain affinities between the psychological landscape of spiritual autobiography and the concept of the state of nature.[11] First, however, we might briefly consider the work of Bunyan to test this thesis in that acknowledged template for spiritual autobiographical fiction, *The Pilgrim's Progress*.

One of the most striking aspects of *The Pilgrim's Progress* is the sheer amount of conflict, both verbal and physical, that takes place over the course of Christian's journey from the City of Destruction to the Celestial City (a point emphasised in our earlier study *Bunyan and Authority*[12]). That space in many ways resembles a state of nature: Christian may receive heavenly help at periodic intervals (most notably from Evangelist), but his physical self is at the mercy of whoever he happens to meet on the road – including such openly hostile figures to his progress as Apollyon, with whom he is forced to fight a pitched battle. For most of the journey, in fact, Christian seems to be in a land without any effective civil authority. He must digress from the road into such sites as Vanity Fair in order to find that kind of authority (although not much to his benefit, since he is jailed there as a threat to the state), and it is clear that for the bulk of the time he is traversing a territory in which he can call on no civil protection when accosted with evil intent.

In essence this is the landscape of a 'warre of every man against every man', where Christian is constantly being tested by figures determined to exert domination over him, whether of a mental or physical variety. He is thrown back on his own devices in the manner of the lone individual in the state of nature, forced to use both his wits and brute physical strength – as in the hand-to-hand combat with Apollyon – to survive. To be a nonconformist is to place oneself in a state of nature in the view of most of one's peers, since one is denying the validity of the civil law when it comes to matters of personal conscience. Again, one can appreciate why Hobbes had so little time for the phenomenon of conscience: sooner or later its assertion will constitute a challenge to central authority and the doctrine of the indivisibility of power on which his discourse of sovereignty rests. Between totalitarianism and conscience lies a differend that the former will always do its best to suppress; equally, the latter can only resist such attempts on its integrity.

There is one crucial element in Christian's state of nature that is not present in Hobbes', and that is God. And not just God, but a God on one's side – the God of Calvinist predestinarian theology, who divides the world into the mutually exclusive categories of the elect and the reprobate, abandoning the latter to their fate in the process. By means of God's grace Christian will be saved from the state of nature, but only after his death: until then he must endure the state of nature that is the world peopled with reprobates, whose nature is so often disposed towards the oppression of the elect. Perhaps the state of nature also obtains in hell, that being a domain where the individual can call on no protection whatsoever from the exercise of arbitrary power against him (although another reading might see hell as a prime example of the perils of absolutism, with the qualification that Satan's power is encompassed by God's absolutism). One might even conjecture that the state of nature applies everywhere except in the ordered kingdom of the Celestial City: the 'wilderness' the narrator refers to in *The*

Pilgrim's Progress' opening sentence seems to be all that the vast majority of mankind will ever experience.[13] That would be consistent with predestinarian theory, which pictures the world as a predominantly reprobate site where the elect, as a forerunner of Bunyan, Arthur Dent, bluntly put it, 'would walke very thinly in the streets'.[14]

Calvinist theology, in its English variant anyway, therefore sees the elect as marooned in a hostile environment, constantly beset with the unwelcome attentions of the reprobate, whose main function is to disrupt the elect pilgrimage towards a state of grace. Difference is encoded within the elect experience from the start. The wilderness of the world is, in effect, a Hobbesian state of nature, where none but the elect can ever feel secure – and then only with the significant qualification of being prey to a constant nagging anxiety over their final spiritual state. Predestinarian theory can never provide a total guarantee of election, and always leaves room for lingering doubt within the individual psychology, as Bunyan himself recognises in his own spiritual autobiography: 'I have continued with much content thorow Grace, but have met with many turnings and goings upon my heart both from the Lord, Satan, and my own corruptions'.[15] The potential electee has nothing but his internal feelings to rely upon that he *is* of the elect, after all, since his election can never be externally validated. Being in the state of nature, that is, the state without God's grace, may in truth prove to be the real fate awaiting him. The landscape of Calvinist predestinarian theory amounts to the state of nature plus a promise of salvation; but a promise only for the very few; a promise that may not be met; and a promise that no-one else can verify. Anxiety is only too understandable a reaction from the individual under the circumstances.

Once removed from England and the 'middle Station' of life that his father so admires and recommends to him as a social ideal, Crusoe, too, is effectively existing in a Hobbesian state of nature, where there is no secure protection for his person.[16] Sea voyages become an apt metaphor for this state, in that the individual is constantly poised on the brink of disaster: at any moment shipwreck is a real possibility and security at best an illusory condition. Almost every time Crusoe sets sail his life is threatened, with storms at sea constituting perpetual reminders of human weakness: 'I expected every Wave would have swallowed us up, and that every time the Ship fell down, as I thought, in the Trough or Hollow of the Sea, we should never rise more'.[17] This is life at the 'edge of chaos', where the individual is sometimes pushed that little bit further and engulfed by chaos itself. The latter concept is derived from complexity theory, which holds that it is the most desirable state for systems to be in. At that point they are at their most creative and adaptable, whereas without that dynamic they tend to stagnate and, eventually, to decline. As the science writers Peter Coveney and Roger Highfield have put it,

> the edge of chaos is a good place to be in a constantly changing world because from there you can always explore the patterns of order that are available and try them out for their appropriateness to the current situation. What you don't want to do is get stuck in *one* state of order, which is bound to become obsolete sooner or later (remember the dinosaurs, or the British Empire, or IBM before the shake-up).[18]

Spiritual autobiography itself, we might say, transcribes existence at the edge of chaos – most particularly in its pre-conversion experience stage, when the individual is consistently brought to the borderline of breakdown where anxiety rules. Election represents a move back towards *psychological* order, although the electee's continued existence within an overwhelmingly reprobate world means that he remains at the edge of chaos in his social relations with the mass of his fellows. Many critics find Crusoe's conversion experience unconvincing, and he certainly continues to challenge God's will in his post-island days by returning enthusiastically to his sea-borne adventures. It could even be argued that Crusoe strives to keep election at bay, in which case his narrative – the first part, certainly – could be seen as an *incomplete* spiritual autobiography. We shall return to the psychological landscape this involves later.

The metaphor above is enhanced by the presence on the open ocean of pirates, whose entire life-style is based on the premise of a 'warre of every man against every man', and who at one point succeed in taking Crusoe captive and treating him as a slave. Crusoe's final shipwreck on his island Despair merely serves to accentuate his vulnerability as an individual at large in a Hobbesian environment, where civil society has no remit. It is a vulnerability further emphasised by the appearance on Despair of the inhabitants of a neighbouring island, Friday's tribe, who pose yet another serious threat to Crusoe's person. What we are subsequently to witness in the narrative is a dialectic between the Hobbesian and Lockean states of nature, with Crusoe striving to reconstruct society in the most inauspicious of circumstances – albeit metaphorically extremely rich and resonant ones for its readers, as the text's subsequent popularity has amply proved. Whether Crusoe's heart lies in settled social existence is, as we shall go on to discuss, a more debatable topic. In many ways he registers as no less reluctant a *zoon politikon* than he does an electee.

This reluctance would form the ground for our objection to Schonhorn's project of '[d]e-mythologizing the "Lockean" Defoe' by turning him into an absolutist ruler:

> Crusoe, then, is no simple Austen squire bent on improving his estate; he is, as we finally see, a monarch whose vision of self and society remains in many ways antithetic to the principles of Whig, Lockean, and contractualist political thought that was dominant in Defoe's time.[19]

Crusoe may well take on some of the trappings of an absolute ruler on occasion, but that does not mean he sees this state as his ultimate objective, or any permanent 'solution' to his problematical relationship with the rest of the human race. Schonhorn's reading only makes sense if we disregard Crusoe's departure from the island, and then, even more so, his extended 'Farther Adventures' (Novak, too, can be criticised on the same grounds as the latter point[20]). If he is a monarch, then he is one who soon loses interest in the role and what it requires of him. Schonhorn's concern is to prove that Defoe himself was, at heart, pro-monarchical, with a 'conservative-royalist thread in the complex weave of his political imagination'.[21] While he puts forward some interesting arguments to support his thesis, it underestimates the subversive, anti-authoritarian side to the author's work. Crusoe's innate restlessness, if nothing else, would cast doubt on such a conservative interpretation of Defoe's fiction. Absentee absolute monarchs are hardly an advertisement for the royalist cause. To reduce *Crusoe* to a defence of 'conservative-royalism' is to lose the work's political complexity. It could be argued that Defoe is contributing to an emergent tradition of republican oppositional discourse, that has accommodated monarchy as the only pragmatic contemporary option.

There is a perpetual conflict of narratives being played out in the text, therefore, with Crusoe seeking to ensure that his own personal narrative is not swamped by the myriad of others present in a state of nature. Periodically that does happen, most notably perhaps in his capture by pirates, and it is instructive that Crusoe seeks to return to the state of nature, as represented by the sea, as a refuge. We might regard his condition of capture and slavery as an extreme form of Hobbesian absolute sovereignty in the submission it demands of the individual, and, as with every other instance of settled existence in Crusoe's life, his natural inclination is to escape from it even if that puts him in a position of some risk. The perils of the sea are preferable to the unconditional surrender of one's personal sovereignty, or, as complexity theory would have it, becoming stuck indefinitely in one state of order.

Once at sea with Xury, his erstwhile fellow slave, Crusoe displays precisely those characteristics required to be successful in the state of nature, exerting domination over his companion (soon to be referred to as his 'boy'), and, when they are picked up by a passing European ship, quite shamelessly exploiting him for personal gain:

> he offer'd me also 60 Pieces of Eight more for my Boy *Xury*, which I was loath to take, not that I was not willing to let the Captain have him, but I was very loath to sell the poor Boy's Liberty, who had assisted me so faithfully in procuring my own. However when I let him know my Reason, he own'd it to be just, and offer'd me this Medium, that he would give the Boy an Obligation to set him free in ten Years, if he turn'd Christian; upon this, and *Xury* saying he was willing to go to him, I let the Captain have him.[22]

Existence in the state of nature encourages such reification of others, given that survival calls for the systematic exploitation of all the resources, the human no less than the natural, that surround one. Moral scruples can play no part in such transactions (Crusoe overcoming what little he has with embarrassing ease in this instance), where the self will always be placed first. Xury's narrative is simply subsumed under Crusoe's own; that being the objective of all such conflicts in the state of nature, to frustrate, and if possible neutralise, the similarly self-seeking narratives of others. The politics of self-interest dictate the course of one's actions, and Crusoe reveals himself to be well versed in the discourse of sovereignty most appropriate to survival in the Hobbesian state of nature – exploit or be exploited, dominate or be dominated.

Crusoe sets out to tame nature, but, as the necessity of maintaining a stronghold to withdraw to would suggest, this is a project whose success must always be limited: 'When I came to my Castle, for so I think I call'd it ever after this, I fled into it like one pursued ... never frighted Hare fled to Cover, or Fox to Earth, with more Terror of Mind than I to this Retreat'.[23] The self is permanently at risk and can never take its safety for granted in such a setting: 'I was exceedingly surpriz'd with the Print of a Man's naked Foot on the Shore, which was very plain to be seen in the Sand: I stood like one Thunder-struck'.[24] An ability to surprise remains a prime feature of the state of nature, keeping the individual isolated – as well as delicately balanced at the edge of chaos. As Soncini has noted of the footprint episode, 'the mere possibility of an encounter with the Other generates deep anxiety and a terror of being devoured, whereas the simpler hypothesis of a fortunate escape from loneliness is immediately discarded'.[25] Little narratives can only ever thrive up to a point in this condition, although existing at the edge of chaos certainly promotes a vivid sense of selfhood. This is something that Hobbes never really addresses in his presentation of the state of nature – the *excitement* that can attend existence in a condition of uncertainty and fear. Hobbes assumes that we flee as if by reflex from the experience of fear, yet it can also exert a fascination that some individuals find not just attractive, but even addictive. Crusoe is one of those individuals.

Crusoe is often seen as a symbol of capitalist entrepreneurialism, and this, too, assumes treating the world as a state of nature in which ruthless competition for control over resources is taken to be normative behaviour. The acquisitive instinct is something that Crusoe cultivates from an early stage, even to the extent of rendering his spiritual 'acquisitions' in double-entry bookkeeping form at one point: *'I am singl'd out too from all the Ship's Crew to be spar'd from Death; and he that miraculously sav'd me from Death, can deliver me from this Condition'.*[26] Predictably enough, Marx emphasised this side of Crusoe's character, remarking in *Capital* that, '[h]is stock-book contains a catalogue of the useful objects he possesses, and finally of the labour-time that specific quantities of these products have on average cost him'.[27] Crusoe continues to display this acquisitive instinct right through to the end of his career, keeping a close eye on his wealth, as well as any opportunities that arise for increasing it significantly.[28] Hence the lure of other voyages that he succumbs to at the conclusion of his first volume of adventures. Marxist theory regards capitalism as akin to the state of nature, and wants to replace it with a more rational, planned society where the means of production are held in common. For Crusoe, however, it is a state of freedom and opportunity to exercise his personal sovereignty, even if it does entail a considerable degree of risk. It is precisely the lack of rule and plan that Crusoe finds attractive, and Marxists, no less than Hobbes before them, have most likely underestimated the possible appeal of living at the edge of chaos. What Crusoe enacts in his own life is the dialogue between the edge of chaos and 'one state of order'; that is, between the state of nature and civil society. He evinces no desire to see the former eclipsed by the latter.

In terms of Calvinist spiritual autobiographical models, Crusoe is no less in a state of nature as regards his psychological development than his forerunners Christian and his author were. Like those two, he finds himself inhabiting an essentially hostile landscape beset with enemies of one kind or other, having no-one to rely on but himself – as well as his faith in a God apparently determined to test him to the limits of his endurance. Marx's comment that Crusoe regards 'prayers and the like ... as recreation' could hardly be wider of the mark in this respect, missing as it does the sheer anxiety that is built into that activity prior to the conversion experience.[29] Life is reduced to a series of trials one suffers through in order to realise one's spiritual, and in Crusoe's case also economic, destiny. It is a situation in which 'the personal is political' clearly applies. Everything that lies outside the self has to be considered threatening by the prospective electee, who is only too aware that the world consists largely of reprobates, each of whom is a potential obstacle to the attainment of his personal objectives. The discourse of personal sovereignty assumes a more or less permanent state of struggle, where difference must be constantly reasserted – no matter how much anxiety this induces in the individual; and this is very much the landscape of Calvinist soteriology.

We might conclude that it is the need to assert difference that drives Crusoe from England yet again at the age of 62, despite the comfortable lifestyle his wealth has brought him. He finds it difficult to settle in English society on his return from the island and remains a social nonconformist to the last, seemingly requiring the test provided by life in the state of nature to experience his personal sovereignty fully. We note how little impact on him marriage has, for example, with the whole experience being dismissed in a casual aside:

> In the mean time, I in part settled my self here, for first of all I marry'd, and that not either to my Disadvantage or Dissatisfaction, and had three Children, two Sons and one Daughter: But my Wife dying, and my Nephew coming Home with good Success from a Voyage to *Spain*, my Inclination to go Abroad, and his Importunity prevailed and engag'd me to go in his Ship, as a private Trader to the *East Indies*.[30]

At this point in the hero's career 'in part' is a highly revealing phrase to use. It is as if Crusoe's 'Inclination' can never really be stifled for long, and, at best, will only ever be held in check awaiting a new set of adventures in far-flung places. His journeys begin again, and, as detailed in *The Farther Adventures*, continue for ten more years before he finally returns to England. The attraction of the edge of chaos proves too strong for Crusoe to resist – his advanced years notwithstanding. As he remarks in the sequel of his desire 'to go abroad again': 'I dream'd of it all night, and my imagination run upon it all day ... I could talk of nothing else'.[31] We have Hobbes turned on his head here, with the state of nature being chosen over civil society, not in spite of, but precisely *because of* the insecurity and uncertainty that it involves. The former yields excitement and a heightened sense of one's identity and difference from others, the latter merely boredom, with neither marriage nor parenthood offering enough of interest to merit more than a few lines of bare factual detail from Crusoe (admittedly, he does provide more information about his married life in *The Farther Adventures of Robinson Crusoe*, although this does have the air of an afterthought).

Both Hobbes and Locke may be proponents of civil society, but Crusoe remains a rebel against settled existence, a figure committed to the conflict of narratives where one's personal sovereignty must be continually reasserted. Here we take issue with Novak's reading of Crusoe as an essentially 'social animal', where the argument is that 'Defoe recognized the benefits of the state of nature, but he believed that the freedom and purity of Crusoe's island were minor advantages compared to comfort and civilization'.[32] Crusoe has an in-built resistance to becoming stuck in one state of order, or comfort, and the state of nature provides an escape route that he is only too happy to access when social existence palls – as inevitably it always will with this restless character, driven as he is by his 'Inclination'. Hobbes wanted to expunge the state of nature from our experience; Locke to construct safeguards to preserve its best features within civil society; for Crusoe, on the other hand, it constitutes an alternative world where he can express himself to best advantage, repeatedly testing just where the edge of chaos lies. Far from being a threat or an unrealisable ideal, the state of nature is for Crusoe a necessary part of his world: without it he would be doomed to the dreaded 'middle station'.

In *The Farther Adventures* Crusoe is given ample opportunity to assert his difference in a hostile world and to continue a precarious existence at the edge of chaos, far from what are to him the stultifying conventions of Western society: a society where mankind is 'living in a daily circulation of sorrow, living but to work, and working but to live, as if daily bread were the only end of wearisome life, and a wearisome life the only occasion of daily bread'.[33] He ranges freely around the globe, experiencing various forms of life from his island through China and Russia, without ever quite allowing himself to sink into one state of order long enough to lose the impetus of his restless 'Inclination'. When he arrives at his island he reassumes his role of ruler, resolving various disputes that have broken out in his absence and reorganising the colony along Christian lines (encouraging the various couples living there to marry, for example). His authority is readily accepted, with the inhabitants declaring themselves 'resolv'd to stay upon the island 'till I came to remove them'.[34] All of this is expeditiously prosecuted in a mere twenty-five days, constituting little more than a brief interlude in Crusoe's ten-year progress. Once again, he is careful to curtail any slide into one state of order: island existence equals stasis to this character.

Soncini's argument on the socio-political significance of the island is worth considering in more detail at this point. She sees a turn from Hobbes to Locke between Crusoe's first and second sojourns on the island, arguing that on his return Crusoe recognises that he can no longer act as an absolute monarch now that property has come into the equation. The island has ceased to be a state of nature and has evolved into a proto-civil society, where the protection of property rights is of more pressing concern to the inhabitants than basic survival. Those rights will only be guaranteed if the Hobbesian model of government is dropped, since under that system, 'Property rights can be altered, limited, or revoked at the sovereign's will'. Soncini goes on to conclude that the 'image of authoritarian kingship which emerges from *Robinson Crusoe* seems therefore to be wholly discredited by the *Farther Adventures*'.[35] In effect, Crusoe accepts his redundancy, and gracefully withdraws. The argument is well constructed and persuasive, but for our purposes somewhat inconclusive. The island episode occupies only a small part of Crusoe's second-volume adventures, and what is most striking from our point of view is that Crusoe so rapidly rejects island life to re-embrace the state of nature. It is not so much that Crusoe acknowledges his redundancy to the newly-constituted civil society, rather that such a society does not fulfil his psychological needs.

On leaving the island Crusoe is rapidly brought back to the very edge of chaos, in the form of an attack on his vessel by a large fleet of native canoes, whose hostile intent is unmistakable. In the ensuing struggle Friday is killed, another salutary reminder of just how finely balanced existence can be outside the bounds of civil society; although by this stage nothing will deter Crusoe from his quest for adventure. He is, as he readily admits, a man 'not cool'd by almost forty years' misery and disappointments, not satisfy'd with prosperity beyond expectation, not made cautious by affliction and distress beyond imitation'.[36] Hardly the words of one supposedly seeking 'the comfort and security of civilization'. The adventures pile up: a spell in Brazil followed by a projected trip to the East Indies, broken by some depressing experiences in Madagascar on the way. A rape of a local woman by one of the sailors prompts an attack on the Europeans, which leads to reprisals of a particularly savage nature that Crusoe goes so far as to compare to Cromwell's massacre of the civilian population of Drogheda. We are returned, in other words, to the state of nature at its very worst – open war, with sudden death an omnipresent possibility. Shortly afterwards, several members of the crew are either killed or captured in Arabia; then Crusoe falls out with the remaining crew over their conduct, and is forced to leave the ship at Bengal. Next, having entered into partnership with another English merchant, he is making voyages to the East Indies and China to amass a new fortune: 'The whole world is in motion, rouling round and round; all the creatures of God, heavenly bodies and earthly, are busy and diligent, why should we be idle?', as his new partner puts it.[37] For early capitalists like Crusoe and his partner, the state of nature is above all a state of opportunity.

The fact that the vessel Crusoe and his partner buy to ply their trade proves to be a stolen one, turning them technically into pirates, merely confirms our sense of the basic insecurity of existence in the state of nature, and how easy it is to be compromised by events. There is also more than a certain amount of irony in observing a figure who has spent so much of his time at sea fleeing from pirates, and has been captured by them at one point, being transformed, however unwittingly, into one himself. The state of nature retains the ability to surprise the individual. Crusoe acts as one would expect such an experienced inhabitant of the state to do; he consults his own self-interest and makes a run for China where he is more likely to be safe from attempts by the Dutch to recover their stolen ship. It is a way of life that has a brutalising effect on those who embrace it, as is graphically illustrated in the episode when attacking Cochin Chinese are repelled by means of boiling pitch. When Crusoe declares himself 'never pleas'd better with a victory in my life', his subsequent pious sentiments that 'I thought it was a sad life, which we must be always oblig'd to be killing our fellow-creatures to preserve' ring decidedly hollow.[38] He has long since learned that survival in the state of nature depends on just such a lack of humanity as the application of boiling pitch signals. Almost anything can be justified in the name of self-interest, and when Crusoe notes at another point that 'I know not what liberties men may take when they are out of reach of the law', we are only too aware that others should fear him for just the same reason.[39]

Crusoe's innate restlessness and love of the dangerous life is further revealed in China, when, after managing to sell his share in the tainted ship, he attaches himself to a caravan making its way overland to Moscow. A series of attacks by fierce Tartars further reinforces the notion of being at the edge of chaos, with the caravan having to traverse a 'wild uncultivated country' inhabited by pagans before it reaches European-controlled territory.[40] Once again we find ourselves in 'the wilderness of this world' and having to rely on our own ingenuity for survival.[41] Snowbound in Siberia, Crusoe is forced to succumb to one state of order for the duration of the winter, but as soon as possible resumes his travels and eventually arrives in Archangel, from where he takes ship to England. Now 72 years old, he claims to have learned 'the value of retirement', but his life as he has presented it to us over the two volumes constitutes a tribute to the state of nature and the attractions of living at the edge of chaos.[42] Right to the end we have a character motivated by the need to assert difference in the name of personal sovereignty, a reluctant *zoon politikon* actively resisting absorption into the body politic.

We might even say that Crusoe's kingdom within is *ruled* by difference. It is noticeable that any society he forms a part of in *The Farther Adventures* – various ships, the island, the overland caravan, winter quarters in Siberia – is only ever temporary in nature. Nonconformism dies hard in him; not even marriage – another temporary arrangepment, as it turns out – can tame him. Crusoe may or may not have reached a state of grace by the end of his adventures (there is still a sense of his adventures forming an incomplete spiritual autobiography), but, no less than Christian, he has convincingly demonstrated his ability to survive in a world peopled largely by reprobates: that alone hints at elect status and the protection of the Calvinist God – a God, we must remember, firmly committed to the cause of difference.

Notes

1   For readings exploring Hobbesian tendencies in *Robinson Crusoe*, see particularly Manuel Schonhorn, *Defoe's Politics: Parliament, Power, Kingship and Robinson Crusoe*, Cambridge, Cambridge University Press, 1991, and Sara Soncini, 'The Island as Social Experiment: A Reappraisal of Daniel Defoe's Political Discourse(s) in *Robinson Crusoe* and *The Farther Adventures*', in Marialuisa Bignami (ed.), *Wrestling with Defoe: Approaches from a Workshop on Defoe's Prose*, Bologna, Cisalpino, 1997, pp. 11-43. Soncini's argument is that Defoe blends Hobbes and Locke 'into an utterly unorthodox eclecticism' where he 'alternatively wears the Hobbesian or the Lockean mask' (pp. 13, 43). Maximilian E. Novak had earlier made a similar point, referring to the 'eclectic originality' of Defoe's 'scheme of natural law', with its incorporation of elements of Grotius and Pufendorf as well as various English theorists (*Defoe and the Nature of Man*, Oxford, Oxford University Press, 1963, p. 2).

2   Daniel Defoe, *The Life and Strange Surprizing Adventures of Robinson Crusoe, of York, Mariner*, J. Donald Crowley (ed.), Oxford, Oxford University Press, 1972, p. 166.

3   Soncini, 'The Island as Social Experiment', p. 24. Peter Hulme has also noted Hobbesian tendencies in Crusoe's treatment of the sailors: 'Only as an absolute despot will Crusoe's composed self enter the social world' (*Colonial Encounters: Europe and the Native Caribbean 1492-1797*, London and New York, Methuen, 1986, p. 208).

4   'The *Labour* of his Body, and the Work of his Hands, we may say, are properly his. Whatsoever then he removes out of the State that Nature hath provided, and left it in, he hath mixed his *Labour* with, and joyned to it something that is his own, and thereby

makes it his *Property*' (Locke, *Two Treatises*, pp. 288-9). Eve Tavor, on the other hand, argues that Crusoe's island constitutes 'an egalitarian society' (*Scepticism, Society and the Eighteenth-Century Novel*, New York, St. Martin's Press, 1987, p. 23).

5   *Robinson Crusoe*, p. 305.

6   *Ibid.*, p. 245.

7   Stuart Sim, *Negotiations with Paradox: Narrative Practice and Narrative Form in Bunyan and Defoe*, Hemel Hempstead, Harvester Wheatsheaf, 1990, p. 245.

8   *Robinson Crusoe*, p. 206. For a discussion of Crusoe's imperialist character see, for example, Pat Rogers, *Robinson Crusoe*, London, George Allen and Unwin, 1979; Martin Green, *Dreams of Adventure, Deeds of Empire*, London, Routledge and Kegan Paul, 1980; John McVeagh, *Tradefull Merchants: The Portrayal of the Capitalist in Literature*, London, Routledge and Kegan Paul, 1981; and Hulme, *Colonial Encounters*.

9   See, for example, G.A. Starr, *Defoe and Spiritual Autobiography*, Princeton, NJ, Princeton University Press, 1965; J. Paul Hunter, *The Reluctant Pilgrim*, Baltimore, Johns Hopkins University Press, 1966; and Sim, *Negotiations with Paradox*.

10   See, for example, Novak, *Defoe and the Nature of Man*, where it is argued that Defoe 'refused to commit himself to a rigid doctrine of predestination' (p. 13). Ian A. Bell has also argued that Defoe's narratives 'cannot ... be wholly assimilated to the world of spiritual autobiography' (*Defoe's Fictions*, London, Croom Helm, 1985, p. 108). Frank Bastian, on the other hand, sees Defoe's Dissenting Academy education as imbuing him with Calvinist principles that he never really loses (*Defoe's Early Life*, London, Macmillan, 1981).

11   Novak also finds links between Calvinism and conceptions of the state of nature, arguing that 'theories of self-interest and self-defence suited ... well with the Calvinistic concept of man in his fallen state' (*Defoe and the Nature of Man*, p. 5).

12   See Sim and Walker, *Bunyan and Authority*, chapter 7.

13   John Bunyan, *The Pilgrim's Progress*, James Blanton Wharey and Roger Sharrock (eds), Oxford, Clarendon Press, 1967, p. 8.

14   Arthur Dent, *The Plaine Man's Path-Way to Heaven*, Amsterdam, Theatrum Orbis Terrarum, 1974, p. 287.

15   John Bunyan, *Grace Abounding to the Chief of Sinners*, Roger Sharrock (ed.), Oxford, Clarendon Press, 1962, p. 96.

16   *Robinson Crusoe*, p. 4.

17   *Ibid.*, p. 8.

18   Peter Coveney and Roger Highfield, *Frontiers of Complexity: The Search for Order in a Chaotic World*, London, Faber and Faber, 1995, p. 273.

19   Schonhorn, *Defoe's Politics*, pp. ix, 154.

20   Novak sees Crusoe's desire to leave the island as being motivated by 'the comfort and security of civilization'; but the character seems curiously loath to relax into these for any length of time (Novak, *Defoe and the Nature of Man*, p. 23).

21   Schonhorn, *Defoe's Politics*, p. 8.

22   *Robinson Crusoe*, pp. 33-4.

23   *Ibid.*, p. 154.

24   *Ibid.*, p. 153.

25   Soncini, 'The Island as Social Experiment', p. 27.

26   *Robinson Crusoe*, p. 66.

27   Karl Marx, *Capital*, vol. I, Ben Fowkes (trans.), Penguin, Harmondsworth, 1976, p. 170.

28   For Stephen Hymer, Crusoe's conduct on the island bears out Marx's theories of primitive accumulation in the early stages of capitalism (see 'Robinson Crusoe and the Secret of Primitive Accumulation', *Monthly Review*, 23 (1971-2), pp. 11-36).

29   *Capital*, I, p. 169.

30   *Robinson Crusoe*, p. 305.

31   Daniel Defoe, *The Farther Adventures of Robinson Crusoe*; in complete edition of *Robinson Crusoe*, London: Everyman, 1945, p. 225.

32   Novak, *Defoe and the Nature of Man*, p. 23. Novak's argument is heavily dependent on the *Serious Reflections*, which come *after* Crusoe has spent almost his entire life avoiding settled existence.

33   *Farther Adventures*, p. 229.

34   *Ibid.*, p. 335.

35   Soncini, 'The Island as Social Experiment', pp. 33, 40.

36   *Farther Adventures*, p. 341.

37   *Ibid.*, p. 359.

38   *Ibid.*, p. 371. Novak is more charitable, seeing the sentiments as representing 'a Christian approach to the problem of self-defence and the laws of nature' (*Defoe and the Nature of Man*, p. 58).

39   *Farther Adventures*, p. 374.

40   *Ibid.*, p. 413.

41   *Pilgrim's Progress*, p. 8.

42   *Farther Adventures*, p. 427. Alan Downie, on the other hand, reads *The Farther Adventures* as an admission on Crusoe's part that his character lacks consistency (see Downie, 'Robinson Crusoe's Eighteenth-Century Contexts', in Lieve Spaas and Brian Stimpson (eds), *Robinson Crusoe: Myths and Metamorphoses*, Basingstoke and London, Macmillan, 1996, pp. 13-27). We would want to reiterate the point made earlier, however, that this is a retrospective judgement, and that Crusoe's adventures as they unfold show the consistency of someone drawn to a life of risk – that is, a life at the edge of chaos. David Trotter argues that what *The Farther Adventures* demonstrates is 'Crusoe's unfitness for ... positions of authority', which is another way of stating his commitment to a life at the edge of chaos, well away from settled society (David Trotter, *Circulation: Defoe, Dickens, and the Economies of the Novel*, Basingstoke and London, Macmillan, 1988, p. 37).

Chapter 10

Manley, Defoe and the Politics of Self-Interest

Manley's *The New Atalantis* adds a gender twist to the debate about the relationship between the state of nature and the nature of the state. Here is a world in which self-interest is rife – much to the detriment of the female sex, for whom the politics of self-interest can be particularly dangerous terrain to negotiate, and the discourse of sovereignty at best ambivalent about their claims. Women have much more to lose than men if their reputation is ever called into question, and have every reason to doubt the moral probity of the male sex in general, for whom seduction is just one large game seemingly devoid of moral content. Sexual double standards manifestly apply in Manley's world: 'Men may regain their reputations, though after a complication of vices – cowardice, robbery, adultery, bribery and murder – but a woman, once departed from the road of virtue, is made incapable of a return'.[1] Although morally loose women do feature in Manley's world, men are clearly the worst offenders, with the author attracting much recent feminist interest in her work in consequence. *The New Atalantis* certainly qualifies as an indictment of masculine ethics: when a certain public figure is revealed to have a 'contempt of self-interest', that alone is enough to turn him into a wonder of the world.[2]

Manley's narrative is also a very self-conscious allegory on the party political struggles of the early eighteenth century, with the author's Tory sympathies registering strongly ('the female writing subject as political agent', as Rosalind Ballaster has described it[3]), and we need to consider the relationship between the latter and the politics of self-interest. We have seen how critical a role self-interest plays in *Robinson Crusoe*, and it looms large in Defoe's other fiction as well, although there it usually functions as a marker of spiritual shortcomings. Thus in *Roxana* the protagonist's obsessive accumulation of wealth through prostitution argues a lack of capacity for grace that presages a bad end – duly delivered by the author in the narrative's chilling *dénouement*. Self-interest in Roxana's case will extend to the murder of her own daughter Susan, who discovers to her cost just how vicious the politics of self-interest can become when she attempts to unmask her mother's disguise. Moll Flanders is another Defoe character well versed in the politics of self-interest, although the moral lesson to be drawn from her narrative is more ambiguous. We shall be comparing the respective treatment of the politics of self-interest, and its impact on gender relations, by these two authors over the course of this chapter.

Manley's allegorical narrative traces the journey made around the island of Atalantis by the Goddess of Justice, Astrea (returning from self-imposed exile on a fact-finding mission), her mother, Virtue, and their guide, Lady Intelligence. Virtue paints a sorry picture of how the island has developed in her daughter's absence, with moral decline visible in all sectors of society: 'Thee they have not mourned for since thy flight, but have constituted a false appearance in the divine Astrea's room, a mock sort of Justice, whom they invoke upon every occasion, without any real regard to right or wrong'.[4] Astrea has a particular obsession with hypocrisy, all instances of which she feels the need to unmask for the edification of the young prince placed in her care to educate, and her self-appointed task will be to determine the discrepancy between the ideal and the real, theory and practice, in Atalantic society:

> I will go to the courts, where justice is professed, to view the magistrate, who presumes to hold the scales in my name, to see how remote their profession is from their practice; thence to the courts and cabinets of princes, to mark their cabal and disingenuity; to the assemblies and alcoves of the young and fair to discover their disorders and the height of their temptations; the better to teach my young Prince how to avoid them, and accomplish him.[5]

Guided by Lady Intelligence, Astrea builds up a body of evidence that places Atalantic society, and particularly Atalantic male society, in a very bad light. It is highly significant that all this evidence is being mediated through female commentators, with Astrea herself standing for the character of Aphra Behn, thus affirming, as Ballaster notes, 'a feminocentric tradition in Manley's work'.[6] Clearly, this is a world morally out of joint, where action is guided almost solely by self-interest; where human nature is distorting the nature of the state. Hypocrisy, we are informed, 'is not the least reigning vice among the illustrious'.[7] Add in the sexual exploitation of the female sex by the male, and we have a morally highly-charged tale on our hands – Frederick Karl's suggestion that 'we may dismiss [*The New Atalantis*] as gossipy and superficially scandalous', notwithstanding.[8]

The vices of the age are apparent wherever the characters look, with Virtue declaiming sadly that 'Human nature is universally corrupted' in island society.[9] The corruption is particularly apparent in the area of sexual relations, and there are numerous tales of the exploitation of women 'truly named unfortunate' to be recounted over the course of the narrative.[10] There is the case of Mademoiselle Charlot, for example, brought up by a politically-influential Duke to be a wife for his son, but eventually seduced by the Duke himself – 'ruined by him that ought to have been her protector!'.[11] Despite being warned by a female friend at court that, 'the first thing a woman ought to consult was her interest and establishment in the world: that love should only be a handle towards it', Charlot allows herself to be drawn into the Duke's schemes, until finally he abandons her to marry another (a familiar refrain in Manley's world).[12] As for Charlot,

> The remainder of her life was one continued scene of horror, sorrow and repentance. She died a true landmark to warn all believing virgins from shipwracking their honour upon (that dangerous coast of rocks) the vows and pretended passion of mankind.[13]

Charlot proves to be only one of a series of 'unfortunate' female victims to the politics of male self-interest, whose tales clutter the narrative (with Manley including herself in the character of Delia). John J. Richetti has complained that Manley's fictions amount to 'nothing more than a series of anecdotes', but it is the sheer profusion of these which indicates the scale of the problem women face in male conduct, with the same tragic events being enacted over and over again.[14] The betrayed Zara, for example, is driven to commit suicide when her married lover Mosco refuses to leave his wife for her, repulsing her with the harsh words: 'True, you have obliged me; I promised to make a marriage after your fashion by cohabitation. I do not think fit to perform it. What of that? Are you the first woman that has gone upon a wrong principle?'.[15] In case after case, the moral is hammered home that the exploited woman 'is made incapable of a return' to normal existence, while the man escapes censure. Zara drowns herself: Mosco returns to the city of Angela to resume his former life. It is in the repetition of such anecdotes that much of the text's power as feminist narrative lies – as Richetti himself implies when he speaks of scandal novelists like Manley dealing in 'effective erotic-pathetic cliche'.[16] Manley's reference to 'the calumny of male-administration' seems only too aptly to describe the female condition.[17]

It is true that women can on occasion be as corrupt as men, as in the case of the Duchess de l'Inconstant, who seduces the impressionable young brother of one of her staff. But whereas women are generally very vulnerable in such a position, the male can turn it to his own advantage, and the young man in question proceeds to exploit the Duchess' contacts to carve out a career for himself at court. In time-honoured male fashion he is soon acting the seducer himself, and inveigling the Duchess into a compromising position with another admirer, in order to have an excuse to break with her and pursue the other relationship. A long, tortuous tale unfolds, with everyone involved invariably looking to their own interests first and foremost, and using others as a mere means to achieve their own ambitious ends. The episode ends badly for the Duchess, who loses her beauty, her fortune (through gaming), and then, through 'amours, with mean ill formed domestics', her reputation as well.[18] Woman's essential vulnerability within a patriarchal system is forcefully brought home to us by such cautionary tales (the victim almost always, as here, being the woman), and it is clear that they have more to fear from a society structured on Hobbesian 'natural' behaviour than men do.

The contrast between the fate of the seduced young man and Mademoiselle Charlot could hardly be more stark, and we are made to realise at an early stage in Manley's narrative that the politics of self-interest is heavily biased towards the male. 'Male-administration' certainly applies in Atalantis: 'How is it possible to hinder the women from believing or the men from deceiving?', Astrea wonders, and in real terms that is a problem that neither she, nor her author, ever satisfactorily resolves.[19] As one wronged woman, Elonora, puts it, 'I was lost before I reflected and, when I did, my reflections came too late, for ... his design terminated not in marriage' (again, an all too familiar refrain).[20] On the basis of that crucial gender difference (which can come to suggest a differend, so incommensurable do the two respective positions seem to be) men can proceed to exploit women at will, with gender relations largely conforming to the Hobbesian state of nature and the strong consistently preying on the weak. Even when women appear to have attained a position of relative power over men, it is usually only transitory until male-administered society finds ways of redressing the balance. Women are simply not equipped to be the stronger sex; biology almost inevitably betrays them, and the presence of a differend suggests itself again.

It becomes clear as we work our way through Manley's narrative that women are generally guilty of nothing more serious than gullibility. They tend to take men at their word, until bitter personal experience proves this to be a mistake – as it almost always does (Charlot, Zara, etc.). Even then, they remain vulnerable in a patriarchally-ordered society, where male lovers can never be depended upon to keep their promises. The Prince deserts the Baroness de Somes, a young widow he has promised to wed when her mourning period expires, to travel on the continent, where he casually marries another instead. The friend who passes on this information is himself trying to win the widow to restore his ruined fortune, although his appearance of virtue hides his real character: 'The Count, who declaims so well, keeps two women for his debauch. He visits 'em by turns'.[21] Male appearance can never really be trusted. This is even more the case when it involves soldiers, who trade on their handsome exterior to seduce the local female population wherever their company is billeted: 'and then to work they go – shave and powder, and on goes the blue or scarlet coat every day. ... Their company marched away, but left I know not how many unborn bastards behind 'em'.[22] In one particularly sombre tale, a young woman who gives birth in secret to an illegitimate child by a soldier, murders the child in panic and is subsequently hanged publicly for the crime. Yet again, the burden of guilt for sexual indiscretion falls entirely on the woman: 'She was a handsome gentlewoman; I wish all young women would take warning by her fall'.[23] The triteness of the sentiments merely serves to point up the injustice of the whole episode; the underlying assumption being that men in general will be deaf to such warnings, so there is no point in addressing them. The attitude of men is well summed up by the notoriously libertine military tribune who supports a law to punish adultery by death: 'he thought they did deserve to die that were such fools to be catched, for, whereas he had but shut the door before, he would be sure to lock it now'.[24] Again, the sense of seduction being a mere game to the male sex is much in evidence.

When women *are* revealed to be corrupt and hypocritical, it is generally in imitation of male behaviour – and after having been sexually or financially exploited by men in the first place. Male behaviour sets the pattern in Atalantic society, and it is based unequivocally on self-interest; with the politics of self-interest dictating that one pursues one's desires to the exclusion of all other considerations, doing and saying whatever is necessary in order to achieve one's objectives. Morality never seems to enter the equation; satisfaction of one's appetites is all that counts. While women can be drawn into this cycle of conduct ('these are prosperous times for vice', after all[25]), eventually they will find themselves to be handicapped – by double-standard morality, for example – in a way that men are not. It remains a high-risk strategy for the female sex to imitate male conduct, with their reputation permanently in danger of exposure if, like the Duchess de l'Inconstant, they fail to be discreet enough in their activities. The gender equivalent of absolute sovereignty is missing in Atalantis, and women are suffering in consequence.

The nature of the state reflects the imperfections of human nature as displayed in Atalantis, with the court riven by factions for whom hypocrisy has become second nature:

> A prince knows not how to distinguish by the out, and are seldom let into the inside. All appears fair to 'em, if he be a good man Who so forward as the atheist in affecting piety? ... There are few honest men found at court. ... None serve there but in prospect of making, advancing, or preserving their fortunes.[26]

In effect, the court is in a state of nature, where everyone seeks their own advantage at the expense of others, and the nation at large has to pay the penalty. Politics is reduced to a perpetual scramble for personal advantage, with the public interest subordinated to the private – and that becomes the crux of Manley's critique of party politics: 'Who in this age would serve without reward?'.[27]

The second volume of *The New Atalantis* delves more deeply into open political satire, with Manley's Tory sympathies coming to the fore. As Jane Spencer, amongst others, has pointed out, however, it is part of Manley's general approach throughout the narrative to mix the sexual and the political; thus 'to accuse her [Whig] targets of sexual intrigues' is consistently to be making political points.[28] The Whig political establishment is mercilessly lampooned by the author, who appears to be taking a particularly firm stand against the politics of self-interest. There is what Ballaster calls an 'unabashed specificity' to these attacks.[29] 'Two renowned politicians' (the Whigs John, Baron Somers, and Charles Montagu, Earl Halifax), for example, whose fortunes have grown during their time in office, are mockingly congratulated for blurring the line between public and private interest:

> The methods they have took to raise their fortune gives us but little hopes that they would have persevered in any principle that should but once appear to be contrary to their interest but, since no such change has arrived, let us charitably applaud 'em, as men remaining true to their first professions, a virtue rarely found in a statesman.[30]

Somers (Lord Artaban) is further criticised for his unforgiving nature and ungovernable temper; the suggestion being that he acts in a manner more akin to the Hobbesian state of nature than the court of a supposedly civilised country. Another Atalantic politician is warned how 'much easier it is to be born great than continue great', and Manley communicates a very jaundiced view of public life in general.[31] The probity of the Count of Valentia (Charles Mordaunt, 3rd Earl of Peterborough) is all the more remarkable in such a context; the Count being fulsomely praised for a 'contempt of self-interest not to be matched by the old Roman and Spartan worthies, free from the modern system that takes up an employment to fill their own coffers'.[32] Valentia harks back to a classical concept of public service, where the individual served the state rather than his own interest, but he is a notable exception to the general party political rule: modern political life otherwise is corruption incarnate.

By the close of the narrative Manley has made it clear that she regards self-interest as a cancer eating away at the heart of Atalantic society, infecting both public and private life. And for every Count of Valentia with his 'contempt of self-interest' there are dozens of Lord Artabans abusing the public trust without scruple. Women are the most obvious victims of this sorry state of affairs, as Manley exhaustively reveals in her litany of 'unfortunates', but its negative effects can be felt throughout the whole nation. Atalantis is a society which presents itself in one way, but acts in another fashion entirely behind the scenes: ostensibly a civilised modern nation with strict moral ideals, in reality it is a state of nature where the strong prey incessantly on the weak and hypocrisy has become a way of life. When it comes to *male* human nature, certainly, Manley has little faith, and Atalantic society stands as an indictment of that phenomenon, with its well-attested capacity for generating endless anecdotes of female emotional distress. Even more to the point, the narrative is, as Spencer has noted, an indictment of the male infantilisation of women in a patriarchal society, and we should rid ourselves of 'the mistaken notion that Manley glorifies female innocence and weakness'.[33]

After some chastening experiences in early life (the product of her feckless husband abandoning her with five young children to care for), the politics of self-interest comes to rule Roxana's life. She proves to be quite ruthless about this, and despite initial misgivings about having to turn to prostitution to survive, rapidly transforms herself into a model entrepreneur who always puts profit first, regardless of what the consequences may be – even to the extent of abandoning her own children in turn, as hindrances to her 'business' dealings. Roxana conducts herself as if she were, for all practical purposes, existing in a state of nature. She lives in permanent dread of the discovery of her true situation, relying on her wits to stay one step ahead of the forces of social convention, which continue to operate according to double-standard morality. The best way to stay ahead is to accumulate as much wealth as she can as quickly as she can, since wealth equals power over others and a greater measure of control over one's life. Roxana's reiterated itemisation of her growing wealth, and use of the real-life character Sir Robert Clayton as her personal investment consultant, indicate where her own priorities lie:

> Let it lie, Madam, *says he*, till the next Year, and then I'll put out your 1400 *l*. together, and in the mean time I'll pay you Interest for the 700 *l*. so he gave me his Bill for the Money, which he told me shou'd be no less than 6 *l*. *per Cent*. Sir *Robert Clayton's* Bill was what no-body wou'd refuse; so I thank'd him, and let it lie; and next Year I did the same, and the third Year Sir *Robert* got me a good Mortgage for 2200 *l*. at 6 *per Cent*. Interest: So I had 132 *l*. a Year added to my Income; which was a very Satisfying Article.[34]

In economic terms anyway hers is a success story, and by the end of the narrative she is a very rich woman indeed.

Yet no matter how rich Roxana may become, she can never consider herself to be entirely safe or able to relax her vigilance – as the arrival on the scene of her abandoned daughter Susan proves. Susan is as determined to trace her parentage as Roxana is to deny it, and refuses to be warned off from her pursuit of her mother: 'for, *in short*, if I was in *England* or *Holland*, she wou'd find me'.[35] Seizing the initiative, Roxana's faithful servant Amy, often seen as the former's unscrupulous *alter ego*, murders Susan (or at least that is strongly implied by Roxana herself after Susan's sudden, and suspiciously convenient, 'disappearance'): a case of the assumption of the executive power to deal with those who threaten us, although here we are seeing its dark side rather than the ethically-defensible situation pictured by Locke in the *Second Treatise*. It is one thing to punish a genuine transgressor who threatens our physical well-being, something else altogether to act so severely against a mere nuisance – particularly one with undeniable moral claims on us. Susan is an embarrassment rather than a physical threat as such, and nothing she does warrants the death penalty that is exacted on her. Roxana's own anguish about the outcome can appear hypocritical as a result, and her own ultimate fall from grace, strongly hinted at in the narrative's closing paragraph, a case of just deserts:

> Here, after some few Years of flourishing, and outwardly happy Circumstances, I fell into a dreadful Course of Calamities, and *Amy* also; the very reverse of our former Good Days; the Blast of Heaven seem'd to follow the Injury done the poor Girl, by us both; and I was brought so low again, that my Repentance seem'd to be only the Consequence of my Misery, as my Misery was of my Crime.[36]

Given such sentiments, Roxana's narrative ultimately registers as somewhat less than an endorsement of the politics of self-interest.

The politics of self-interest certainly infect gender relations in *Roxana*, too, although here it appears to be the heroine who is taking the initiative – admittedly, largely as a means of self-defence after her formative early experiences at the hands of her husband. Roxana's intention seems to be to take the game to the male sex, in order to avoid the possibility of sexual exploitation. By doing so, she undercuts much of the power that the male sex has over women, with her goal being to turn herself into a 'Man-Woman', an entity transcending gender, and thus, Roxana hopes, manipulation by others:

> I knew no Reason the Men had to engross the whole Liberty of the Race ... it was my Misfortune to be a Woman, but I was resolv'd it shou'd not be made worse by the Sex; and seeing Liberty seem'd to be the Men's Property, I wou'd be a *Man-Woman*; for as I was born free, I wou'd die so.[37]

Roxana is never seduced; instead, she uses men as a means to an end – the improvement of her personal fortune. Here is a woman who has gone well beyond 'believing' male rhetoric. Unlike Manley's female characters, she is immune to male deception and takes a clinical view of sexuality as a mere business transaction to be exploited for all it is worth. Whereas Manley's heroines invariably display weaknesses when engaging in the politics of self-interest, Roxana ditches all emotional baggage the better to compete with her male rivals for power. There is a single-mindedness about her that not even Moll Flanders can match. Roxana reaches a state where 'Avarice cou'd have no Pretence', yet she avidly continues to amass wealth through prostitution, despite idly wondering '*What am I a Whore for now?*'.[38]

Aspiring to become a 'Man-Woman' is a way of trying to alter the balance of power within a patriarchal society that operates much like the state of nature, where the strong, generally the men, prey on the weak, generally the women. Roxana achieves a considerable degree of success in her venture, with Sir Robert Clayton teasing her about her '*Amazonian*' inclinations, while nevertheless respecting her decision to use them as a basis for a business ethos: 'Sir *Robert* laugh'd heartily at me, but gave over offering any more Arguments ... he applauded my Way of managing my Money, and told me, I shou'd soon be monstrous rich'.[39] The implication seems to be that whatever furthers one's economic self-interest is, by definition, the right course of action to pursue – although Sir Robert is unaware of the source of Roxana's investment capital. Nevertheless, economic self-interest seems to be cutting across the whole notion of morality, with Roxana calling society's bluff in terms of both its moral pretensions and its hypocrisy. If the body *is*, as Locke claims, property, then there seems to be no moral objection to Roxana's deployment of it as a courtesan, if that is economically beneficial to her. Biology here works, for once, to a woman's advantage.

The victory over biology is only temporary, however, and eventually it reasserts itself in conventionally restrictive fashion when Susan re-enters Roxana's life; at which point the insecurity associated with the state of nature, gender-based or otherwise, returns with a vengeance to plague Roxana: 'the Blast of Heaven seem'd to follow the Injury done the poor Girl by us both'. As we have already seen with the heroine of *Love Letters*, those who live according to the state of nature will eventually fall victim to it; no-one can escape its disadvantages indefinitely. Roxana's avoidance of a marriage contract can be interpreted as a rejection of contractually-based civil society in general; in which case her fate becomes an argument against embracing the ethics of the state of nature. Roxana must accept the consequences of failing to take the Lockean route out of the latter condition, although it has to be acknowledged that, as far as women are concerned, patriarchy remains a less than attractive prospect. Caught between moral anarchy and male domination, Roxana becomes a highly symbolic representative of the socio-political tensions within early eighteenth-century English culture. Through observing Roxana's career we become very aware of significant gaps in the discourse of sovereignty (personal and political), and, indeed, of the presence of some particularly intractable differends within it: differends which become more insistent as we analyse the impact of the politics of self-interest on gender relations. Defoe offers us no easy answers to the dilemma women face in this respect either.

Moll Flanders, too, can be considered to be, *de facto*, in a state of nature for most of her highly eventful career. First, as an orphan put into service; then, as a thief; finally, as a condemned convict in Newgate, subsequently transported to the new world of the Virginian plantations as indentured labour. Maltreatment by various men in her early life places Moll in a compromising position, where she is forced back on her wits to survive:

> I resolv'd, therefore, as to the State of my present Circumstances; that it was absolutely Necessary to change my Station, and make a new Appearance in some other Place where I was not known, and even to pass by another Name if I found occasion.[40]

Neither female servants nor unattached women without personal fortunes – both categories into which Moll falls at one time or other – have many options open to them in such a severely patriarchal society, and eventually she drifts into a life of crime. That life proves to have all the characteristics of the Hobbesian state of nature: permanent personal insecurity, a relentlessly competitive environment enacting the 'warre of every man against every man', and the never-ending need to accumulate wealth and possessions in order to protect oneself, for example. Moll differs from Roxana in being a far less ruthless personality, who retains at least a measure of her humanity despite her precarious social position. As a case in point, she is more open to the play of her emotions, which sometimes cause her to act against her own best, economic, interests. Men are not simply a resource to be exploited for her, although she does treat selected individuals that way on those occasions when the economic need arises. Drunken men are fair game, and Moll is not above robbing children either, if her livelihood demands it. Moll can, and does, fall in love, and although this makes her less competitive in a 'male-administered' world, it also makes her more human; as we can see when her 'Lancashire husband', Jem, deserts her to prevent her from being dragged down into a life of poverty with him:

> Nothing that ever befel me in my Life, sunk so deep into my Heart as this Farewel: I reproach'd him a Thousand times in my Thoughts for leaving me, for I would have gone with him thro' the World if I had beg'd my Bread.[41]

For all her redeeming features, however, Moll is thrown into some desperate situations which severely test her survival skills – therefore her ability to heed the politics of self-interest. Her imprisonment in Newgate is a prime example of such trials. Once inside, she is indeed returned to a state of nature, where personal security is routinely violated and none of her fellow inmates can be trusted. Newgate truly replicates the anarchy of a war of all against all, compressing all the worst aspects of Moll's society to demonstrate just how vulnerable the individual can be in that condition:

> 'tis impossible to describe the terror of my mind, when I was first brought in, and when I look'd round upon all the horrors of that dismal Place: I look'd on myself as lost ... the hellish Noise, the Roaring, Swearing and Clamour, the Stench and Nastiness, and all the dreadful cloud of Afflicting things that I saw there; joyn'd together to make the Place seem an Emblem of Hell itself, and a kind of an Entrance into it.[42]

We might see Newgate as standing for a microcosm of the new entre-preneurial capitalism with the markedly Hobbesian bias it imparts to human relations. In such conditions of intense competition only the very fittest survive, and that demands that the politics of self-interest take precedence. Moll can play that card when required, and we might well question the sincerity of her eventual religious 'conversion' in Newgate on those grounds It is certainly in Moll's interest to repent, or, being more cynical, to give the appearance of repentance (as hinted at by the 'editor' in his preface to the tale[43]), since repentance holds out the hope of commutation of her sentence from public execution to transportation to the colonies. Re-pentance carries no guarantees, but lack of repentance manifestly does – hanging at Tyburn. Transportation carries no guarantees either, but it is enough of a life-line to continue to prosecute the politics of self-interest. Moll takes full advantage of that life-line, eventually managing to obtain her freedom and set up as a planter herself; the first step on the road to amassing a fortune, and the greater sense of personal security this brings to the individual.

The spiritual autobiographical structure of the narrative brings Moll within the framework of the Calvinist state of nature, where, post-conversion, she can be assumed to take her place in the ranks of the elect within a world peopled largely by hostile, elect-threatening, reprobates. Again, it is certainly in one's self-interest to be in the category of the elect rather than the reprobate, and the character's deployment of spiritual auto-biographical conventions might be a ruse to gain our sympathy, when we ought more correctly to be condemning her criminal tendencies (theft, incest, and bigamy, for starters). The conventions of spiritual autobiogra-phy allow for repeated instances of sinful behaviour, and help to disguise the politics of self-interest by endowing them with a sense of theologically-sanctioned destiny – something that Roxana, to her intense frustration, can never achieve, no matter how much she reflects on her situation. The de-gree of authorial irony with regard to Moll's 'solution' to her plight in Newgate, however, is always open to question (she does suggest, as one critic has put it, a 'conveniently underdeveloped, sense of morality' much of the time[44]). J. Paul Hunter's reading of Defoe and Richardson as 'classic examples of writers who often got old and new loyalties powerfully mixed up and who therefore send quite mixed signals in their plots as well as their appeals', is worth acknowledging in this respect.[45] *Moll* is certainly a more complex narrative situation than that presented by Manley, where there is a more obvious critique of the politics of self-interest taking place.

The politics of self-interest have a marked effect on gender relations in each of these authors, although Manley makes us more aware of the general socio-political context in which they are conducted, and the way in which acting according to the state of nature can distort the nature of the state. For all her critique of male human nature, however, Manley suggests a certain qualified optimism: at least the problem has been identified, and women alerted to the rhetorical malpractice of the male race. A solution of sorts, with overtones of feminist separatism, is put forward in the guise of the Cabal, whose members eschew male society in protest at the injustices of male-administration. While he shows us the pressures women are subjected to in a capitalist patriarchal society, Defoe suggests a greater capacity for subterfuge in the female character. Both Moll and Roxana resist rather better than the average Manley heroine does, and both reveal a certain talent for survival within a state of nature framework – although of course this must always leave us less than secure in our person. To return to a point made earlier, too, Defoe seems rather more interested in the spiritual aspect of self-interest than the strictly political – although the spiritual does have political implications none the less.

Perhaps the major difference between the two authors is that Manley regards the state of nature as something like a male conspiracy against women, whereas Defoe treats it as a more widespread social problem (exacerbated by the new economic order) that puts us all at risk – women admittedly more than men, but not exclusively so. Either way, gender relations are profoundly affected when there is any reversion to a state of nature, and the discourse of sovereignty is at its most tangled when it has to deal with what looks increasingly like the 'differend' encoded in gender. Entry into that discourse remains the most intractable of tasks for the female sex.

Notes

1   Delarivier Manley, *Secret Memoirs and Manners of Several Persons of Quality, of both Sexes. From the New Atalantis, an Island in the Mediterannean*, Rosalind Ballaster (ed.), Harmondsworth, Penguin, 1992, p. 45.
2   *Ibid.*, p. 268.
3   Ballaster, *Seductive Forms*, p. 120.
4   *New Atalantis*, p. 5.
5   *Ibid.*, p. 8.
6   Ballaster, *Seductive Forms*, p. 115.
7   *New Atalantis*, p. 81.

8   Frederick Karl, *A Reader's Guide to the Development of the English Novel in the Eighteenth Century*, London, Thames and Hudson, 1975, p. 4.
9   *New Atalantis*, p. 11.
10   *Ibid.*, p. 26.
11   *Ibid.*, pp. 39-40.
12   *Ibid.*, p. 40.
13   *Ibid.*, p. 45.
14   John J. Richetti, *Popular Fiction before Richardson: Narrative Patterns 1700-39*, Oxford, Clarendon Press, 1969, p. 121.
15   *New Atalantis*, p. 129.
16   Richetti, *Popular Fiction before Richardson*, p. 125.
17   *New Atalantis*, p. 47. Rosalind Ballaster's reference note suggests that the pun may well have been deliberate on Manley's part (*Ibid.*, p. 276).
18   *Ibid.*, p. 25.
19   *Ibid.*, p. 228.
20   *Ibid.*, p. 165.
21   *Ibid.*, p. 81.
22   *Ibid.*, p. 83.
23   *Ibid.*, p. 84.
24   *Ibid.*, p. 229.
25   *Ibid.*, p. 101.
26   *Ibid.*, p. 110.
27   *Ibid.*, p. 135.
28   Jane Spencer, *The Rise of the Woman Novelist: From Aphra Benn to Jane Austen*, Oxford and New York, Blackwell, 1986, p. 53.
29   Ballaster, *Seductive Forms*, p. 123.
30   *New Atalantis*, p. 263.
31   *Ibid.*, p. 266.
32   *Ibid.*, p. 268.
33   Spencer, *The Rise of the Woman Novelist*, p. 116.
34   Daniel Defoe, *Roxana, or, The Fortunate Mistress*, Jane Jack (ed.), Oxford, Oxford University Press, 1964, p. 169.
35   *Ibid.*, p. 321.
36   *Ibid.*, pp. 329-30.
37   *Ibid.*, p. 171.
38   *Ibid.*, pp. 202, 203.
39   *Ibid.*, p. 171.
40   Daniel Defoe, *The Fortunes and Misfortunes of the Famous Moll Flanders*, G.A. Starr (ed.), Oxford, Oxford University Press, 1971, p. 76.
41   *Ibid.*, p. 153.
42   *Ibid.*, pp. 273-4.
43   '[S]he liv'd it seems, to be very old; but was not so extraordinary a Penitent, as she was at first'; *Ibid.*, p. 5.
44   Howard L. Koonce, 'Moll's Muddle: Defoe's Use of Irony in *Moll Flanders*', *Journal of English Literary History*, 30 (1963), pp. 377-94 (p. 380).
45   J. Paul Hunter, *Before Novels: The Cultural Contexts of Eighteenth-Century English Fiction*, New York and London, W. W. Norton, 1990, p. 134.

Chapter 11

Bolingbroke: Party and the State of Nature

In the view of one leading scholar, Jacobitism is *the* salient factor of early eighteenth-century literary and political culture. According to Howard Erskine-Hill recent scholarship in eighteenth-century studies has discredited the notion that the Glorious Revolution was a watershed event leading to the secularisation of society and parliamentary democracy. The Glorious Revolution was not a precedent that made possible the American and French revolutions. 'Lockeian contractualism' did not represent a political consensus; neither did civic humanism. The latter was an important if subordinate aspect of cultural, intellectual and political life in the Augustan period. 'Patriarchalism and providentialism were not less strong than before, they may have been stronger'.[1]

Erskine-Hill is right to state that contract theory as read through Locke was not the force in the early eighteenth century it has for a long time been assumed to be.[2] Civic humanism, however, needs to be given more regard in the works of the period's leading political and literary figures, as does acceptance of the notion that patriarchalism and providentialism strengthened during the years between the Glorious Revolution and the Jacobite rebellion of 1745. We shall now consider the political writings of Bolingbroke in relation to Whig and Tory ideas about the state of nature in the age of Walpole, and to assess the crucial significance of civic humanism in relation to opposition prose and poetry between 1720 and 1745. Vital to the dialogue that took place between oppositional factions in early eighteenth-century political and literary writings is the manner in which patriarchalism and providentialism were challenged in direct ways. *Cato's Letters*, Bolingbroke's *Dissertation upon Parties* (1733-4), *On the Spirit of Patriotism*, and *The Idea of a Patriot King*,[3] Pope's *Essay on Man* and Thomson's *Liberty*, were engaged in a dialogic debate about the nature of political obligation that borrowed extensively from the canon of civic humanism and classical republicanism. In this respect, Bolingbroke's Toryism shared distinct characteristics with the overt Whiggism of *Cato's Letters* written by Gordon and Trenchard. In his *Dissertation upon Parties* Bolingbroke makes it apparent that the distinctions separating Whigs from Tories were generated in the Exclusion debates of the later seventeenth century, and in a contemporary context are no longer applicable:

> The power and majesty of the people, an original contract, the authority and independence of Parliament, liberty, resistance, exclusion, abdication, deposition; these were ideas associated, at that time, to the idea of a Whig, and supposed by every Whig to be incommunicable, and inconsistent with the idea of a Tory. Divine, hereditary, indefeasible right, lineal succession, passive obedience, prerogative, non-resistance, slavery, nay and sometimes property too, were associated in many minds to the idea of a Tory, and deemed incommunicable and inconsistent in the same manner, with the idea of a Whig.[4]

Divisions between parties, Bolingbroke claims, are by now no longer sustainable, and all must labour for the common good. Bolingbroke's distinctions between Whig and Tory are a little disingenuous, however, as it is the aristocratic, Old Whig ideology, and not the new mercantile and middle class Whiggism associated with Walpole's administration with which he finds common cause.[5] In his attempt to break down the differences between the Old Whigs and the Tories, Bolingbroke is seeking to emphasise parties of a different colour and create a country opposition to the court.

In many ways this is the rhetoric of aristocratic republicanism associated primarily with the later prose works of Milton, Sidney's *Discourses on Government*, and Robert Molesworth's *An Account of the History of Denmark*. The latter work, in particular, like Bolingbroke's *Dissertation*, is a scathing condemnation of the rule of the Stuarts. Bolingbroke is relentless in his criticism of hereditary divine right as it is manifested in the words and actions of the early Stuarts in particular. In the *Dissertation* he describes divine right and 'all those exalted notions, concerning the power and prerogative of kings, and the sacredness of their persons', as constituting 'a system of absurdity as had never been heard of in this country, till that anointed pedant [James I] broached them'.[6] Such an attitude needs to be taken into consideration before contending, as Erskine-Hill and Jonathan Clark do, that eighteenth-century Britain was governed by discourses of 'patriarchalism and providence'. In his *Account of Denmark*, Molesworth argues that the nobility are the natural guardians of liberty and he points to the invidious state of Danish politics, where the commons have allied themselves with a clergy that believes in passive obedience and a king who has absolutist pretensions. The end result is that 'an absolute prince' now oppresses the people.[7] Like Sidney and Neville, Addison also refers to the close links made by ancient historians between moral virtue, political probity and the lessons to be learnt from the past.[8] Recourse to historical argumentation through references to the classical past and also to the ancient constitution, stood in marked contrast to the kind of Whig political theory which emphasised instead 'the highly rationalised, ahistorical idiom of Locke's choice, natural law'.[9] For commentators such as Zook, Harro Hopfl, and Martyn Thompson, Locke's ahistorical natural law methodology, is an example of 'philosophical' as opposed to 'constitutional contractarianism'.[10] As for Addison's hatred of the commonwealth, this may well be true with reference to the government of the 1650s; however, figures such as Bolingbroke and Addison, seemingly diverse in their political affiliations, borrow heavily from a visibly republican vocabulary and echo later English republicanism in its language of reform and consent. Like the republican writers of the 1650s and 1690s, Bolingbroke resorts to history in order to ground an argument that in its sentiments requires checks and balances against arbitrary power. His opinion of James II is a case in point:

> A professed, zealous papist, in full and quiet possession of the throne, and, instead of any provision being made, or any measures taken against him, the notion and the exercise of the prerogative at an extravagant height, were such circumstances as laid the nation almost at the mercy of the King.[11]

The blame for the Revolution of 1688-9, says Bolingbroke, lies at the door of the Tories, who 'acted on the most abject principles of submission to the King, and on those of hereditary right.' The Whigs, on the other hand, who had 'law, example and reason for them', sought to limit the succession and maintain the right of resistance. Only in the immoderate manner in which they sought to defend these principles by illegally usurping the rights of Parliament, were they extravagant in their 'spirit of licence'.[12]

Bolingbroke rejects absolutely the 'slavish principles of passive obedience and non-resistance' and believes wholeheartedly that the nature of the Stuart state with all of its patriarchal and providentialist assumptions is iniquitous. Such ideas, he goes on to assert, were unequivocally rejected by 'Not only the laity, but the clergy', who 'embraced and co-operated in the deliverance which the Prince of Orange brought them'. Accordingly, political man acts in keeping with his interests. Common cause between Whigs and Tories was motivated by necessity and self-interest, which in the case of the Glorious Revolution was given ethical probity in that it was also perceived to be in pursuit of the common good. Bolingbroke sees necessity and self-preservation as being 'the great laws of nature' and in defence of principle it is perfectly acceptable to 'dispense with the strict observation of the common forms of any particular constitution'.[13] The events of the Glorious Revolution re-established the monarchy on its proper basis, bringing it 'back to the first principles'. Bolingbroke argues that if indefeasible hereditary right is to be accepted as the governing principle in politics and is to exist as 'a right independent of the community'; if 'passive obedience and non-resistance' are to exist as 'an allegiance unconditional', then it should surprise no one if tyranny quickly follows. The Glorious Revolution made it apparent that 'The principles by which [a king] governs are plainly original contracts. His institution is plainly conditional, and he may forfeit his right to allegiance, as undeniably and effectually, as the subject may forfeit his right to protection'. Like Harrington, Bolingbroke is unequivocal in his belief that the laws of the land are the 'sole springs from whence the prince can derive his pretensions, and the people theirs'. The nature of the constitution is such, that any attack on liberty justifies active resistance.[14]

The concept of the citizen and his willingness to place himself under a just prince is a key feature of political writing from the 1650s onwards, and is completely in line with the writings of Harrington, Milton, Sidney, Toland, Moyle and Addison. The volume, as well as the quality of such writing questions severely any blanket assumptions about the universal acceptance of patriarchalism and providence. Resistance to an unjust prince is a duty as well as a right. In *Oceana* Harrington writes that 'The corruption of monarchy ... is called tyranny', and 'If one man be sole landlord of territory, or overbalance the people ... his empire is absolute monarchy'. If force is used to change the nature of the existing order, and 'if it be at the devotion of a prince, it is tyranny'.[15] In *The Freeholder* Addison is lavish in his praise of George I. At the same time, however, the negative portrait he paints of the later Stuart monarchs serves as a stark point of contrast and also as a warning. Moreover, despite his panegyrics to the house of Hanover, Addison argues that George carefully safeguards 'civil liberties', because the constitution '*directs*' him to do so.[16] In this respect Addison and Bolingbroke are at one with writers such as Robert Molesworth, who argue that 'tis a true, though but a melancholy Reflection, that our late *Kings* have undid us, and breeding us up as narrow-spirited as they could, made us consider ourselves as proscribed from the world in every sense'.[17]

Bolingbroke's Ciceronian rhetoric, with its emphasis on truth, virtue, reason and liberty, is consistent throughout the *Dissertation*. The manner of Bolingbroke's intellectual borrowing created a strange confluence of ostensibly oppositional ideologies joining together reluctant bedfellows. In the words of David Armitage, '"Court Whigs" became counterposed to "Country Tories", and the so-called Old Whigs who were committed to the neo-republican constitutional Whiggism of the 1690s joined forces with the Tories in an uneasy oppositional alliance'. Bolingbroke, the ostensibly arch-Tory Jacobite became, in his *Dissertation upon Parties*, the purveyor of a post-revolutionary Old Whig ideology.[18] A political theory of aristocratic supremacy underpinned by the legitimising intellectual force of classical thought, primarily Ciceronian political ideas filtered through Renaissance humanism, and a belief in the natural superiority of his own class, were other factors that attracted Bolingbroke to the state of nature advocated by those writers associated with Old Whig political philosophy: 'The efforts of moneyed men to ascend the social scale were an act of rebellion against the natural order of things. The landed men were the natural leaders of civic life and to alter this arrangement was to threaten the whole fabric of society'. The defence of position and property is central to the Whig recourse to natural rights, though as we shall discover below this is severely limited and should not be confused with any democratic impulse.[19] It is this perhaps that makes Old Whig rhetoric with its republican overtones and trenchant defence of property so attractive to Bolingbroke. In the works of such writers republican thought becomes the means of providing the necessary checks and balances that are required to guarantee the liberties of the subject. This is especially the case when republican idioms are blended with theories of the ancient constitution. The ancient constitution protected the rights of parliament and prescribed the extent of royal power, whilst simultaneously denying 'universal and inalienable rights' for all men.[20]

In terms of government, quasi-republican ideas with particular regard to consent are invoked by those writing from a Whig perspective in order to encourage 'reform and perfection' rather than revolution. As Addison in *The Freeholder* would have it:

> I consider myself as one who gives my consent to every law which passes: a freeholder in our government being of the nature of a citizen of Rome in that famous commonwealth; who by the election of a tribune, had a kind of remote voice in every law that was enacted. So that a freeholder is but one remove from a legislator, and for that reason ought to stand up in defence of those laws, which are in some degree of his own making. For such is the nature of our happy constitution, that the bulk of the people virtually give their approbation to every thing they are bound to obey, and prescribe to themselves those rules by which they are to walk.[21]

Elsewhere in *The Freeholder* Addison argues that reading and learning the lessons of history is the foundation of 'good laws', and is the best means of 'detecting conspiracies' and 'crushing seditions and rebellions'. In much the same manner Toland, in his preface to Harrington's *Works*, praises the writers 'invidiously nicknam'd Commonwealthmen', for their valiant rescue of 'our ancient government from the devouring Jaws of Arbitrary Power', and through 'excellent Laws ... set bounds to the Will of the King ... that render him the more safe, equally binding up his and the Subjects hands from unjustly seizing one another's prescribed rights or Privileges'.[22] Addison makes it clear that moral virtue is explicitly linked to political responsibility, as only by safeguarding morality can one hope 'to promote the safety, welfare, and reputation of the community in which we are born, and of the constitution under which we are protected'.[23] In *Cato's Letters*, Trenchard and Gordon make the very same point. Consent is essential to the formation of government, 'if not of every subject, yet of as many as can compel the rest'. Legitimate government derives its strength from 'the laws and constitutions of the society, of which the governors themselves are but the members'.[24] Patriotism in Addison's view is the preserve of those who are stakeholders in their country. Accordingly, 'One is apt to suspect, that the passion for liberty, which appears in a Grub-Street patriot, arises only from his apprehensions of a gaol; and that, whatever he may pretend, he does not write to secure, but to get something of his own'.[25] Patriotism itself naturally arises out of a 'Spartan or Roman Virtue'. Such a view of the exclusivity of democratic participation is very close to Sidney in his remarks on popular government: if 'that is pure democracy, where the people in themselves, and by themselves, perform all that belongs to government, I know of no such thing; and if it be in the world, I have nothing to say for it'.[26] Harrington too had no time for the levelling tendencies of popular political rhetoric.[27] Neville, also, in his *Plato Redivivus* gives short shrift to the masses. For Neville, allowing the majority to participate in politics is to invite disaster, 'these being less sober, less considering, and less careful of the public concerns'.[28]

In this process the Ciceronian and Catonic ideal of public service and obligation, properly restricted to those who are fit to rule, is central. As Bolingbroke himself put it, without Cato and Cicero the theory and fact of Roman liberty would not have survived Catiline's conspiracy had not 'Cicero defended them, abetted by Cato and the best'.[29] In Bolingbroke's eyes Cicero appears to be the complete statesman – not only was Cicero's oratory unsurpassed, but his political skills were paramount. Cicero is revealed in Bolingbroke's essay *On the Spirit of Patriotism* as a politician standing head and shoulders above his contemporaries. Nor is this due to his pre-eminent reputation as an orator. Eloquence alone is no guarantee of political success. Eloquence alone would not have saved Roman liberty. Indeed,

> if [Cicero] had not united by skill and management, in the common cause of their country, orders of men the most averse to each other; if he had not watched all the machinations of the conspirators in silence, and prepared a strength sufficient to resist them at Rome, and in the provinces, before he opened this scene of villainy to the senate and the people: in a word, if he had not made much more use of political prudence, that is, of the knowledge of mankind, and of the arts of government, which study and experience give, than of all the powers of his eloquence,

then Cicero would have been ineffective as a protector of Rome against Catiline.[30] Throughout his political writings Bolingbroke makes considerable play of classical history, Greek and Roman polities, the actions of the great politicians such as Demosthenes and Cicero, as well as drawing upon the reign of the Stuarts to make sense of current events. The past is continually used as a window on the present. Far from being an important though secondary strand to Jacobitism in the years between the rebellions of 1715 and 1745, civic humanism was the common glue that bound together disparate political and cultural ideas. The vocabulary and idiom of classical virtue was the primary language in which politics was discussed in the period; borrowing from classical sources to lend credibility to one's political ideas was commonplace. The language of classical republican virtue and political behaviour was transformed from the 1670s onwards into a respectable form of addressing abuses of power in the Augustan period.

'Truth, virtue and liberty' are in Bolingbroke's eyes the trinity of qualities most appropriate for a statesman. These are qualities that lie at the heart of Cicero's handbook of effective estate management, *De Officiis*, book one of which carefully elaborates the four cardinal virtues that govern the structure of the entire volume. Cicero believed that it is mankind's primary function to act for self-preservation. This includes the defence of life and body and the freedom to organise communally for mutual safety. This is derived from man's access to reason, his ability to think historically for the common good, and 'by seeing with ease the whole course of life' he can prepare for 'whatever is necessary in living it'.[31] The investigation and search for truth leads man to a higher condition by allowing free rein to his intellect. This in itself breeds greatness of spirit and encourages man to labour for the common good.

These themes of self-preservation and the common good, are similarly picked up by Pope in his *Essay on Man*: 'Thus Nature gives us (let us check our pride) / The virtue near our vice ally'd; / *Reason* the bypass turns from good to ill / And Nero rules a Titus, if he will'. And again in Epistle III where Pope demonstrates that it is in an original prelapsarian state of nature that 'Self-love and social at her birth began'.[32] Pope seems remarkably close to Cicero here:

> Everything that is honourable arises from one of four parts: it is involved either with perception of truth and with ingenuity; or with preserving fellowship among men; ... or with the greatness and strength of a lofty and unconquered spirit; or with order and limit in everything that is said and done (modesty and restraint are included here).[33]

As Epistle III of Pope's *Essay* develops, the poet makes it clear that in a prelapsarian world 'All vocal beings hymn'd their equal God', and Heav'n's attribute was Universal Care, / And man's prerogative to rule, but spare'. Although Locke is rarely evoked directly in the political literature of the period, in the spirit of equality with which Pope depicts an original state of nature there seems to be an echo of Locke's *Second Treatise*. Locke opens chapter 2 of that text by declaring that mankind in an original state of nature is perfectly free 'to order their actions and dispose of their Possessions and Persons as they think fit ... without asking leave, or depending upon the Will of any other Man'. Moreover,

> A *State* also *of Equality* [exists], wherein all the Power and Jurisdiction is reciprocal, no one having more than another: there being nothing more evident, than that Creatures of the same species and rank promiscuously born to all the same advantages of Nature, and the use of the same faculties, should also be equal one amongst another without Subordination or Subjection, unless the Lord and Master of them all, should by any manifest Declaration of his Will set one above another, and confer on him by an evident and clear appointment an undoubted Right to Dominion and Sovereignty.[34]

Mankind ruled the natural world with benevolence, says Pope; postlapsarian man, however, demonstrates the extent to which modern man has fallen: 'Who, foe to Nature, hears the general groan, / Murders their species, and betrays his own'.[35] Yet, as Howard Erskine-Hill has rightly stated, Pope's poem does not map the degeneration of man, but his postlapsarian progress. In this respect, of all the models he follows in the poem – Lucretius, Cicero and Vitruvius – it is Cicero to whom Pope is the closest.[36] For Pope, states were formed and kings created to preserve the 'common int'rest', not out of any Filmerian notions about the origins of patriarchal rule. Monarchy is based upon consent. According to one commentator, Pope finds merit in both Lockeian and Filmerian positions regarding the origin of government.[37] Given Pope's highly visible involvement with partisan positions in the cultural and political pamphlet wars of the period, he maintains a high degree of what Cicero refers to in the quote above as moderation and restraint. In his assertion that the preservation of political fellowship amongst men is instinctual as well as reasonable, Pope addresses the main theme of Bolingbroke's *Dissertation*. The case for such influence has been made persuasively by Brean Hammond: '*An Essay on Man* brought Bolingbroke and Pope closer than they had ever been. Apart from the philosophical cross-fertilization … it is possible to read parts of the poem as a promulgation of Bolingbrokean political principles'.[38] Similarly, the maintenance of order, the use politically of temperance and self-control, are also themes that run through Bolingbroke's text.

In *Liberty: A Poem in Five Parts* (1735-6), Thomson too draws on a historiographical framework to depict a state of nature in a process of continual change. In Part One he unfavourably compares modern Rome with its classical republican past:

> The Great republic see! That glowed sublime,
> With the mixed freedom of a thousand states;
> Raised on the thrones of kings her curule chair,
> And by her fasces awed the subject world.
> See busy millions quickening all the land,
> With cities thronged, and teeming culture high:
> For nature then smiled on her free-born sons,
> And Poured the plenty that belongs to men.[39]

Thomson describes classical Rome as a kind of utopian ideal akin to the prelapsarian state of nature that Pope accords to human society at the beginning of Epistle III of his *Essay on Man*. Moreover, as Part One reaches its conclusion, a warning is extended to England regarding the dangers she faces if licence overtakes liberty and the lessons of history are ignored. Like a wide range of other Whig writers to whom we have already referred, Thomson makes it crystal clear that if liberty is not safeguarded by due attention paid to the laws of the land, then tyranny is inevitable. Thomson's picture of liberty in Britain is governed by the manner in which he envisages a land where 'king and people [are] equal bound / By guardian laws' to which Liberty herself gives the fullest blessing.[40] The pastoral and utopian theme is again picked up at the beginning of Part Two when Thomson looks in detail at Greece where Liberty lived, 'First, in the dawn of time' where 'Few were offences, properties, and laws'. In a similar fashion to Pope, Thomson portrays a world in ancient Greece that embodied 'justice', 'reason' and 'equity'. This polity in its most ideal state is ruled by a 'Father-Senate', a term that despite its paternal appearance is not concerned with making a case for patriarchy, but instead points to the senate as the father of assemblies where collective wisdom is gathered and justice and equity are dispensed.[41] Nevertheless, one should be careful, the entire tone of Thomson's poem is one that offers warnings: '*Liberty*'s admonitory strength lies in the gloomy possibility that Britain may and perhaps must go the same way as Rome'.[42] Thomson is glossing classical history in the same sense as Bolingbroke is. One must learn the lessons of the past in order not to repeat mistakes in the present.

As we have seen with reference to the events of the Glorious Revolution, Bolingbroke makes it apparent that a healthy alliance between right-thinking Whigs and Tories facilitated the removal of a prince who was threatening liberty. Pope's *Essay on Man* is dedicated to Bolingbroke and elaborates a state of nature that is close to the latter's political ideas on the condition of political obligation and responsibility. That man's natural condition is social, is reiterated in Epistle IV:

No Bandit fierce, no Tyrant mad with pride,
No cavern'd Hermit, rests self-satisfy'd.
Who most to shun or hate Mankind pretend,
Seek an admirer, or would fix a friend.

To strive for the common good, is 'the Universal Cause' of man, 'And makes what happiness we justly call / Subsist not in the good of one, but all'.[43] For Pope 'ORDER is Heav'n's first law' and the natural consequence of this is social, economic and political hierarchy. Consequently all live together within a *concordia discors* 'that is postulated throughout Pope's poem'.[44] As Christine Gerrard has recently argued, 'the extent of Pope's involvement with Patriot Whig politics and the Hanoverian Frederick raises questions about the traditional equation of Pope with Toryism, and more recently Toryism of a discernibly Jacobean flavour'.[45]

The necessary events of the Revolution, says Bolingbroke in his *Dissertation*, should have brought the political nation to a state of perfection. That they did not, and that liberty still remains insecure, is testified to by the continuing presence of a standing army, the attendance of which during the reign of James II was a constant threat: 'Nothing can be more absurd than to maintain that any government ought to make use of the same expedient to support itself, as another government, on the ruins of which this government stands, was subverted for using'.[46] This was part and parcel of seventeenth-century arguments calling for shorter parliaments, a war against parliamentary corruption, and higher standards in public life. A standing army, its diminution and preferably its disbanding, was a constant bugbear from Cromwell's time onwards and raged fiercely during the reigns of James II and also William III. Other grievances included the manner in which the crown was using its power of patronage to build up a powerful and subservient Court party.[47] In this, the tenth letter to *The Craftsman*, Bolingbroke makes great play of the distinction between 'constitution' and 'government'. In defining the two Bolingbroke states that the former consists of 'that assemblage of laws, institutions and customs, derived from certain fixed principles of reason, directed to certain fixed objects of public good, that compose the general system, according to which the government hath agreed to be governed'. Government, on the other hand, is a matter of practical application. Given the contractual state of nature that has hitherto been the main thrust of his argument, it is important to Bolingbroke that the constitution is protected by a government that is committed to virtue, reason, truth and liberty. As Shelley Burtt has argued, 'With liberty resting on nothing more nor less than the maintenance of a mixed constitution, properly balanced, the people's virtue becomes nothing more nor less than love for the good constitution, as Bolingbroke has defined it'.[48] Bad government arises from the perversion of the constitution, 'the rule by which our princes ought to govern at all times; government is that by which they actually do govern at any particular time'.[49]

From here Bolingbroke proceeds to illustrate, without stating it outright, that the current government falls dramatically short of public probity, virtue, truth and reason. Instead, like Manley, Bolingbroke argues that they are the epitome of Hobbesian self-interest, greed, and the pursuit of power and privilege at any cost. Once achieved, power and profit must be protected, a process that leads inevitably to 'infamy and guilt'. The target here is the administration led by Walpole, popularly perceived as being steeped in corruption. Such men 'may bear the semblance of affection for their prince, and zeal for his government', but in reality are the ruination of the constitution. The constitution, in other words, is only as effective as the government that has been entrusted to protect it. From here Bolingbroke moves the argument back to the origin of political obligation and in the process once again takes the stick to patriarchal and providential theories of political organisation. Beginning with the Greek legislators – Solon and Lycurgus, the Roman *decemviri*, the Saxon king Edgar, and the English Renaissance thinkers, Bacon and Hooker – Bolingbroke makes it all too clear that wherever liberty lay unprotected the condition of man was miserable. The lesson that history has taught is that mankind has had to struggle to reject 'the yoke' that has been placed upon them, or at least to make it 'sit easy on their necks'.[50]

Except for those rare instances in history when the prince invested with arbitrary rule is virtuous, the struggle between the 'spirit of liberty and the spirit of dominion' must be ongoing. An arbitrary prince with a superior intellect places liberty in 'the utmost danger': an inferior prince leaves the door open to unscrupulous men. Such men are 'friends to the government and enemies to the constitution'.[51] Parliament is supposed to be the guardian of liberty. Once this institution has been perverted by unscrupulous men, however, 'we return into that state, to deliver or secure us from which Parliaments were instituted'. If Parliament is shaken by a king or his minister 'the constitution totters', and if this keystone is removed, 'our constitution falls into ruin'. Bolingbroke goes on to state that his hypothetical case of a ruined constitution in some future age is all too possible 'by what we may observe in our own'.[52] Nor was he alone in thinking so. This is precisely the point made by Trenchard and Gordon in *Cato's Letters*. In an essay entitled *The terrible Tendency of publick Corruption to ruin a State exemplified in that of Rome, and applied to our own*, we are informed that 'Rome, the nurse of heroes, the mistress of nations, the glory of empires, and the source, the standard, and pattern of virtue and knowledge, has fallen into the abyss of "corruption and impiety" [...] All for the want of publick spirit'. Rome fell because the pursuit of pleasure usurped temperance and:

> Private regards extinguished that love of liberty, that zeal and warmth, which their ancestors had shown for the interest of the publick; luxury and pride became fashionable; all ranks and orders of men tried to outvie one another in expense and pomp; and when, by so doing, they had spent their private patrimonies, they endeavoured to make reprisals upon the publick; and having before sold everything else, they at last sold their country.[53]

Bolingbroke's 'aristocracy of talent' provides one check to the moneyed and upstart class that he believed had no right to political power. As we have seen, the pursuit of power by such men is driven by greed. In *Liberty*, Part Three, in a passage about Rome that could just as easily be about England in 1735, Thomson states that the pursuit of wealth for its own sake and the aggrandisement of 'stupid *Self*', resulted in '*Roman Virtue*' being 'slacken'd into Sloth'; / Security relax'd the softening State; / And the broad Eye of Government lay clos'd'. The result was that the common good and the law were sacrificed to economic gain, the rage of party and 'Licence unrestrain'd.[54] Whereas *Cato's Letters* warns against corruption in the early and mid-1720s, it was Bolingbroke's and Thomson's belief that by the decade following the nation was already deeply steeped in it.

Peter Miller has argued that Cicero's 'analysis of the relationship between the good and the useful (*honestum* and *utile*) in *De Officiis* was constructed to serve best the public good'. Given the centrality of Cicero's works to the intellectual formation of the medieval and early modern political mind, it is little wonder that his works were adapted to suit a wide variety of positions regarding nature and natural law before, during, and beyond our period.[55] We have noted in previous chapters how Milton and Dryden, writing at the height of a constitutional crisis in the 1650s and late 1680s, drew freely on Cicero to justify and legitimise positions that were completely incompatible. The common good, frequently read through Cicero and adapted to suit the prevailing political conditions, was constantly invoked by a range of writers from all points on the political spectrum, and demonstrates the extent to which political ideas during this period were fluid.

Notes

1   Howard Erskine Hill, *Poetry of Opposition and Revolution*, pp. 58-59. Erskine-Hill's primary historical source for this assertion is J.C.D. Clark, *English Society, 1688-1832*, first published in 1985. This text has been recently revised substantially and its chronology extended, with a subsequent change in title to *English Society, 1660-1832*, Cambridge, Cambridge University Press, 2000. On Jacobitism generally in the eighteenth century see Paul Kleber Monod, *Jacobitism and the English People, 1688-78*, Cambridge, Cambridge University Press, 1989, and in relation to poetry in the early eighteenth century, see Murray G.H. Pittock, *Poetry and Jacobite Politics in Eighteenth-Century Britain and Ireland*, Cambridge, Cambridge University Press, 1994.

2   See Kenyon, *Revolution Principles*.

3   David Armitage (ed.) *Bolingbroke: Political Writings*, Cambridge, Cambridge University Press, 1997. All further references to Bolingbroke's writings unless otherwise stated are to this edition.

4   Bolingbroke, *Dissertation upon Parties*, p. 5. It is little wonder that Bolingbroke has much to say about the Exclusion Crisis and the Glorious Revolution, as the 1680s are the golden age of radical Whig writings on the subject of sovereignty, the origins of government and the demands of political obligation, providing a rich literature. The heart of the fight against patriarchy was the Whig recourse to natural law. See Ashcraft, *Revolutionary Politics*, pp. 183, 190.

5   On the divergence between Whigs in the aftermath of the Glorious Revolution, see Mark Goldie, 'The Roots of True Whiggism, 1688-94', in *History of Political Thought* 1 (1980), pp. 195-236.

6   Bolingbroke, *Dissertation*, p. 13.

7   Robert Molesworth, *An Account of Denmark: As it was in the Year 1692*, London, Timothy Goodwin, 1738, pp. 39-47.

8   *The Freeholder*, No. 5, 23 December 1715, in *The Works of the Right Honourable Joseph Addison*, London, Cadell and Davies, 1811, I-VI; *Works*, VI, p. 20.

9   Melinda Zook, 'Early Whig Ideology, Ancient Constitutionalism, and the Reverend Samuel Johnson', *Journal of British Studies* 32 (1993), pp. 139-65 (p. 140), and more extensively, her *Radical Whigs and Conspiratorial Politics in Late Stuart England*, University Park, PA, Pennsylvania State University Press, 1999; Goldie, 'The Roots of True Whiggism'.

10   Zook, 'Early Whig Ideology', p. 153; see also Harro Hopfl and Martyn Thompson, 'The History of Contract as a Motif in Political Thought', *American Historical Journal* 84 (1979), pp. 919-44 (p. 941).

11   *Dissertation upon Parties*, p. 62.

12   *Ibid.*, p. 54.

13   *Ibid.*, pp. 76, 81.

14   *Ibid*, pp. 82-5.

15   Harrington, *Political Works*, p. 164.

16   *The Freeholder*, No. 2, 26 December 1715, in *Works*, VI, p. 8. Emphasis added.

17   Molesworth, *An Account of Denmark*, p. vii.

18   Armitage, Introduction, *Bolingbroke: Political Writings*, pp. xi, xv. See also: Nicholas Phillipson, 'Politics and politeness: Anne and the early Hanoverians' in Pocock *et. al.* (eds) *The Varieties of British Political Thought*, pp. 211-45 (pp. 232-33). Isaac Kramnick, *Bolingbroke and his Circle*, Cambridge, MA, Harvard University Press, 1968. Shelley Burtt, *Virtue Transformed: Political Argument in England, 1688-1740*, Cambridge, Cambridge University Press, 1992, chapter 5.

19   H.T. Dickinson, *Bolingbroke*, London, Constable, 1970, p. 207; idem., *Liberty and Property: Political Ideology in Eighteenth-Century Britain*, London, Methuen, 1977, pp. 57-89; M.M. Goldsmith, 'Liberty, Virtue and the Rule of Law, 1689-1770', in Wooton, (ed.), *Republicanism, Liberty and Commercial Society*, pp. 197-232 (pp. 210-13).

20   Dickinson, *Liberty and Property*, p. 61.

21   *The Freeholder*, No. 1, 23 December 1715 in *Works*, VI, p. 4.

22   John Toland, *The Oceana and other Works of James Harrington, Esq. Collected, Methodiz'd, and Reviewed, with An Exact Account of his Life Prefix'd by John Toland*, London, Printed for John Millar, 1737, p. vii.

23   *The Freeholder*, No. 5, 6 January 1716, in *Works*, VI, pp. 20, 23.

24   *Cato's Letters: or, Essays on Liberty, Civil and Religious, and other Important Subjects* by John Trenchard and Thomas Gordon, Ronald Hamowy (ed.), Indianapolis, IN, Liberty Fund, 1995, I-II; I, p. 414.

25   *The Freeholder*, No. 1, 23 December 1715 in *Works*, VI, p. 4.

26   Sidney, *Discourses*, p. 189.

27   Harrington, *Political Works*, pp. 233-39. As Davis has remarked, Harrington was keen to preserve the supremacy of a 'propertied aristocracy'; see 'Equality in an unequal commonwealth: James Harrington's republicanism and the meaning of equality', in Gentles *et. al.* (eds), *Soldiers, Writers and Statesmen*, pp. 229-42 (p. 231).

28   Neville, *Plato Redivivus*, p. 101. On the survival and transmission of republican ideas from the seventeenth to the eighteenth century see the following: Blair Worden, 'The Revolution of 1688-9 and the English Republican Tradition', in Jonathan I. Israel (ed.), *The Anglo-Dutch Moment: Essays on the Glorious Revolution and its World Impact*, Cambridge, Cambridge University Press, 1991, pp. 241-77 (p. 248); idem., 'English Republicanism', in Burns and Goldie (eds.), *The Cambridge History of Political Thought*, pp. 443-75; 'Part One' of Wootton (ed.), *Republicanism, Liberty and Commercial Society*, pp. 45-193. Pocock, *The Machiavellian Moment*; idem., *Virtue Commerce and History: Essays on Political Thought and History, chiefly in the Eighteenth Century*, Cambridge, Cambridge University Press, 1985; Skinner, *Liberty Before Liberalism*.

29   Bolingbroke, *On the Spirit of Patriotism*, p. 205. Bolingbroke's admiration for Cato is qualified. He believed that Cato did liberty a great disservice by committing suicide at Utica and giving up the cause. *Ibid.* See James Thomson's *Liberty*, Part III, ll. 465-9 for Cicero's defence of liberty: 'all the force, / All the State-wielding magic of his tongue; / And All the thunder of my CATO'S zeal', James Sambrook (ed.), *Liberty, The Castle of Indolence, and Other Poems*, Clarendon, Oxford University Press, 1986. All further references to Thomson's poetry are to this edition. Although he is on strong ground regarding the negative portraits of Augustus, Howard Weinbrot overstates considerably the case when he argues that Cicero was reviled in the early eighteenth century. See his *Augustus Caesar in Augustan England: the Decline of a Classical Norm*, Princeton, NJ, and London, Princeton University Press, 1978, pp. 15-17. For a recent corrective to Weinbrot's thesis see Peter Miller, *The Common Good: Empire, Religion and Philosophy in Eighteenth-Century Britain*, Cambridge, Cambridge University Press, 1994, pp. 21-87.

30   Bolingbroke, *On the Spirit of Patriotism*, p. 214.

31   Cicero, *On Duties*, p.6.

32   Pope, *Essay on Man*, in *The Twickenham Edition of the Poems of Alexander Pope*, I-XI, III.i, Maynard Mack (ed.), Epistle II. 195-8; my italics. See also ll. 172-4; Epistle III.iv. ll. 158-9. All further references to Pope's poem are to this edition, hereafter abbreviated to *Essay* in the footnotes. Brean Hammond believes that this passage is a rejection of the Hobbesian view that 'the state of nature was a state of warring confusion' *Pope and Bolingbroke: A Study in Friendship and Influence*, Columbus, MO, University of Missouri Press, 1984, p. 87.

33   Cicero, *On Duties*, p. 7.

34   Locke, *Two Treatises*, p. 269.

35   Pope, *Essay*, III.iv. ll. 156, 159-60; ll. 163-4.

36   Howard Erskine-Hill, 'Pope on the origins of society', in *The Enduring Legacy: Alexander Pope, Tercentenary Essays*, G.S. Rousseau and Pat Rogers (eds), Cambridge, Cambridge University Press, 1988, pp. 79-89; pp. 87-8.

37   Erskine-Hill, 'Pope on the origins of society', p. 89.

38   The best study of Pope's relationship with Bolingbroke is Hammond, *Pope and Bolingbroke*, p. 58; see chapter 5, where Hammond argues that the case for Bolingbroke's influence on Pope is very strong. See also, G.S. Rousseau and Marjorie Hope Nicholson, *This Long Disease My Life: Alexander Pope and the Sciences*, Princeton, NJ, Princeton University Press, 1968. For an opposite view regarding influence, see Maynard Mack's preface to the Twickenham edition.

39   Thomson, *Liberty*, Part One, ll. 52-6.

40   *Ibid.*, ll. 318-19.

41   *Ibid.*, Part Two, ll. 3-12.

42   Christine Gerrard, *The Patriot Opposition to Walpole: Politics, Poetry and National Myth, 1725-1742*, Clarendon, Clarendon Press, 1994 pp. 132-3. A much narrower focus on Thomson's Whig Patriotism can be found in Glynis Ridley, 'The Seasons and the Politics of Opposition', in Richard Terry (ed.), *James Thomson: Essays for the Tercentenary*, Liverpool, Liverpool University Press, 2000, 93-116. See also, James Sambrook, *James Thomson: A Life, 1700-1748*, Oxford, Oxford University Press, 1991. Bertrand J. Goldgar, *Walpole and the Wits: The Relation of Politics to Literature, 1722-1742*, Lincoln, NA, and London, University of Nebraska Press, 1976, pp. 142-45.

43   Pope, *Essay on Man* Epistle IV. ii, ll. 41-4, 35, 27-8.

44   *Ibid.*, ll. 49-55; n., p. 133.

45   Gerrard, *The Patriot Opposition*, p. 68.

46   Bolingbroke, *Dissertation upon Parties*, p. 92.

47   W.A. Speck, *Stability and Strife: England, 1714-1760*, London, Arnold, 1977, pp. 222-3.

48   Burtt, *Virtue Transformed*, p. 92.

49   Bolingbroke, *Dissertation upon Parties*, p. 88.

50   *Ibid.*, p. 89.

51   *Ibid.*, p. 91.

52   *Ibid.*, pp. 94, 95.

53   *Cato's Letters*, I, pp. 128-32; 128, 130.

54   Thomson, *Liberty*, Part Three, ll. 379-80, 383-5.

55   Peter Miller, *Defining the Common Good*, p. 6.

Chapter 12

Henry and Sarah Fielding: Hobbes Restated

Hobbes saw self-interest as the governing fact of human psychology, and if ever a fictional world reflected this belief it was that of Henry Fielding, and to a significant extent that of his sister Sarah, too. Fielding's fear of a collapse into anarchy (the second Jacobite rebellion constituting his version of the 'disorders of the present times') underpins his fictional masterpiece *Tom Jones*, which, for all its humour, might be described as a case of Hobbes restated. While it may be true, as C.J. Rawson points out, that Fielding 'mainly disliked Hobbes', that same critic also reminds us that '[i]deas of the natural depravity of man were certainly in wide circulation' in the period, and it is this general discourse to which Fielding is responding: a discourse in which Hobbesian theories have long since been assimilated.[1] It is a world teetering on the brink of anarchy for much of the time, and, as Fielding perceives it, crying out for the kind of moral leadership that Tom, after his apprenticeship in the ways of that world, is equipped to provide; the hero having 'acquired a discretion and prudence very uncommon in one of his lively parts' by the narrative's conclusion.[2] Such discretion and prudence stand out in a nation currently experiencing the bizarre problem of a Protestant-supported rebellion in favour of a Catholic pretender, an event which sums up the irrationality of humankind at large for the author.[3] Tom's innate good nature, for all his various character lapses as a young man, is seen to be infinitely preferable to the grasping and cunning nature that prevails amongst his fellows. Johnson's objection to Boswell's claim that Fielding provides us with life-like characters, 'Why, Sir, it is of very low life', misses the point that, as far as Fielding is concerned, low moral standards are the norm in his society and it would be foolish to pretend otherwise.[4] Here we must part company with Martin C. Battestin's view that 'Fielding took a predominantly optimistic view of human nature'.[5]

The rarity of Tom's nature is enough to elevate him to the moral high ground; a fact duly recognised by his circle of acquaintances after he settles down with Sophia:

> And such is their condescension, their indulgence, and their beneficence to those below them, that there is not a neighbour, a tenant or a servant, who doth not most gratefully bless the day when Mr Jones was married to his Sophia.[6]

Fear of unconstrained human nature motivates Fielding's narrative project much in the way that it does Hobbes'. Unless subject to fairly strict control (if admittedly less authoritarian than that recommended by Hobbes), humankind generally will seek to exploit and swindle each other in the cause of naked self-interest. Every stop on Tom's journey to London provides ample proof of this trait in the actions of innkeepers and their staff, who set to with a will to fleece each and every traveller who comes within their orbit:

> but here we are obliged to disclose some maxims which publicans hold to be the grand mysteries of their trade. The first is, if they have anything good in their house (which indeed very seldom happens) to produce it only to persons who travel with great equipages. Secondly, to charge the same for the very worst provisions, as if they were the best. And lastly, if any of their guests call but for little, to make them pay a double price for everything they have; so that the amount by the head may be much the same.[7]

Between unscrupulous publicans and the ever-present threat posed by highwaymen, being on the road is akin to returning to the state of nature (as Christian had discovered beforehand in his tortuous progress through the 'wilderness of this world'). Respect for the other is in very short supply if one is a traveller, and discretion and prudence in human conduct mostly conspicuous by their absence. Fielding's landscape might be described as a moral wilderness, and all the humour that he extracts from this state of affairs merely serves to reveal the depth of human wickedness that goes to make it so. One of the critical questions that Fielding poses for us is: what capacity does humanity have for reform? Sadly, given basic human nature, the answer appears to be, very little. Although some critics have identified a libertarian strain in Fielding's thought, it has to be placed in the context of a more generalised scepticism regarding intrinsic human worth.[8] If *Tom Jones* is, as Battestin has claimed, a narrative defence of the 'argument from design', then it is a design that the majority of humankind actively seems to be resisting.[9]

The Man of the Hill represents the point at which the humour stops; his sourness eliciting at least a grain of sympathy from the reader, given the former's first-hand experience of the personal tragedies that unfettered self-interest can precipitate. Extreme though his reaction may be, the Man of the Hill's observation that 'there is scarce any human good without its concomitant evil' captures the essence of Fielding's world (as well as recalling Calvin's jaundiced view of humanity).[10] In that world morality is constantly threatened and the individual is rarely more than a step away from disaster: 'a man may be as easily starved in Leadenhall market as in the deserts of Arabia'.[11] With a catalogue of wicked actions behind him in his own youth, the Man of the Hill stands as a salutary reminder of human moral weakness: a more representative figure of his society than Tom will ever be. Certainly, his comments about the behaviour of servants during his travels in Europe, where, amongst others, *'laquais a louange* are sure to lose no opportunity of cheating you', chime in with the narrator's general perception of that same class in England.[12]

Positioned at the centre of the narrative in structural terms, the Man of the Hill is at the centre in symbolic terms also; his character revealing the power that self-interest can exert over us, as well as our apparent inability to do anything very constructive about this even when we come to realise its drawbacks.[13] Even his withdrawal from society is egocentric in nature, as he moves from exploiting his fellow human beings to treating them as corrupt beyond all possible redemption. He remains at the centre of his own little world in each case, passing sweeping judgement on humanity from his own embittered perspective:

> Man alone, the king of this globe, the last and greatest work of the Supreme Being, below the sun; man alone hath basely dishonoured his own nature; and by dishonesty, cruelty, ingratitude, and treachery, hath called his Maker's goodness in question, by puzzling us to account how a benevolent being should form so foolish and so vile an animal.

Tom, as is his wont, argues for a more positive, broadly benevolist, approach, criticising the Man of the Hill for 'taking the character of mankind from the worst and basest among them' rather than from 'among the best and most perfect individuals of that species'.[14] Yet we have long since recognised that Tom is in a minority in his optimistic outlook (Fielding himself hardly follows Tom's advice), and he is a conspicuous failure in 'making a convert' to his philosophy in this instance.[15] If the Man of the Hill really is representative of the mass of mankind ('not an Individual, but a Species', in Fielding's formulation[16]) then that is a very significant failure, and one that hardly bodes well for a future in which Tom is to become a social role model. Between rampant self-interest and chronic pessimism about human nature there is not a great deal of room for moral manoeuvre. When Tom and the Man of the Hill part it leaves an interesting loose end in Fielding's scheme. It will take more than Tom's good nature to reform humankind, and self-interest, pessimism, and cynicism will continue to require strict policing.[17]

Ian A. Bell acknowledges that loose end, arguing that 'neither Tom nor the Man of the Hill achieves full narrative authority', and that we are to interpret their exchanges as part of the more general negotiation between narrator and reader that, for Bell, lies at the heart of Fielding's narrative project.[18] Rather than seeing this as a stalemate, however, where the Hobbesian and benevolist positions are both equally viable, we would want to argue that this demonstrates the need to find more effective methods of containing Hobbesianism. It will simply require stronger measures than Tom recommends here. The scale of the problem set by human nature for those on the side of order is revealed to us in this episode. It is also worth noting, too, that when it comes to the Jacobite rebellion, Tom and the Man of the Hill are completely in agreement – a point we shall return to below, when discussing the role of that event in the narrative.

Tom is one of a select band of individuals in his world who is not motivated solely by self-interest, with Sophia and Allworthy being other notable exceptions to what seems a general social rule whereby others are used as means rather than ends in themselves. Neither compassion nor self-sacrifice is much in evidence amongst Tom's fellow citizens. Ultimately Tom will be made to realise just how unreliable and untrustworthy humanity at large is, but it will be a long and often painful process before he reaches that state of awareness – including a spell in jail on a trumped-up charge as part of his trials. In the main, human relations fall into a recognisably Hobbesian pattern, where individuals are constantly vying to establish a sense of superiority over their fellows; some leverage, no matter how small, by which to improve their own position in the general scramble for power. Unlike Manley, Fielding does not regard self-interest as an essentially male trait, and there are numerous examples of the self-interested female to be found throughout *Tom Jones*. Lady Bellaston is a striking case: a sexual predator who uses Tom as a sexual object much in the way that the male sex invariably does the female in *The New Atalantis* or *Love Letters*. Tom's trusting, open nature is in stark contrast to the calculating wiles of Lady Bellaston, who is far removed from the vulnerability found in the average Manley heroine. The moral seems to be that self-interest is an almost universal trait that takes no account of gender; nor of class either, with similar behaviour to Lady Bellaston's being found at all points on the social scale – Molly Seagrim is not without her share of wiles, for example, in using her body in an attempt to improve her social prospects.

Sexual relations in general in *Tom Jones* take the form of power struggles, with individuals all too often using others as a means to an end in this area, too. Blifil's conduct in the aftermath of his disgrace, when he exiles himself to a northern county, is only too typical of the calculation that goes into such matters in the inveterately self-seeking temperament: 'He is also lately turned Methodist, in hopes of marrying a very rich widow of that sect, whose estate lies in that part of the kingdom'.[19] The money will be used to further Blifil's political career, and it is clear that he is not to be diverted from his self-seeking path through life by what he regards as a mere temporary setback. Blifil will continue to operate as if he were in a state of nature, with politics providing an apt context for his world-view, this being an area where the struggle for ascendancy never ceases and morality is at best highly pragmatic in form. He has the soul of a predator, and if he outstrips his fellow characters in the narrative in this respect, it has to be said that it is largely a matter of degree that is involved: predatory instincts lurk under the surface of the vast majority of the inhabitants of Fielding's world. Perhaps this is never put as succinctly as it is by the narrator of Fielding's *Jonathan Wild*, who points out that we hate and fear those we have gained any advantage over, 'from an apprehension that the person whom we have ourselves greatly injured will use all possible endeavours to revenge and retaliate the injuries we have done him'.[20] Assume the worst of others and then act accordingly: that appears to be the watchword to adopt in human affairs.

The hero is once again the exception to the general rule when it comes to sexual conduct, and is presented as the object of female sexual desire rather than as someone exploiting women for his own nefarious purposes: 'I have been guilty with women, I own it; but am not conscious that I have ever injured any – nor would I, to procure pleasure to myself, be knowingly the cause of misery to any human being'.[21] If Tom is guilty with women, Fielding leaves us in little doubt that it is largely the women's fault in being unable to resist this 'picture of Adonis', as Lady Bellaston admiringly describes him to his face.[22] So irresistible does he prove to be that women are willing to reverse the usual rules of courtship in their pursuit of him, projecting Tom into a series of morally compromising situations that hinder his cause. In sexual terms at least, Tom might be seen to be existing at the edge of chaos until marriage with Sophia produces the one state of order that is Fielding's social ideal: the Aristotelian 'golden mean' where all aspects of human nature are in proper balance.

Fielding simply glosses over female vulnerability in the sexual arena, giving us a gallery of sexual adventurers instead. Bridget Allworthy may have an illegitimate child, but the fact can be hidden away and life goes on as normal with no apparent emotional aftermath. Molly Seagrim's various sexual exploits are treated in a light-hearted manner, although we are only too aware of what the most likely fate to befall such a figure from her social class would be in that age – prostitution, with all its grim consequences. The projected marriage with Partridge that the author mentions in a closing aside, was hardly the norm for someone with Molly's sexual history. Lady Bellaston is portrayed as the one in control in her relationship with Tom, to the extent of turning him into a kept man:

> so that by her means he was now become one of the best-dressed men about town, and was not only relieved from those ridiculous distresses we have before mentioned, but was actually raised to a state of affluence beyond what he had ever known.[23]

Again, as with Bridget Allworthy, Lady Bellaston has the social and financial power to protect herself and maintain an air of respectability no matter what she does; but one cannot help wondering about the emotional effects of such liaisons, which Fielding never really explores with any great conviction. Appearances are what count instead; thus Molly Seagrim is to be manoeuvred into marriage with Partridge, significantly enough 'through the mediation of Sophia', in order to disguise the facts of Tom's youthful indiscretions.[24] Fielding makes it appear that women use and abuse others in much the same way that most men do, as if sexual relations were one large state of nature demanding self-seeking behaviour from all. Women's disadvantage in the discourse of sex at the time is simply hidden from our view, unless one reads against the grain as in Molly's case. Fielding hardly encourages us to do that, however, and the narrative tends to impress female cunning upon us rather than female vulnerability, with Lady Bellaston's machinations against Sophia setting a pattern.[25] It is a far cry from the world of Defoe's heroines, where, as Bell points out, we are made very aware that their 'sexuality continually jeopardises their yearnings for security and survival'.[26]

Fielding specifically alludes to recent political 'disorders' in the Man of the Hill episode. The Man of the Hill is a staunch defender of the Protestant religion who recounts his experiences in the Glorious Revolution, where he takes up arms against King James after deciding that 'no real security can ever be found against the persecuting spirit of Popery, when armed with power, except the depriving it of that power'.[27] Escaping from capture by the king's side at one point, he finds himself returned to a state of nature by the breakdown in the political situation and having to fend for himself in the wild:

> At last, after rambling several days about the country, during which the field afforded me the same bed and the same food which nature bestows on our savage brothers of the creation, I at length arrived at this place, where the solitude and wildness of the country invited me to fix my abode.[28]

It is not until the success of the Glorious Revolution is announced that he can safely show himself abroad again, thus providing hard evidence of the basic insecurity of natural existence as claimed by Hobbes. The fact that the Man's capture was as a result of betrayal by one of his closest associates is further proof of the vulnerability of the individual in such a situation, where no-one can be trusted and personal control of one's sovereignty is no guarantee of one's safety.

The Man's arguments against King James engage directly with the notions of sovereignty put forward by both Hobbes and the Whigs. Unlike Hobbes, he refuses to accept that the king has the right to dictate the nature of the religious settlement in the nation, justifying the Monmouth Rebellion by 'the danger to which the Protestant religion was so visibly exposed under a Popish prince'. This is a danger by which the Man feels 'seriously affected' at a personal level – enough to prompt him to resist his ruler.[29] When it comes to Catholicism at least, conscience, that ultimate court of appeal for the nonconformist temperament, and the source of so much trouble for the political establishment over the previous century, reasserts itself even within the ranks of conformity. It would appear that sovereignty is no longer a question of Filmerian or Hobbesian obedience for apologists of the latter position. Between Protestantism and Catholicism lies a differend that even absolute sovereignty cannot suppress, and a purist interpretation of Hobbes becomes more difficult to defend. The latitudinarianism ascribed to Fielding by Battestin becomes apparent at such junctures, although it is worth noting that Bernard Harrison is at pains to clear Fielding of any suspicion of *moral* latitudinarianism.[30] Harrison considers Battestin's reading to be somewhat simplistic overall: 'The amiably *bien pensant* latitudinarian simpleton who emerges from this summary is not recognisable as the savage satirist whose irony Coleridge thought superior to Swift's'.[31] Yet if we think of latitudinarianism as signalling intellectual flexibility regarding the complexity of moral matters, rather than, as Harrison implies, lack of moral depth, then it is not incompatible with the ethical seriousness that Harrison is seeking to establish in Fielding.

Latitudinarian benevolism and scepticism are in constant dialogue in Fielding, as he wrestles to find ways of keeping self-interest under control. We find a spectrum of response rather than mutually exclusive positions.

The case for absolute sovereignty is considered by the narrator in the episode involving the King of the Gypsies, a successful exponent of political absolutism whom Tom comes to admire after observing his administration of justice in action. While conceding that absolute monarchy at its best is as close to perfect government as we are likely to attain, the point is also forcefully made that few men have the necessary qualities – to wit, moderation, wisdom, and goodness – to succeed in that taxing office, and that 'absolute power, vested in the hands of one who is deficient in them all, is likely to be attended with no less a degree of evil'.[32] The Gypsy King may represent the acceptable face of absolutism, but Satan, as the narrator subtly informs us, is as much an absolute monarch in his own dominions as any earthly king might claim to be in his, and as justified by Scripture in assuming divine right over his subjects. Filmer is dispensed with in favour of the current English political system, for all its obvious faults: 'it will be much wiser to submit to a few inconveniences arising from the dispassionate deafness of laws, than to remedy them by applying to the passionate open ears of a tyrant'. It is an argument for the preservation of the status quo, but it takes place against the disturbing backdrop of corrupt human nature: 'the examples of all ages show us that mankind in general desire power only to do harm, and, when they obtain it, use it for no other purpose'.[33] The Hobbesian vision is validated by such an assessment, even if the author swerves away from a Hobbesian clinical solution to the problem (although as Bell has pointed out, the author himself 'takes the liberty to act as the absolute monarch of his fictional world'[34]). What is clear is that mankind cannot be left to its own devices, and that we are in dire need of wise magistrates to keep us in check. It is a call for diffusion of power, but diffusion within a specific social class, which collectively wields sovereignty over unregenerate mankind: a case of Hobbes modified, but his relevance tacitly acknowledged. Some do manage to rise above self-interest – but precious few. Harrison's point that, while 'Fielding had, after all, some reason to feel pessimistic about the prevalence of common humanity ... his pessimism was not absolute', is worth noting; although it is also worth noting that Fielding puts his faith in a ruling elite to deal with the causes of that pessimism.[35] Tom will take his place within that elite in due course.

Tom's own situation in the current 'disorders' is, as is so often the way with such events, a confused one. His travelling companion Partridge turns out to be a Jacobite, and mistakenly assumes that Tom is of the same political persuasion when a quarrel between Jones and an army officer, over Sophia's honour, is transposed by popular rumour into a political disagreement. Taken for a supporter of the Pretender, Tom is in reality no less firm in his Protestant belief than the Man of the Hill, as he makes clear when he informs that figure of the persistence of Jacobite sympathies in the country:

> it has often struck me as the most wonderful thing I ever read of in history, that so soon after this convincing experience, which brought our whole nation to join so unanimously in expelling King James, for the preservation of our religion and liberties, there should be a party among us mad enough to desire the placing of his family again on the throne.

The Man of the Hill is in perfect agreement with Tom on this critical issue, railing against the 'monstrous extravagances' of human nature that could allow this to happen.[36] *Contra*-Bell, at this point the figures *jointly* achieve 'full narrative authority', especially given the author's well-attested antipathy to the Jacobite cause.[37] Given the fact that in many respects it *is* a Protestant rebellion on behalf of a Catholic prince (in Calvinist Scotland, particularly so[38]), Tom's apparent support would not necessarily strike anyone as paradoxical. Partridge himself is no Catholic, and only too willing to believe the word of a Catholic priest that 'Prince Charles was as good a Protestant as any in England'.[39] Squire Western, too, is unmistakably Jacobite in sympathy, with his toasts to 'the king over the water' and diatribes against 'the Hanover rats' now ruling the nation, without being any the less conventionally Anglican in his religious observance.[40] He includes the local clergy in his social circle, with Parson Supple, for example, being one of his regular dinner guests.

The world of *David Simple* is very similar to that of *Tom Jones*, inhabited as it is mainly by deeply egocentric, unreliable and cynical individuals, motivated almost exclusively by self-interest. David's quest to find true friendship amongst his fellow men merely proves the extent to which self-interest is the dominant trait of the time, and his limited success indicates just how isolated he is in his society: an innocent abroad in a world of hypocrisy that infects even his closest relatives, with his own brother not above taking financial advantage of him over the matter of his father's will. David's final testament in volume two is that of a broken man, forced to acknowledge the essential corruption of the society around him – a corruption he has experienced repeatedly at first-hand over the course of his chequered career:

> When I revolve in my Thoughts all my past Life, the Errors of my Mind strike
> me strongly. The same natural Desire for Happiness actuated me with the rest
> of Mankind: But there was something peculiar in my Frame; for the Seeds of
> Ambition or Avarice, if they were in me at all, were so small they were im-
> perceptible.[41]

The implication is clear: most of humanity *is* actuated by ambition and avarice, those public markers of the self-interested personality. David Simple
and his small circle of friends constitute a notable exception to normal
human conduct (an elect group, one might say), which falls within Hobbesian parameters. In one sense Sarah's vision is even bleaker than her
brother's, in that in her world there seems to be a dearth of wise magistrates
to keep humanity under control: no-one like Tom turns up to provide a role
model for us at the last. Unlike *Tom Jones*, *David Simple* ends on a note of
deep despair, with self-interest manifestly in the ascendancy in human
affairs, and most likely set to be so for the foreseeable future. The simple
will prove no match for the cunning, and the cunning are manifestly in the
majority.

David's quest draws him into London life in all its teeming variety,
and he quickly finds that he cannot trust to appearances anywhere in the
city. This is a world in which, he is informed, '*a good Man*' is someone
whose sharp practice in business dealings keeps him one step ahead of his
adversaries; 'a Place, where Riches were esteemed Goodness, and Deceit,
Low-Cunning, and giving up all things to the love of Gain, were thought
Wisdom'.[42] It is also a world where David will be cheated out of his intended wife by a suitor who can offer her father more money for her
person:

> He said, as she had hitherto been a very obedient Girl, he hoped she would
> still continue so. He owned he had ordered her to encourage Mr. *Simple's* Ad-
> dresses, because at that time he appeared to be a very advantageous Match for
> her; but now when a better offered, she would, he said, be certainly in the
> right to take the Man she could get most by.[43]

Soon enough, Miss Nanny Johnson is admitting to a confidante that, 'I will
have the Riches, that is positive', even though her new husband-to-be is a
singularly unattractive prospect, being old and ugly.[44] David's reaction on
accidentally overhearing these sentiments sums up the gulf that is opening
up between himself and the rest of humanity: 'Love, Rage, Despair, and
Contempt alternatively took possession of his Mind'.[45] His dilemma is that
he continues to trust to appearances, where in reality London life offers

only the most superficial veneer of civil society over a ruthless state of nature. David's highly developed moral sensibility is redundant in a world driven by vanity and greed. Nanny Johnson comes to a bad end, rapidly regretting her decision and then dying shortly after her husband from an infection caught from him; but despite her experience, vanity and greed will continue to be the mainsprings of individual human behaviour, with most only too happy to 'have the Riches', no matter what the emotional expense may be.

David encounters a stream of self-regarding rogues as he moves through London society; such as Spatter, with his 'Delight in *abusing* People', including David behind his back; Varnish, a practised exponent of obseqiousness; and assorted self-important coffee-houses habitues, or '*Set of No-bodies*', as Spatter, characteristically uncharitably but most likely also quite accurately, refers to them.[46] While David does meet some like-minded individuals on his travels – Cynthia, Camilla, and Valentine, for example (the basis for his later circle) – their various narratives merely reinforce our sense of a world in which hypocrisy reigns and humankind in the mass is not to be trusted. Thus Cynthia is reduced to a humiliating state of dependence by her refusal to marry a man she does not love, causing her father to cut her out of his will, leaving her penniless on his death. It is entirely characteristic of the mores of this society, that her sisters, far from taking pity on her plight, are positively gleeful about it, treating it as a crucial advantage gained instead. Camilla and Valentine have their father turned against them by their stepmother, who 'spent her whole Time, in considering which way she should best carry on her pernicious Schemes' to alienate them from the family unit and their father's affections.[47] David also meets the unfortunate Isabelle, who retires to a nunnery after having been caught up in a complex emotional tangle between several lovers that leads to rash actions, death and disaster. The few sensitive individuals in David's world seem to be at the mercy of the insensitive majority, against whom they have precious little defence. What Linda Bree calls 'the self-annihilation of victimhood' lies in wait for the former.[48] It is not a particularly inspiring picture of humankind that is being offered for our inspection.

David is patently someone who does not want to exist at the edge of chaos, and his whole career is an attempt to find that elusive state of order in which self-interest fades away and human beings can with confidence place trust in each other. In such a state appearances can be relied upon, and there is no need to search for ulterior motives in the actions of one's peers. David manages to create his own little narrative unit of friendship, where trust in each other prevails, but it can never be more than an anomaly within the overarching grand narrative of self-interest that rules his society: as Gillian Skinner has observed, 'true benevolence is rare indeed in David's world'.[49] Like the elect in a spiritual autobiographical context, David's unit is fair game for predatory reprobates, and will be forced to live at the edge of chaos in terms of its relations with that dominant social group. Death comes to seem a welcome release from an uncaring world, and there is little of solace to be taken from David's fate:

> I chuse to think he is escaped from the Possibility of falling into any future Afflictions, and that neither the Malice of his pretended Friends, nor the Sufferings of his real ones, can ever again rend and torment his honest Heart.[50]

In the face of unregenerate human nature, all that the author can recommend to us is stoicism, with her earlier paeans to 'Tenderness and Benevolence (which alone can give any real Pleasure)' in the narrative's first part, seeming like so much wishful thinking.[51] The state of nature soon demolishes any such pretensions, and we are left to contemplate David's defeat at the hands of his relentlessly cunning peers. There seems to be a Gresham's Law operating within human nature whereby the bad inexorably drives out the good, and David becomes its most conspicuous victim.

The last volume unfolds an almost unrelieved tale of woe, in which we observe human goodness, as represented by David and his friends, almost systematically being extinguished. Despite the loss of much of their fortune through the likely 'Roguery of their Agent', David and his circle nevertheless prosper for a time, until a series of crippling reverses brings home 'the Truth of that Observation, so common both in the Writings and Conversations of Mankind, namely, "That solid and lasting Happiness is not to be attained in this World"'.[52] David becomes embroiled in a lawsuit when a malicious claim is made against the estate left to him by his uncle, and after several years of legal wrangling finds himself nearly reduced to penury by the loss of the case and the huge lawyer's bills it has generated. Then in an attempt to repair their declining fortunes, Valentine and Cynthia move to Jamaica, thus dispersing the circle of friends, to David's great regret. Valentine dies on the island of a fever, and Cynthia is subsequently swindled out of her estate by a crooked lawyer (Spencer's claim that Cynthia has been endowed by her author 'with intelligence and a competence in dealing with the evils of the world that prevents her from ever really becoming its victim', sits rather oddly with this latter occurrence[53]). David's wife, Camilla, dies before Cynthia arrives back in England, and David by then has fallen into his final illness. Various examples of mean and petty behaviour towards David and his circle by pretended friends punctuate this sad litany of events, and it is clear that David is fighting a losing battle against the dark side of human nature. At almost every turn he meets with duplicity, as if humanity collectively has decided to make a concerted effort to break his spirit. Mr. and Mrs. Orgeuil prove to be hypocrites of the first order, more concerned about the death of their unpleasant lap-dog than David's loss of Camilla. Compassion is once again in notably short supply, and others of selective interest only. The human race stands revealed as essentially reprobate in nature, and David's true place, like Christian's, lies beyond a world which more and more comes to resemble the City of Destruction in its inability to recognise the need for moral reformation. What we witness over the narrative of *David Simple* is, if anything, progressive moral decline.

The actions of the majority of the characters in *David Simple* suggest there is a fiercely competitive strain in human nature that prevents goodness from ever establishing itself as a dominating force in human affairs. Self-interest does not just seek to deflect goodness from its objectives, but actively to destroy it, taking a grim pleasure in any success it has in doing so. All that remains of goodness at the narrative's end is to be found in Cynthia, a forlorn figure bereft of all her friends and cheated out of her husband's estate, and David's daughter, committed to Cynthia's care in the hope that she can be 'protected from any Insult to which Youth and Beauty, joined with Poverty, might subject her'.[54] How successful this new little narrative is likely to be we can only speculate, the author choosing to 'draw the Veil' over the increasingly desperate vision of humanity's prospects that her story presents.[55] The portents are less than promising, however, with the author emphasising that youth and beauty are 'the Objects of the Pursuit, or rather Persecution not only of all the abandoned amongst Men, but of all the envious amongst Women'.[56] The failure of David's project resonates well beyond his individual situation to become an indictment of human nature, about which it has been made abundantly clear we should harbour no illusions. David and his circle make no converts to their cause, and remain an isolated and inward-looking group, ill equipped to deal with the deviousness of their fellow human beings. The sheer accumulation of wicked actions is depressing, and moral reformation seems the most distant of hopes as the veil is drawn over David's unfortunate history. For Skinner, the end of the narrative constitutes the triumph of 'the early modern commercial world' over 'the sentimental community'; which, from another perspective, is to say the triumph of the state of nature.[57] When Malcolm

Kelsall sees David's plight as proceeding from his 'timidity', 'stupidity' and 'naivete' in the face of the new social order, a similar point is being made.[58]

The impression we are left with in both narratives is of a society where anarchy is only just being held at bay – the anarchy that follows on from the ceaseless clash of opposing self-interests. Human behaviour, in the main, conforms to the Hobbesian model ('mankind in general desire power only to do harm'), with society turning a blind eye to such behaviour most of the time. In *Tom Jones* there is a relatively optimistic ending to the social critique (enough for Skinner to consider it a 'novel of sentiment'[59]); in *David Simple* a deeply pessimistic one, but each author communicates a strong sense of a world in which the social bond is very weak and the veneer of civilisation dangerously thin. For every repentant Man of the Hill there is a multitude of amoral, unscrupulous individuals, 'abandoned' men and 'envious' women, pursuing their own ends at the expense of others, and regarding that as the natural state of affairs. Just underneath the surface of most human behaviour the state of nature rules – and not even a repentant Man of the Hill can do much about that. Appropriating a phrase of the eighteenth-century divine Robert South, Battestin notes how a 'perpetual deliverance' of his characters from disaster is the hallmark of Fielding's fiction, and illustrative of its desire to impose order on events.[60] Yet we might also note that the need for perpetual deliverance is created by the perpetual deviousness of the mass of humankind, and that there is every reason to believe that such deviousness will continue unabated, periodic deliverances notwithstanding.

Henry Fielding suggests more relish for the battle to keep this strain of our natures contained than his sister does, but he is no less aware of the scale of the effort required: the Aristotelian balance being aimed for can never be considered anything more than precarious. Tom may reach a state of relative security, but the conditions that created Blifil, Black George, and, for that matter, Lady Bellaston, too, still obtain when the narrative has run its course. With Sarah, however, comes the bleaker conclusion that there is not enough will to impose a Hobbesian solution on such an unjust society. David dies a martyr to human venality, and with him, it would appear, goes any real hope of a society based on compassion and fellow feeling. We fear for the fate of his daughter under the circumstances. It is a particularly sombre note on which to end a disquisition on the prospects for friendship in one's society, and an indication of just how deeply engrained the period considers self-interest to be in human nature. Well into the eighteenth century Hobbes continues to speak very directly to his successors, who can find his unremittingly pessimistic view of human nature very hard to overcome, given that their study of social relations seems to provide so much confirmation of Hobbes' basic tenets. Hobbes restated is Hobbes apparently vindicated in his cyncism.

Notes

1   C.J. Rawson, *Henry Fielding and the Augustan Ideal Under Stress: 'Nature's Dance of Death' and Other Stories*, London and Boston, Routledge and Kegan Paul, 1972, p. 19. As Rawson points out, a more obviously Hobbesian thinker in this period is the fourth Earl of Chesterfield.

2   Henry Fielding, *The History of Tom Jones, A Foundling*, John Bender and Simon Stern (eds), Oxford and New York, Oxford University Press, 1996, p. 871.

3   In an earlier draft of this episode (printed in the current Penguin edition), the disgust at mankind's irrationality comes out even more clearly in the Man of the Hill's comment that, 'a Protestant rebellion in favour of a Popish prince! The folly of mankind is as wonderful as their knavery' (*The History of Tom Jones, A Foundling*, R.P.C. Mutter (ed.), Harmondsworth, Penguin, 1966, p. 387).

4   James Boswell, *Life of Johnson*, R.W. Chapman (ed.), Oxford and New York, Oxford University Press, 1980, p. 480.

5   Martin C. Battestin, *The Moral Basis of Fielding's Art: A Study of 'Joseph Andrews'*, Wesleyan University Press, Middletown, CT, 1959, p. 55.

6   *Tom Jones*, p. 871.

7   *Ibid.*, pp. 372-3.

8   See, for example, Angela Smallwood, *Fielding and the Woman Question: The Novels of Henry Fielding and Feminist Debate 1700-1750*, Hemel Hempstead, Harvester, 1989.

9   See Martin C. Battestin, *The Providence of Wit: Aspects of Form in Augustan Literature and the Arts*, Oxford, Clarendon Press, 1974, chapter 5.

10   *Tom Jones*, p. 400. Battestin, on the other hand, sees in the Man of the Hill's misanthropy a critique 'of both Hobbes and the Calvinists' (*The Moral Basis of Fielding's Art*, p. 56).

11   *Tom Jones*, p. 400.

12   *Ibid.*, p. 417.

13   The importance we are according this episode clashes quite sharply with Ian Watt's reading of it as merely one of several 'excrescences' that mar the generally smooth unfolding of Fielding's plot (Ian Watt, *The Rise of the Novel: Studies in Defoe, Richardson and Fielding*, London, Chatto and Windus, 1957, p. 268).

14   *Tom Jones*, p. 420.

15   *Ibid.*, p. 421.

16   Henry Fielding, *The History of the Adventures of Joseph Andrews*, Douglas Brooks-Davies (ed.), Oxford, Oxford University Press, 1970, p. 168.

17   Fielding himself is not above following the cause of self-interest and cynicism, even at the expense of his reputation. He went from being a vociferous opponent of Robert Walpole's ministry to an apologist, with suspicious haste. Pat Rogers' assessment is fairly acid: 'we must not whitewash his conduct; he changed sides, it appears, less on

account of ideology than in order to pay his bills' (*Henry Fielding: A Biography*, Paul Elek, London, 1979, pp. 112-13).

18 Ian A. Bell, *Henry Fielding: Authorship and Authority*, London and New York, Longman, 1994, p. 200.

19 *Tom Jones*, p. 869.

20 Henry Fielding, *The Life of Mr. Jonathan Wild the Great*, David Nokes (ed.), Harmondsworth, Penguin, 1982, p. 133.

21 *Tom Jones*, p. 661.

22 *Ibid.*, p. 711.

23 *Ibid.*, p. 633.

24 *Ibid.*, p. 870.

25 Not all critics see Fielding's portrayal of women in a negative light. Smallwood, for example, argues that he is in dialogue with a tradition of 'rationalist-feminist polemic' in seventeenth- and eighteenth-century thought (*Fielding and the Woman Question*, p. 2).

26 Ian A. Bell, 'Crusoe's Women: Or, the Curious Incident of the Dog in the Night-Time', in Spaas and Stimpson (eds), *Robinson Crusoe: Myths and Metamorphoses*, pp. 28-44 (p. 38).

27 *Tom Jones*, p. 413.

28 *Ibid.*, p. 416.

29 *Ibid.*, p. 413.

30 'Fielding's view of human nature generally coincided with that of the latitudinarians in its over-all optimism' (Battestin, *The Moral Basis of Fielding's Art*, p. 84).

31 Bernard Harrison, *Henry Fielding's Tom Jones: The Novelist as Moral Philosopher*, London, Sussex University Press, 1975, p. 23.

32 *Tom Jones*, p. 586.

33 *Ibid.*, p. 587.

34 Bell, *Henry Fielding: Authorship and Authority*, p. 210.

35 Harrison, *Henry Fielding's Tom Jones*, p. 51.

36 *Tom Jones*, p. 414.

37 The final edition of Fielding's satirical publication *The Jacobite's Journal* (Number 49, Saturday, November 5, 1748), explained the author's intentions as follows: 'A strange spirit of Jacobinism, indeed of Infatuation, discovered itself at the latter End of the Year 1747, in many Parts of this Kingdom ... As it seemed necessary to apply some Remedy, in order to stop the Progress of this dangerous, epidemical Madness at so critical a Season; so none seemed more proper, or likely to be more effectual than Ridicule' (Fielding, *The Jacobite's Journal and Related Writings*, p. 424).

38 As Rogers has remarked, 'the Jacobites were able to recruit many Scottish supporters amongst solid protestant folk whose dislike of England hinged on the terms of the Union forged in the year of Fielding's birth' (*Henry Fielding: A Biography*, p. 143).

39 *Tom Jones*, p. 381.

40 *Ibid.*, pp. 294, 280.

41 Sarah Fielding, *The Adventures of David Simple*, Malcolm Kelsall (ed.), Oxford and New York, Oxford University Press, 1987, p. 430.

42 *Ibid.*, pp. 29, 30.

43 *Ibid.*, p. 34.

44 *Ibid.*, p. 37.

45 *Ibid.*, p. 39.

46   *Ibid.*, pp. 82, 91.
47   *Ibid.*, p. 151.
48   Linda Bree, *Sarah Fielding*, New York: Twayne, 1996, p. 39.
49   Gillian Skinner, *Sensibility and Economics in the Novel, 1740-1800: The Price of a Tear*, Basingstoke and London, Macmillan, 1999, p. 16.
50   *David Simple*, p. 432.
51   *Ibid.*, p. 305.
52   *Ibid.*, pp. 314, 315.
53   Spencer, *The Rise of the Woman Novelist*, p. 94. Bree, too, talks about Cynthia's intellectual qualities, regarding her as 'a stronger and more positive figure than the nominal hero, David' (*Sarah Fielding*, p. 39).
54   *David Simple*, p. 427.
55   *Ibid.*, p. 432.
56   *Ibid.*, p. 427.
57   Skinner, *Sensibility and Economics*, p. 30.
58   Malcolm Kelsall, Introduction to Sarah Fielding, *David Simple*, p. xv.
59   Skinner, *Sensibility and Economics*, p. 15.
60   Battestin, *The Providence of Wit*, p. 161.

Conclusion: The Narratives
of Sovereignty

Our survey of the discourse of sovereignty from the Civil War through to the aftermath of the second Jacobite rebellion, has revealed how critical a role theories of the state of nature played in the intellectual life of the period. The various narratives of sovereignty we have been examining ultimately constitute a series of dialogues with the principle of self-interest. It is a principle which provokes strong responses in the seventeenth and eighteenth centuries: avid support from radical Whig theorists and assorted nonconformists, condemnation from ideologically more conservative figures. A political divide opens up over this issue, with radicals and nonconformists emphasising the positive aspects of self-interest, whereas conservatives generally can only see its drawbacks. The reader is invited to choose between a liberating personal autonomy on the one hand or a terrifying anarchy on the other. Depending on one's starting point, basic human nature is either something enthusiastically to be promoted or something drastically to be curbed, and the nature of the state that is put forward for our consideration will reflect that fundamental conception of individual psychology – whether providing structures to support the development of personal autonomy or for the active suppression of anarchy.

We can identify a pessimistic and an optimistic strain of thought on human nature which dictates how the civil state will be constructed. For Hobbes and the absolutists, the fear is of man's propensity to revert to a 'nasty, brutish and short' condition of existence, where no individual is ever safe for any length of time in the face of the threat posed by unchecked self-interest. This is an omnipresent threat to a thinker like Hobbes, shocked by the events of a civil war followed by regicide. Although less extreme in their outlook, both Filmer and Dryden feel that God's order is being questioned by any challenge that is offered to traditional models of sovereignty, as represented by the Stuart monarchy. Tradition, supported by biblical precedent, presents a powerful case for that monarchy, but one that eventually fails them. The arguments for absolutism may still be there after the Glorious Revolution but they are soon being modified to meet changing political circumstances, where the Stuart monarchy has been exiled to the fringes of British political life, and no longer has a coherent support base on which to call. Even a proto-absolutist like Henry Fielding cannot be brought to defend the Stuart cause – especially when the complicating factor of Catholicism is taken into account.

The matter is further complicated by writers such as Behn, who respond to patriarchal assumptions and support of the Stuarts in what sometimes can seem to be an ambivalent fashion. Self-interest in the private sphere of sexual relations, as read through texts such as *The Rover* and *Love Letters*, is perceived by Behn in positive terms, whilst the texts simultaneously uphold political patriarchy of a Filmerian persuasion in the public sphere of monarchical sovereignty. Behn appears to recognise no obvious tensions between the public and private domains. The state of nature she posits is one that draws upon conservative political thought in the former and extreme individualism in the latter. *Love Letters* in particular captures this dualism as the heroine leads a libertine sex life, acting from motives that are clearly predicated upon self-satisfaction and self-advancement. In a text that is a thinly-veiled allegory of the politics of the 1680s, Behn throws her weight emphatically behind the absolutist claims of the later Stuarts. When we turn to Manley, however, self-interest in the sexual sphere is seen to be essentially a male prerogative, and a specifically female pessimism regarding the state of nature asserts itself. In yet another thinly-veiled allegory, it is made clear by Manley that the corruption of contemporary politics is directly attributable to the absence of any effective check on male self-interest. The masculine phrase regime has swamped the feminine, and society at large suffers in consequence.

On the optimist wing, from the Levellers and Diggers onwards we have arguments that press the case of the individual, and the 'people' (even if this sometimes can be a limited category by our standards), against the machinations of institutional authority, with Locke and Sidney holding out the heady prospect of popular revolt if our sovereign rights are abused by the powers-that-be. While this can be overstated in twenty-first century terms (Whig radicalism still has its limits), there is no denying that an anti-absolutist narrative of sovereignty is systematically being constructed over our period, and that the relationship between individual and state is being rigorously rethought. As we have observed, this is a debate that soon infiltrates literary discourse. From Dryden onwards, writers of fiction have competing narratives of sovereignty to choose from, and the traditional, absolutist-inclined, model is no longer commanding the uncritical, largely reflex, support of the populace. The discourse of sovereignty is now generating differences that the Stuart monarchy and its supporters cannot resolve by appeal to the Bible or traditional cultural practices. Self-interest has become a site of cultural conflict, but increasingly it is one that the optimists are coming to dominate: Robinson Crusoe's appeal extends far more widely than does Tom Jones'.

It is important to emphasise how embedded in the politics of the period all the theories of the state of nature considered in this study were. At no point are we dealing with an abstract philosophical discourse. Hobbes and the Levellers were responding to the Civil War; Winstanley, Harrington, and Milton to the uncertainties of the Commonwealth settlement; Locke, Sidney, Behn, and Dryden to the Exclusion Crisis as it gained momentum. Meanwhile a host of other theorists were raiding the Bible for guidance as to how to resolve the various other political crises that arose over the turbulent years between the Civil War and the Hanoverian succession. This extends to the alliances between Whig and Tory opposition to Walpole in the 1720s and 1730s. In every case there is a specific political context for which the theory is designed. It is noticeable, however, how deeply Hobbes' basic model of the state of nature infiltrates the discourse of the time. Hobbes may not have had much direct influence on the practice of government in the later seventeenth or early eighteenth century, even amongst the absolutist constituency (where, as we have seen, Filmer was more likely to be the model adopted), but something of his worst-case scenario about human nature seems to form the background for much of the contemporary debate about the nature of the state. If only implicitly, the radicals are trying to disprove the worst-case scenario advanced by Hobbes and to present self-interest as a positive socio-political characteristic worthy of encouragement. Self-interest for such theorists, is a force for social good that should be allowed to express itself: Robinson Crusoe, for all his character faults, is where the future lies (although, as Manley makes us aware, women might wonder where this leaves them in the discourse of sovereignty). For sceptics like the Fieldings, however, self-interest is the great enemy of the social order that it is in our collective interest to maintain. It is a more benevolent absolutism than Hobbes was propounding that is being recommended in Henry Fielding's case, but it is a form of absolutism nevertheless, which accepts the worst-case scenario as a live possibility capable of occurring at any moment if we are not vigilant. The tradition of suspicion stemming from Hobbes is alive and well in the aftermath of the second Jacobite rebellion, therefore, with the 'strange spirit' of that movement, as Fielding described it in *The Jacobite's Journal*, still very much in the air.

Repeatedly throughout the texts we have been addressing, one notes attempts by writers from all points on the political spectrum to come to terms with what is a rapidly developing and very fluid process of change. In the 1720s and 1730s, for instance, the arch-Tory of the early eighteenth century, Henry St. John, Viscount Bolingbroke, borrows extensively from a republican and Whig canon of political literature to launch his attack on Walpole's administration. Bolingbroke's tactics testify to the power of such writing to survive its immediate political context and remain relevant in the public sphere years after the events that initiated their creation. Writers such as Bolingbroke, and indeed all of the figures that we have focused upon over the century from the 1640s to the 1740s, saw themselves as acting in the public interest. They drew upon a common classical heritage in order to do so. Across the period, the most constant source for writers such as Milton, Harrington, Dryden, and Bolingbroke, notwithstanding the fact that they were often divided ideologically, was the writings of the Roman philosopher and rhetorician, Cicero. It is the latter's model of the state of nature, linked as it is to theories of the common good, that can be felt most clearly.

The optimistic and pessimistic discourses on human nature are still in conflict when our period ends, and continuing to generate differends and incommensurable phrase regimes: Robinson Crusoe and Tom Jones remain irreconcilable in their cultural outlooks, highly symbolic representatives of a radical and reactionary political tradition respectively. It is the state of nature which has provided much of the impetus for this debate, with, to return to Lovejoy's breakdown of the concept, the anthropological having been assimilated into the cultural and the political. In real terms, this means that the personal becomes an integral part of the discourse of sovereignty, and, in many ways, the prime site where differends are contested and incommensurable phrase regimes clash. If nothing else, actions taken 'for the love of our Selves' have wider cultural support from the Glorious Revolution settlement onwards – a phenomenon which proves a boon to a rising generation of novelists, for whom the conflict between self and society becomes the very stuff of their narrative endeavours. Whether in the literary or the political arena, narratives of sovereignty will continue to thrive on the tension between the personal and the social that is arguably the most enduring legacy of the seventeenth-century's debate over the state of nature.

Bibliography

Achinstein, Sharon (1994), *Milton and the Revolutionary Reader*, Princeton University Press, Princeton, NJ.

Addison, Joseph (1811), *The Works of the Right Honourable Joseph Addison*, Cadell and Davies, London.

Ashcraft, Richard (1986), *Revolutionary Politics and Locke's Two Treatises of Government*, Princeton University Press, Princeton, NJ.

Aylmer, G.E. (ed.) (1972), *The Interregnum: The Quest for Settlement 1646-1660*, Macmillan, London and Basingstoke.

Bacon, Francis (1998), *The History of the Reign of King Henry VII*, Brian Vickers (ed.), Cambridge University Press, Cambridge.

Bailyn, Bernard (1982), *The Ideological Origins of the American Revolution*, Harvard University Press, Cambridge, MA.

Ballaster, Rosalind (1992), *Seductive Forms: Women's Amatory Fiction from 1684 to 1740*, Clarendon Press, Oxford and New York.

Barker, Arthur (1940), *Milton and the Puritan Dilemma, 1641-1660*, University of Toronto Press, Toronto.

Bastian, Frank (1981), *Defoe's Early Life*, Macmillan, London.

Battestin, Martin C. (1959), *The Moral Basis of Fielding's Art: A Study of 'Joseph Andrews'*, Wesleyan University Press, Middletown, CT.

— (1974), *The Providence of Wit: Aspects of Form in Augustan Literature and the Arts*, Clarendon Press, Oxford.

Behn, Aphra (1992), *Works*, I-V, Janet Todd (ed.), Pickering and Chatto, London.

— (1996), *Love Letters Between a Nobleman and his Sister*, Janet Todd (ed.), Penguin, Harmondsworth.

— (1998), *Oroonoko and Other Writings*, Paul Salzman (ed.), Oxford University Press, Oxford.

Bell, Ian A. (1985), *Defoe's Fictions*, Croom Helm, London.

— (1994), *Henry Fielding: Authorship and Authority*, Longman, London and New York.

Bignami, Marialuisa (ed.) (1997), *Wrestling with Defoe: Approaches from a Workshop on Defoe's Prose*, Cisalpino, Bologna.

Bloom, Harold (1973), *The Anxiety of Influence*, Oxford University Press, New York.

Bolingbroke, Viscount Henry St. John (1997), *Political Writings*, David Armitage (ed.), Cambridge University Press, Cambridge.

Boswell, James (1980), *Life of Johnson*, R.W. Chapman (ed.), Oxford University Press, Oxford and New York.

Bree, Linda (1996), *Sarah Fielding*, Twayne, New York.

Bruce, Susan (ed.) (1999), *Three Early Modern Utopias: Utopia, New Atalantis, The Isle of Pines*, Oxford University Press, Oxford.

Bunyan, John (1962), *Grace Abounding to the Chief of Sinners*, Roger Sharrock (ed.), Clarendon Press, Oxford.

— (1967), *The Pilgrim's Progress*, James Blanton Wharey and Roger Sharrock (eds), Clarendon Press, Oxford.

Burnet, Gilbert (1823), *History of His Own Time*, I-VI, Clarendon Press, Oxford.

Burns, J.H. and Goldie, Mark (eds) (1994), *The Cambridge History of Political Thought, 1450-1700*, Cambridge University Press, Cambridge.

Burtt, Shelley (1992), *Virtue Transformed: Political Argument in England, 1688-1740*, Cambridge University Press, Cambridge.

Bywaters, David (1991), *Dryden in Revolutionary England*, University of California Press, Berkeley, Los Angeles, CA and London.

Chappell, Vere (ed.) (1999), *Hobbes and Bramhall on Liberty and Necessity*, Cambridge University Press, Cambridge.

Charles I (1966), *Eikon Basilike: The Portraiture of His Sacred Majesty in His Solitude and Sufferings*, Philip A. Knatchel (ed.), Ithaca University Press, Ithaca, NY.

Chernaik, Warren (1995), *Sexual Freedom In Restoration Literature*, Cambridge: Cambridge University Press.

— (1999), 'Civil Liberty in Milton, the Levellers and Winstanley', *Prose Studies*, 22, pp. 101-20.

Cicero (1991), *On Duties*, M.T. Griffin and E.M. Atkins (eds), Cambridge University Press, Cambridge.

Clark, J.C.D. (2000), *English Society, 1660-1832*, Cambridge University Press, Cambridge.

Collinson, Patrick (1986), 'The Monarchical Republic of Elizabeth I', *Bulletin of the John Rylands Library*, 69, pp. 394-424.

Conniff, James (1982), 'Reason and History in Early Whig Thought: The Case of Algernon Sidney', *Journal of the History of Ideas*, 43, pp. 397-416.

Cooper, Anthony Ashley, Earl of Shaftesbury, *A Letter From a Person of Quality To His Friend in the Country*, in Joyce Lee Malcolm (ed.) (1999), *The Struggle for Sovereignty: Seventeenth-Century English Political Tracts*, I-II, Liberty Fund, Indianapolis, IN.

Cope, Kevin L. (ed.), (2000), *1650-1850: Ideas, Aesthetics, and Inquiries in the Early Modern Period*, vol. 5, AMS Press, New York.

Coppe, Abiezer (1987), *Selected Writings*, Andrew Hopton (ed.), Aporia Press, London.

Coveney, Peter and Highfield, Roger (1995), *Frontiers of Complexity: The Search for Order in a Chaotic World*, Faber and Faber, London.

Davis, J.C. (1981), *Utopia and the Ideal Society: A Study of English Utopian Writing, 1516-1700*, Cambridge University Press, Cambridge.

Defoe, Daniel (1945), *The Farther Adventures of Robinson Crusoe*, Everyman, London.

— (1964), *Roxana, or, the Fortunate Mistress*, Jane Jack (ed.), Oxford University Press, Oxford.

— (1971), *The Fortunes and Misfortunes of the Famous Moll Flanders*, G.A. Starr (ed.), Oxford University Press, Oxford.

— (1972), *The Life and Strange Surprizing Adventures of Robinson Crusoe*, J. Donald Crowley (ed.), Oxford University Press, Oxford.

Dent, Arthur (1974), *The Plaine Man's Path-Way to Heaven*, Theatrum Orbis Terrarum, Amsterdam.

Dickinson, H.T. (1970), *Bolingbroke*, Constable, London.

— (1977), *Liberty and Property: Political Ideology in Eighteenth-Century Britain*, Methuen, London.

Dryden, John, (1956-), *The Works of John Dryden*, H.T. Swedenborg, *et al* (eds), I-XX, University of California Press, Berkeley, CA and London.

Dunn, John (1969), *The Political Thought of John Locke*, Cambridge University Press, Cambridge.

Eachard, John (1672), *Mr Hobbs's State of Nature Considered*, London.

Evelyn, John (1959), *Diary*, E.S. De Beer (ed.), Oxford University Press, Oxford.

Fielding, Henry (1966), *The History of Tom Jones, A Foundling*, R.P.C. Mutter (ed.), Penguin, Harmondsworth.

— (1970), *The History of the Adventures of Joseph Andrews*, Douglas Brooks-Davies (ed.), Oxford University Press, Oxford.

— (1974), *The Jacobite's Journal and Related Writings*, W.B. Coley (ed.), Clarendon Press, Oxford, 1974.

— (1982), *The History of the Life of the Late Mr. Jonathan Wild the Great*, David Nokes (ed.), Penguin, Harmondsworth.

— (1996), *The History of Tom Jones, A Foundling*, John Bender and Simon Stern (eds), Oxford University Press, Oxford and New York.

Fielding, Sarah (1987), *The Adventures of David Simple*, Malcolm Kelsall (ed.), Oxford University Press, Oxford and New York.

Filmer, Sir Robert (1949), *Patriarcha and Other Political Works of Sir Robert Filmer*, Peter Laslett (ed.), Blackwell, Oxford.

— (1991), *Patriarcha and Other Writings*, Johann P. Sommerville (ed.), Cambridge University Press, Cambridge.

Fink, Zera S. (1962), *The Classical Republicans: An Essay in the Recovery of a Pattern of Thought in Seventeenth-Century England* (2nd ed.), Northwestern University Press, Evanston, IL.

Fish, Stanley (1997), *Surprised by Sin: The Reader in Paradise Lost*, Macmillan, London.

Fraser, Antonia (1979), *King Charles II*, Weidenfeld and Nicholson, London.

Gentles, Ian, Morrill, John and Worden, Blair (eds) (1998), *Soldiers, Writers, and Statesmen of the English Revolution*, Cambridge University Press, Cambridge.

Gerrard, Christine (1994), *The Patriot Opposition to Walpole: Politics, Poetry and National Myth, 1725-1742*, Clarendon Press, Oxford.

Glassey, Lionel K. J. (ed.) (1997), *The Reigns of Charles II and James VII & II*, Macmillan, London.

Goldgar, Bertrand J. (1976), *Walpole and the Wits: The Relation of Politics to Literature, 1722-1742*, University of Nebraska Press, Lincoln, NA and London.

Goldie, Mark (1980), 'The Roots of True Whiggism, 1668-94', *History of Political Thought*, 1, pp. 195-236.

— (1983), 'John Locke and Restoration Anglicanism', *Political Studies*, 31, pp. 61-85.

Greaves, Richard L. (1986), *Deliver Us from Evil: The Radical Underground in Britain, 1660-1663*, Oxford University Press, Oxford.

— (1990), *Enemies Under his Feet: Radicals and Nonconformists in Britain, 1664-1677*, Stanford University Press, Stanford, CA.

— (1992), *Secrets of the Kingdom: British Radicals from the Popish Plot to the Revolution of 1688-89*, Stanford University Press, Stanford, CA.

Green, Martin (1980), *Dreams of Adventure, Deeds of Empire*, Routledge and Kegan Paul, London.

Hammond, Brean (1984), *Pope and Bolingbroke: A Study in Friendship and Influence*, University of Missouri Press, Columbus, MO.

Hammond, Paul (1999), *Dryden and the Traces of Classical Rome*, Clarendon Press, Oxford.

Hampsher-Monk, Ian (1976), 'The Political Theory of the Levellers: Putney, Property and Professor Macpherson', *Political Studies*, 24, pp. 397-422.

Hampton, Jean (1986), *Hobbes and the Social Contract Tradition*, Cambridge University Press, Cambridge.

Harrington, James (1977), *The Political Works of James Harrington*, J.G.A. Pocock (ed.), Cambridge University Press, Cambridge.

Harris, Tim (1993), *Politics Under the Later Stuarts: Party Conflict in a Divided Society*, Longman, Harlow.

Harris, Tim, Goldie, Mark, and Seaward, Paul (eds) (1990), *The Politics of Religion in Restoration England*, Blackwell, Oxford.

Harrison, Bernard (1975), *Henry Fielding's Tom Jones: The Novelist as Moral Philosopher*, Sussex University Press, London.

Harth, Philip (1993), *Pen for a Party: Dryden's Tory Propaganda and its Contexts*, Princeton University Press, Princeton, NJ.

Hill, Christopher (1958), *Puritanism and Revolution: Studies in Interpretation of the English Revolution*, Secker and Warburg, London.

— (1977), *Milton and the English Revolution*, Faber, London.

— (1984), *The Experience of Defeat: Milton and Some Contemporaries*, Faber, London.

Hill, Howard Erskine (1996), *Poetry of Opposition and Revolution: Dryden to Wordsworth*, Clarendon Press, Oxford.

Hobbes, Thomas (1946), *Leviathan, Or, The Matter, Forme, and Power of a Commonwealth Ecclesiasticall and Civill*, Michael Oakeshott (ed.), Blackwell, Oxford.

— (1991), *Leviathan, Or, The Matter, Forme, and Power of a Common-wealth Ecclesiasticall and Civill*, Richard Tuck (ed.), Cambridge, Cambridge University Press.

— (1969), *Behemoth, or The Long Parliament*, Ferdinand Tonnies (ed.), Frank Cass, London.

— (1983), *De Cive: Philosophicall Rudiments Concerning Government and Society*, Howard Warrender (ed.), Clarendon Press, Oxford.

— (1994), *Human Nature and De Corpore Politico*, J.C.A. Gaskin (ed.), Oxford University Press, Oxford.

— (1999), *Treatise of Liberty and Necessity*, in Vere Chappell (ed.), *Hobbes and Bramhall on Liberty and Necessity*, Cambridge University Press, Cambridge.

Hobby, Elaine (1999), 'Winstanley, Women and the Family', *Prose Studies*, 22, pp. 61-72.

Holmes, Geoffrey (1993), *The Making of a Great Power: Late Stuart and Early Georgian Britain, 1660-1722*, Longman, Harlow.

Holstun, James (1987), *A Rational Millennium: Puritan Utopias of Seventeenth-Century England and America*, Clarendon Press, Oxford.

— (ed.) (1992), *Pamphlet Wars: Prose in the English Revolution*, Frank Cass, London.

— (1999), 'Communism, George Hill and the *Mir*: Was Marx a Nineteenth-Century Winstanleyan?', *Prose Studies*, 22, pp. 121-48.

Hopfl, Haro, and Thompson, Martyn (1979), 'The History of Contract as a Motif in Political Thought', *American Historical Journal*, 84, pp. 919-44.

Houston, Alan Craig (1991), *Algernon Sidney and the Republican Heritage in England and America*, Princeton University Press, Princeton, NJ.

Hughes, Derek (1981), *Dryden's Heroic Plays*, Macmillan, London.

Hulme, Peter (1986), *Colonial Encounters: Europe and the Native Caribbean 1492-1797*, Methuen, London and New York.

Hunter, J. Paul (1966), *The Reluctant Pilgrim*, Johns Hopkins University Press, Baltimore.

— (1990), *Before Novels: The Cultural Contexts of Eighteenth-Century English Fiction*, W.W. Norton, New York and London.

Hutner, Heidi (ed.) (1993), *Rereading Aphra Benn: History, Theory and Criticism*, University of Virginia Press, Charlottesville, VA and London.

Hutton, Ronald (1985), *The Restoration: A Political and Religious History of England and Wales, 1658-1667*, Oxford University Press, Oxford.

— (1989), *Charles II: King of England, Scotland and Ireland*, Oxford University Press, Oxford.

Hymer, Stephen (1971-2), 'Robinson Crusoe and the Secret of Primitive Accumulation', *Monthly Review*, 23, pp. 11-36.

Israel, Jonathan I. (ed.) (1991), *The Anglo-Dutch Moment: Essays on the Glorious Revolution and its World Impact*, Cambridge University Press, Cambridge.

Jones, J.R. (1978), *Country and Court: England, 1658-1714*, Edward Arnold, London.

Jordan, Mathew (2001), *Milton and Modernity: Masculinity and Paradise Lost*, Palgrave, London.

Karl, Frederick (1975), *A Reader's Guide to the Development of the English Novel in the Eighteenth Century*, Thames and Hudson, London.

Keeble, N.H. (1987), *The Literary Culture of Nonconformity in Later Seventeenth-Century England*, Leicester University Press, Leicester.

Kelsey, Sean (1997), *Inventing a Republic: The Political Culture of the English Commonwealth, 1649-1653*, Manchester University Press, Manchester.

Kenyon, J.P. (1958), *Robert Spencer, Earl of Sunderland, 1641-1702*, Longman Green, London and New York.

— (1977), *Revolution Principles: The Politics of Party 1689-1720*, Cambridge University Press, Cambridge.

— (1985), *Stuart England* (2nd ed.), Penguin, Harmondsworth.

King, Dr. William (1818), *Political and Literary Anecdotes of His Own Times*, John Murray, London.

Kishlansky, Mark A. (1979), *The Rise of the New Model Army*, Cambridge University Press, New York and Cambridge.

— (1996), *A Monarchy Transformed: Britain 1603-1714*, Penguin, Harmondsworth.

Knights, Mark (1994), *Policy and Opinion in Crisis*, Cambridge University Press, Cambridge.

Koonce, Howard L. (1963), 'Moll's Muddle: Defoe's Use of Irony in *Moll Flanders*', *Journal of English Literary History*, 30, pp. 377-94.

Kramnick, Isaac (1968), *Bolingbroke and his Circle*, Harvard University Press, Cambridge, MA.

Latour, Bruno (1993), *We Have Never Been Modern*, Catherine Porter (trans.), Harvester Wheatsheaf, Hemel Hempstead.

Lieb, Michael, and Shawcross, John T. (eds) (1974), *Achievements of the Left Hand: Essays on the Prose of John Milton*, University of Massachusetts Press, Amherst, MA.

Locke, John (1988), *Two Treatises of Government* (rev. ed.), Peter Laslett (ed.), Cambridge University Press, Cambridge.

Loewenstein, David (2001), *Representing Revolution in Milton and his Contemporaries: Religion, Politics and Polemics in Radical Puritanism*, Cambridge University Press, Cambridge.

Loewenstein, David, and Turner, James Grantham (eds) (1990), *Politics, Poetics and Hermeneutics in Milton's Prose*, Cambridge University Press, Cambridge.

Loftis, John (ed.) (1979), *The Memoirs of Anne, Lady Halkett, and Ann, Lady Fanshawe*, Oxford University Press, Oxford.

Lord, George deF. (ed.) (1968), *Poems on Affairs of State*, I-VII, Yale University Press, New Haven, CT and London.

Lovejoy, A.O. (1948), *Essays in the History of Ideas*, Johns Hopkins University Press, Baltimore.

Ludlow, Edmund (1894), *Memoirs*, I-II, C. H. Firth (ed.), Clarendon Press, Oxford.

MacLean, Gerald (ed.) (1995), *Culture and Society in the Stuart Restoration: Literature, Drama, History*, Cambridge University Press, Cambridge.

Macpherson, C.B. (1962), *The Political Theory of Possessive Individualism*, Oxford University Press, Oxford.

Malcolm, Joyce Lee (1999), *The Struggle for Sovereignty: Seventeenth-Century English Political Tracts*, I-II, Liberty Fund, Indianapolis, IN.

Manley, Delarivier (1992), *Secret Memoirs and Manners of Several Persons of Quality, of both Sexes. From the New Atalantis, an Island in the Mediterannean*, Rosalind Ballaster (ed.), Penguin, Harmondsworth.

Marshall, Alan (1999), *The Age of Faction: Court Politics, 1660-1702*, Longman, Harlow.

Marx, Karl (1976), *Capital*, vol. I, Ben Fowkes (trans.), Penguin, Harmondsworth.

McVeagh, John (1981), *Tradefull Merchants: The Portrayal of the Capitalist in Literature*, Routledge and Kegan Paul, London.

Miller, John (1973), *Popery and Politics in England, 1660-1668*, Cambridge University Press, Cambridge.

— (1985), *Restoration England: the Reign of Charles II*, Longman, London and New York.

Miller, Peter (1994), *The Common Good: Empire, Religion and Philosophy in Eighteenth-Century Britain*, Cambridge University Press, Cambridge.

Milton, John (1953-82), *The Complete Prose Works* , I-VIII, Don Wolfe, *et al.* (eds), Yale University Press, New Haven, CT and London.

— (1971), *Complete Shorter Poems*, John Carey (ed.), Longman, Harlow.

— (1971), *Paradise Lost*, Alastair Fowler (ed.), Longman, Harlow, 1971.

— (1991), *Political Writings*, Martin Dzelzainis (ed.), Cambridge University Press, Cambridge.

Mintz, Samuel I. (1962), *The Hunting of Leviathan*, Cambridge University Press, Cambridge.

Molesworth, Robert (1738), *An Account of Denmark: As it was in the Year 1692*, Timothy Goodwin, London.

Monod, Paul Kleber (1989), *Jacobitinism and the English People, 1688-1788*, Cambridge University Press, Cambridge.

Nedham, Marchamont (1656), *The Excellency of a Free State*, London.

Neville, Henry (1647), *The Parliament of Ladies*, London.

— (1969), *Plato Redidivus or, A Dialogue Concerning Government*, in Caroline Robbins (ed.), *Two English Republican Tracts: Plato Redivivus or, A Dialogue Concerning*

Government by Henry Neville; An Essay upon the Constitution of the Roman Government by Walter Moyle, Cambridge University Press, Cambridge.

— (1999), *The Isle of Pines*, in Susan Bruce (ed.), *Three Early Modern Utopias: Utopia, The New Atalantis, The Isle of Pines*, Oxford University Press, Oxford.

Newlyn, Lucy (1993), *Milton and the Romantic Reader*, Clarendon Press, Oxford.

Norbrook, David (1999), *Writing the English Republic: Poetry, Rhetoric and Politics, 1627-1660*, Cambridge University Press, Cambridge.

Novak, M.E. (1963), *Defoe and the Nature of Man*, Oxford University Press, Oxford.

Ogg, David (1956), *England in the Reign of Charles II* (2nd ed.), Oxford University Press, Oxford.

Paine, Thomas (1969), *The Rights of Man*, Henry Collins (ed.), Penguin, Harmondsworth.

Parker, Samuel (1669), *Discourse of Ecclesiastical Polity*, London.

Petegorsky, David W. (1972), *Left-Wing Democracy in the English Civil War: A Study of the Social Philosophy of Gerrard Winstanley*, Haskell House, New York.

Phillipson, Nicholas, and Skinner, Quentin (eds) (1993), *Political Discourse in Early Modern Britain*, Cambridge University Press, Cambridge.

Pincus, Steven C.A. (1996), *Protestantism and Patriotism: Ideologies and the Making of Foreign Policy, 1650-1668*, Cambridge University Press, Cambridge.

Pittock, Murray G.H. (1994), *Poetry and Jacobite Politics in Eighteenth-Century Britain and Ireland*, Cambridge University Press, Cambridge.

Pocock, J.G.A. (1972), *Politics, Language and Time: Essays on Political Thought and History*, Methuen, London.

— (1975), *The Machiavellian Moment: Florentine Political Thought and the Atlantic Republican Tradition*, Princeton University Press, Princeton, NJ.

— (1985), *Virtue, Commerce and History: Essays on Political Thought and History, Chiefly in the Eighteenth Century*, Cambridge University Press, Cambridge.

— (ed.) (1993) (with Schochet, Gordon J., and Schwoerer, Lois G.), *The Varieties of British Political Thought, 1500-1800*, Cambridge University Press, Cambridge.

Pope, Alexander (1939-69), *The Twickenham Edition of the Poems of Alexander Pope*, I-XI, John Butt, *et al.* (eds), Methuen, London.

Rapaport, Herman (1983), *Milton and the Postmodern*, University of Nebraska Press, Lincoln, NA.

Rawson, C.J. (1972), *Henry Fielding and the Augustan Ideal Under Stress: 'Nature's Dance of Death' and Other Stories*, Routledge and Kegan Paul, London and Boston.

Richetti, John J. (1969), *Popular Fiction before Richardson: Narrative Patterns 1700-39*, Clarendon Press, Oxford.

Robbins, Caroline (1959), *The Eighteenth-Century Commonwealthman: The Transmission, Development and Circumstance of English Liberal Thought from the Restoration of Charles II until the War with the Thirteen Colonies*, Harvard University Press, Cambridge, MA.

— (ed.) (1969), *Two English Republican Tracts: Plato Redivivus or, A Dialogue Concerning Government by Henry Neville; An Essay upon the Constitution of the Roman Government by Walter Moyle*, Cambridge University Press, Cambridge.

Rogers, G.A.J., and Ryan, Alan (1988), *Perspectives on Thomas Hobbes*, Clarendon Press, Oxford.

Rogers, Pat (1979), *Henry Fielding: A Biography*, Paul Elek, London.

— (1979), *Robinson Crusoe*, George Allen and Unwin, London.

Rousseau, G.S., and Nicholson, Marjorie Hope (1968), *'This Long Disease My Life':
Alexander Pope and the Sciences*, Princeton University Press, Princeton, NJ.

Rousseau, G.S., and Rogers, Pat (1988), *The Enduring Legacy: Alexander Pope, Tercentenary Essays*, Cambridge University Press, Cambridge.

Sambrook, James (1991), *James Thomson: A Life, 1700-1748*, Oxford University Press, Oxford.

Schenk, W. (1948), *The Concern for Social Justice in the Puritan Revolution*, Longman Green, London and New York.

Schonhorn, Manuel (1991), *Defoe's Politics: Parliament, Power, Kingship and Robinson Crusoe*, Cambridge University Press, Cambridge.

Scott, Jonathon (1988), *Algernon Sidney and the English Republic, 1623-1677*, Cambridge University Press, Cambridge.

— (1991), *Algernon Sidney and the Restoration Crisis, 1677-1683*, Cambridge University Press, Cambridge.

— (2000), *England's Troubles: Seventeenth-Century English Political Instability in European Context*, Cambridge University Press, Cambridge.

Scott, Sir Walter (1985), *Redgauntlet*, Kathryn Sutherland (ed.), Oxford University Press, Oxford.

Seaward, Paul (1989), *The Cavalier Parliament and the Reconstruction of the Old Regime 1661-1667*, Cambridge University Press, Cambridge.

Sharpe, Kevin, and Zwicker, Steven N. (eds) (1998), *Refiguring Revolution: Aesthetics and Politics from the English Revolution to the Romantic Revolution*, University of California Press, Berkeley, Los Angeles, CA and London.

Sidney, Algernon (1996), *Discourses Concerning Government*, Thomas G. West (ed.), Liberty Fund, Indianapolis, IN.

Sim, Stuart (1990), *Negotiations with Paradox: Narrative Practice and Narrative Form in Bunyan and Defoe*, Harvester Wheatsheaf, Hemel Hempstead.

— and Walker, David (2000), *Bunyan and Authority: The Rhetoric of Dissent and the Legitimation Crisis in Seventeenth-Century England*, Peter Lang, Bern and New York.

Skinner, Gillian (1999), *Sensibility and Economics in the Novel, 1740-1800: The Price of a Tear*, Macmillan, Basingstoke and London.

Skinner, Quentin (1996), *Reason and Rhetoric in the Philosophy of Hobbes*, Cambridge University Press, Cambridge.

— (1998), *Liberty Before Liberalism*, Cambridge University Press, Cambridge.

Smallwood, Angela (1989), *Fielding and the Woman Question: The Novels of Henry Fielding and Feminist Debate 1700-1750*, Harvester Wheatsheaf, Hemel Hempstead.

Smith, David L. (1994), *Constitutional Royalism and the Search for Settlement, 1640-1649*, Cambridge University Press, Cambridge.

Smith, Hilda L. (1998), *Women Writers and the Early Modern British Political Tradition*, Cambridge University Press, Cambridge.

Smith, Nigel (1994), *Literature and Revolution in England, 1640-1660*, Yale University Press, New Haven, CT and London.

— (1999), 'Gerrard Winstanley and the Literature of Revolution', *Prose Studies*, 22, pp. 47-60.

Spaas, Lieve, and Stimpson, Brian (eds) (1996), *Robinson Crusoe: Myths and Metamorphoses*, Macmillan, Basingstoke and London.

Speck, W.A. (1977), *Stability and Strife: England, 1714-1760*, Arnold, London.

Spencer, Jane (1986), *The Rise of the Woman Novelist: From Aphra Benn to Jane Austen*, Blackwell, Oxford and New York.

Starr, G.A. (1965), *Defoe and Spiritual Autobiography*, Princeton University Press, Princeton, NJ.

Summers, Claude J., and Pebworth, Ted-Larry (1999), *The English Civil Wars in the Literary Imagination*, University of Missouri Press, Columbia, MO and London.

Syme, Ronald (1939), *The Roman Revolution*, Oxford University Press, Oxford.

Tacitus (1996), *The Annals of Imperial Rome*, Michael Grant (ed.), Penguin, Harmondsworth.

Tavor, Eve (1987), *Scepticism, Society and the Eighteenth-Century Novel*, St. Martin's Press, New York.

Terry, Richard (ed.) (2000), *James Thomson: Essays for the Tercentenary*, Liverpool University Press, Liverpool.

Thomson, James (1986), *Liberty, the Castle of Indolence, and Other Poems*, James Sambrook (ed.), Clarendon Press, Oxford.

Todd, Janet (1989), *The Sign of Angellica: Women, Writing and Fiction, 1660-1800*, Virago, London.

Toland, John (ed.) (1737), *The Oceana and Other Works of James Harrington, Esq. Collected, Methodiz'd, and Reviewed, with An Exact Account of his Life Prefix'd by John Toland*, A. Millar, London.

Trenchard, John, and Gordon, Thomas (1995), *Cato's Letters: or, Essays on Liberty, Civil and Religious, and Other Important Subjects*, Ronald Hamowy (ed.), Liberty Fund, Indianapolis, IN.

Trevor-Roper, Hugh (1989), *Catholics, Anglicans and Puritans*, Fontana, London.

Trotter, David (1988), *Circulation: Defoe, Dickens, and the Economies of the Novel*, Macmillan, Basingstoke and London.

Tuck, Richard (1979), *Natural Rights Theories: Their Origin and Development*, Cambridge University Press, Cambridge.

Tyrrell, James (1681), *Patriarcha non Monarcha*, R. Baldwin (Written in 1681, published in 1694), London.

Underdown, David (1971), *Pride's Purge*, Clarendon Press, Oxford.

Vane, Sir Henry (1656), *A Healing Question Propounded and Resolved*, (Reprinted in Sir Walter Scott, (ed.) Somers Tracts, [London: T. Cadell and W. Davies, 1809-15] 13 volumes, volume 6).

Waldock, Arthur John Alfred (1947), *Paradise Lost and its Critics*, Cambridge University Press, Cambridge.

Watt, Ian (1957), *The Rise of the Novel: Studies in Defoe, Richardson and Fielding*, Chatto and Windus, London.

Webster, John (1988), *The Duchess of Malfi*, John Russell Brown (ed.), Manchester University Press, Manchester.

Wedgewood, C.V. (1983), *The Trial of Charles I*, Penguin, Harmondsworth.

Wehrs, Donald R. (1992), '*Eros*, Ethics, Identity: Royalist Feminism and the Politics of Desire in Aphra Benn's *Love Letters*', *Studies in English Literature*, 32, pp. 461-78.

Weinbrot, Howard (1978), *Augustus Caesar in Augustan England: The Decline of a Classical Norm*, Princeton University Press, Princeton, NJ and London.

White, R.S. (1996), *Natural Law in English Renaissance Literature*, Cambridge University Press, Cambridge.

Winn, James Anderson (1987), *John Dryden and his World*, Yale University Press, New Haven, CT and London.

Winstanley, Gerrard (1973), *The Law of Freedom and Other Writings*, Christopher Hill (ed.), Penguin, Harmondsworth.

— (1973), *The Works of Gerrard Winstanley*, George H. Sabine (ed.), Russell and Russell, New York.

Index